Horn and Banner

Horn and Banner

*Rituals for the
Northern Tradition*

Compiled by Raven Kaldera

Hubbardston, Massachusetts

Asphodel Press
12 Simond Hill Road
Hubbardston, MA 01452

Horn and Banner: Rituals for the Northern Tradition
© 2012 Raven Kaldera
ISBN: 978-0-9825798-9-3

Cover Photo © 2011 Thorskegga Thorn

All rights reserved. Unless otherwise specified,
no part of this book may be reproduced in any form
or by any means without the permission of the author.

Printed in cooperation with
Lulu Enterprises, Inc.
860 Aviation Parkway, Suite 300
Morrisville, NC 27560

*To all the good folk
of Iron Wood Kindred,
past and present,
and especially for Jon Norman
whose innocence and enthusiasm
we will miss forever.
Rest in Hela's arms, Jon,
And may you find peace.*

Contents

Beginnings
Creating Sacred Space: Opening Rites 1
World Creation Opening 3
Jormundgand Opening Ritual 4
Four Directions and Nine Worlds: 5
Cosmological Opening Rite 5
Warding Rite of the Four Directions 7
Divide And Conquer: Advanced Group Liturgical Design. 11

Rites of Passage
Ritual to Bless a Newborn 25
Seven-Year Rite 28
A Note On Coming-Of-Age Rites 31
Coming of Age Rite for a Girlchild 33
Rite of Passage for a Boychild 37
Rite of Passage for an Ergi Child 41
Runic Handfasting Rite 46
Frigga Wedding Rite 50
Vanir Wedding Rite 55
Handparting Rite 57
Vanir Ritual for the Joining of Families 58
A Note On Funerals 60

Seasonal Rites
Candlemas Creation Rite 64
Oimelc Candle Rite 67
Charming of the Plough Ritual 70
Ostara Rite 71
Northern Tradition Beltane Rite 73
Litha Rite for Frey and Freya 75
Northern Tradition Lammas Rite 77
Equinox Ritual for Idun 82
Winternights Ritual 85
Mother Night Ritual 89
Blutmonath Journey to Helheim 92
Sun Wheel Rite For Yule 105

Rituals for Gods

- Rite of the Tides 112
- Rite of the Nine Mermaids 114
- Solitary Ritual to Angrboda 131
- Solitary Rite for Baldur and Nanna 134
- Bragi's Ritual for Public Speaking 136
- Sacred Well Rite for Eir 137
- Freyr: A Man To Man Rite 139
- Four Directions Rite for Freya 143
- Forseti Ritual, in Two Parts 147
- A Blót to Frigga 150
- Frigga Blot 159
- Ritual for Jormundgand 168
- Loki Rite 170
- Evening Ritual to Mani 173
- Well of Wisdom Seidh Ritual For Mimir 175
- Devotional Rite for Njord 179
- Three Norns Ritual 181
- Walpurgisnacht Ritual for Odin 183
- Ritual In Honor Of Woden 188
- Devotional Rite for Sigyn 192
- Skadhi Blót 194
- Sunna Rite 201
- Farmer's Thorrablot 203
- Ritual to Tyr 204
- Oathing Rite for Ullr 206

Rituals for Many Purposes

- Rite of Yggdrasil 211
- Three and Three Protection Rite 221
- Warding Rite for Gerda 225
- Needfire Ritual 230
- Anglo-Saxon Blessing Rite 236
- Evening Rite of the Five Elements 244
- Rite for the Land 249
- Earth Healing Rite For Jord 251
- Acre Bot Ritual, Modernized 253
- Rune Creation Ritual 259
- Rune Tree Rite 264

Holda Housecleaning Rite 267
A Meal Blessing 269
Fidelity Ritual for Sif 272
A Northern-Tradition Sauna Ritual 277
Ritual for Healing of the Body 282
Thirteen Maidens Graduation Ritual 288
Heimdall Ritual for Blessing a Guard 295
Mordgud's Ritual for Blessing a Guard.............................. 297
Standing In The Shadows Rite 299
Chaining Fenris: A Ritual to Bind The Inner Beast 302
Hela's Rite of Unbinding 307
Solitary Rite for the Ancestors 313
Ancestor Ritual of the Four Directions 315
Bloodline Curse Aversion Rite for Hyndla 318
Ritual for Elevating the Troubled Dead 321
Ritual for Frith 326

foreword

To the casual observer, the form of the rituals found within modern Norse Neo-Paganism would seem to be fairly straightforward – one would assume that rituals from Àsatru or other forms of Northern European pagan reconstructionism[1] would find a place here as well. This is not always the case. Traditional Heathen rituals mainly fall into two categories: *blót* and *sumbel*. The former usually indicates a formal offering or sacrifice of some sort on the part of a family or community, while the latter term generally refers to a round of toasts made by a group in honor of a god or gods, ancestors, and/or honored persons living or dead.[2] Few solitary rituals appear to be used in mainstream Heathenry, and those that exist are due more to simple necessity than anything else – for example, when a Heathen finds him- or herself geographically isolated from others of the same faith and thus must make offerings or mark holy days alone. However, the strong emphasis on group observation in Àsatru/Heathen religious practice is not necessarily a part of all forms of Norse/Germanic paganism, which may be far less community- or kin-focused than concerned with the individual's unique relationship to his or her gods.

Many of those who have chosen to adopt the "Northern Tradition Pagan"[3] label – or who have merely chosen not to use "Àsatruar" or "Heathen" to describe themselves – may look to other sources than the accepted "lore" and related secondary academic sources for inspiration concerning rituals both personal and communal. As many modern Norse/Germanic religionists ultimately come to their beliefs through a

---

[1] "Reconstructionism" refers to those pagan religious traditions which seek to accurately recreate the practices, world-view, and beliefs of pre-Christian Europe via primary sources such as mythological poetry and contemporary accounts, or secondary sources such as academic interpretations of archaeological finds. Àsatru, Nova Romana, and Hellenismos are three such examples of modern reconstructionist pagan belief.

[2] *Exploring the Northern Tradition* by Galina Krasskova pp. 147-153, New Page Books 2005.

[3] This term was coined by the editor of this book, and refers to "reconstructionist-derived" Norse/Germanic Neo-Pagan practice and belief. A more detailed definition may be found here: http://www.northernpaganism.org/general/northern-tradition-paganism-heathenry.html

Wiccan or Neo-Pagan background after first leaving their birth religion, these approaches may vary. Some people shy away from anything which is reminiscent of Wiccan-inspired religious practice, while others feel free to incorporate a certain amount of modern Wicca-based ritual concepts (such as the "calling of quarters" and casting a circle) into their current practices. Still others may look further afield to unrelated cultures for inspiration, or combine several approaches depending on the occasion. Whatever the case, there seems to be much less tendency among non-reconstructionist, Norse-influenced Pagans (as opposed to strictly reconstructionist Heathens) to limit their rituals solely to the usual *sumbel* or *blót* formats.

Within traditional Heathenry, there is also less emphasis on the presence of the gods in worshipers' lives than there is among less traditional Northern Tradition Pagans or other Norse/Germanic religionists. This is not to argue or infer that such experience is totally lacking among those in more traditional circles, of course. However, in reconstructionist Heathenry one's personal relationships with the gods are not generally considered as important as one's relationships with one's ancestors, family, and community. Also, in reconstructionist Heathenry the luck and welfare of the group, family, or community is paramount versus that of the individual.[4]

In contrast, many non-reconstructionist Norse Pagans, Northern Tradition Pagans, and less traditional Heathens may find themselves in close, direct relationships with deities and spirits which do not always have an example from history or mythology to use as a justification. Deities may require specific and exacting behavior or observations from Their devotees, ancestors may not care whether or not one's blood descends from the "correct" ethnic group,[5] and personal or political inclinations may cause friction with more conservative groups.

---

[4] *Exploring the Northern Tradition* by Galina Krasskova pp. 141-145.
[5] "Folkishness" or "Folkism" is the belief that the indigenous religious traditions of one's ancestors are the best for a person to adopt for themselves, rather than converting to a "foreign" religion, such as Christianity for non-Hebrews or Middle Easterners. Folkish Heathens argue that those of non-Northern European descent should not be Heathen, but instead should follow "the gods of their own ancestors." It should be noted that not all Heathens subscribe to this belief, and there is much debate over whether or not Folkism is merely another name for racism.

Many non-reconstructionists may find themselves unwelcome in more strictly traditional venues where either their preferred deities or their emphasis on the welfare of the individual versus the group may clash with the goals of hard-line reconstructionists. Rather than consider these situations aberrant and thus to be shunned, it is the opinion of this writer that it is better to meet the Powers on Their own terms. After all, there is no rule or law stating that the gods (or the ancestors, for that matter) are obligated to behave in ways that reflect our current understanding of the ancient history and customs of pre-Christian Europe.

The rituals in this book have been compiled as both a guide for handling various occasions that do not fit neatly into either *blót* or *sumbel* format, and as an inspiration for readers to create their own unique rites, with an eye towards immanent and personal experience of the Holy Ones and of the various Powers. They were contributed by people from a wide range of backgrounds, from "fringe" Heathens to avowed Neo-Pagans to those who prefer not to use any of the aforementioned labels at all. There are both group and solitary rites, rituals of worship and rituals of purpose. In any case, all of the ceremonies included here were created by actual, living devotees of the Norse/Germanic gods, for love and honor of the Holy Ones, the ancestors, and the living spirits of the Nine Worlds, and for us to acknowledge our place among Them. May they bless and enhance your life, luck, and understanding of the Powers that be.

ELIZABETH VONGVISITH
MAY, 2012

Beginnings

Creating Sacred Space: Opening Rites
Raven Kaldera

Creating sacred space is an important part of ritual – in fact, it's the very first thing that we do. It's especially important, I believe, for a community to have one to three standard "opening" rituals which are short, simple, and clearly signaling to a group of people that Sacred Space Is Now Opening Up. The rite should ideally work well at the beginning of any ritual, with any deities invoked, which is why I've not included any that center around the invocation of one particular god, with the exception of the one that calls on the Duergar of the Four Directions.

Wiccan and Wiccan-derived groups generally start with something around the four elements – earth, air, fire, and water, which are symbols common to most Neo-Pagans. Because I've been asked for it frequently, I did write an opening rite that deals in these symbols, with a Nordic slant. I also include here my favorite opening, which is in Anglo-Saxon, and a couple of others as well. Some are very short, finished in only a couple of minutes. Some are longer. Opening rites don't need to be elaborate; they need only be riveting to the attention, and understandable in their symbolism.

Anglo-Saxon Warding

I use this as my standard space-warding, whether that's before a group ritual, a personal rite, or a working with clients. It is derived from the last verse of the Anglo-Saxon *Song of the Nine Sacred Herbs*, and is made to be used with *recels* – a burning stick of dried, bound plant matter, the Northern Tradition version of "smudge". I generally prefer to use mugwort or juniper – the sacred recaning plants of northwestern and northeastern Europe respectively. The Anglo-Saxon words are:

> *Gif ænig attor cume eastan fleogan*
> *oððe ænig norðan cume, oððe ænig suðan cume,*
> *oððe ænig westan ofer werðeode.*
> *Ic ana wat ea rinnende*
> *þær þa nygon nædran nean behealdað,*
> *Motan ealle weoda nu wyrtum aspringan,*
> *Sæs toslupan, eal sealt wæter,*
> *ðonne ic þis attor of ðe geblawe.*

The words translated into modern English are:

> If any poison comes flying from the east,
> Or if any comes from the north,
> Or if any comes from the south,
> Or any from the west over the people,
> I know a running stream
> And there the nine poisons one beholds,
> But from the weeds new herbs spring up!
> The seas part, all salt water,
> And now this poison from you I blow!

Start by waving the stick in the four directions, as you call each one on the first three lines. Then circle it around you. End after you finish singing the last line by actually blowing on the smoking recaning stick, directing the smoke where it seems more appropriate.

Pronunciation of Old English is a matter of much debate. The truth is that we are not completely certain how many of the vowels were pronounced, and different experts have slightly differing opinions. At any rate, I have reconstructed the pronunciations as best I can. For a simple recording of the entire song (not just the last verse), in order that you might learn it, you can check on the online herbal on my Northern Shamanism website at http://www.northernshamanism.org/herbal/song.html and just listen for the last verse. If you'd like to own it, my CD with this song (and others), *Nine Sea Songs*, is available for online ordering at: http://asphodelpress.com/ntshamanism.html. This is in no way a professional CD, just me and a guitar and drum, but it will give you an idea of the song tune and pronunciation.

World Creation Opening
Raven Kaldera

For this rite, you will need a candle (symbolizing the fire of Surt and Muspellheim); a chalice of ice water (symbolizing the ice and rivers of Niflheim); a cup of cow's milk (symbolizing Audumhla's gift); and a large bowl with a few stones in it (symbolizing Ymir). Ideally, this rite should start in darkness. The officiant says:

> For the worlds were born in fire and in ice.
> First there was ice, over mountain's stone.

Pour the ice water over the stones.

> Then the darkness was rent asunder,
> And fire came forth from Ginnungagap.

Light the candle.

> Fire and ice met, and ice became water,
> And Life grew in places unexpected,
> Life was nourished from Source unexpected.

Pour the cup of milk over the stones.

> So began Life, which led to Death,
> Yet brought forth Life again, endlessly.
> As they began, so we go on,
> Between heat and cold, darkness and light,
> Between fire and ice as of old.

Step back and begin whatever rite you choose.

Jormundgand Opening Ritual
Raven Kaldera

For this rite, one person runs around the perimeter of the group with a stick, flying from which is a long green serpent made of fabric or some other appropriate material. The runner circles the people three times, while a speaker in the center says:

> As the Serpent swims the endless seas
> Round Midgard's many, so we are surrounded
> By ward, by will, by Wyrd's wending way.
> As it is bound and boundary, so we are bounded
> By guardian Gods who look with love each day
> Upon our hearts, and so we hail them high:
> Returning love for love, from roots to sky.

This is a good rite to open a blot or faining, where the folk will hail specific Gods, or where many Gods will promptly be hailed around a circle and given libation.

Four Directions and Nine Worlds:
Cosmological Opening Rite
Raven Kaldera

This rite is vaguely parallel to Neo-Pagan circle castings, although it does not necessarily denote space through which one cannot pass (unless that is the intent of the caster). It is especially useful for group workings in an intrafaith context, where there will be people from different Neo-Pagan traditions present, or for the opening to a ritual that is mixed-tradition – Northern Tradition and some other Neo-Pagan context. If a shorter rite is needed, only the first four lines can be used.

The rite can be done by one person, or by different people in the different directions. The caster(s) can use props – blades, wands, etc. – or simply lift their arms in celebration. If props are used, we might suggest four hammers tied with appropriately colored ribbons for the Duergar of the Four Directions, a horn of mead poured out for Asgard, something glittery for Ljossalfheim, earth for Vanaheim, a stone blade for Jotunheim, a long green or blue ribbon for Midgard, a flame for Muspellheim, a forged iron implement for Svartalfheim, a bowl of ice water for Niflheim, and stones for Helheim. Alternately, a libation could be carried around and a little poured out at each stop.

~ ~ ~ ~

To begin, face the East and say:

    Hail Austri, Guardian of Sunna's Rising!
    Anchor us in all our beginnings!

Face the South and say:

    Hail Sudri, Guardian of Sunna's Height!
    Anchor us in all our creations!

Face the West and say:

    Hail Vestri, Guardian of Sunna's Passing!
    Anchor us in all our dreaming!

Face the North and say:

    Hail Nordri, Guardian of Mani's Riding!
    Anchor us in all our endings!

Face the East and say:

Hail to the Powers of the Sky!
May the blessed ones of Asgard guard us from beyond the bend of Bifrost!

Face the South and say:

Hail to the Powers of Light!
May the Alfar of Ljossalfheim guard us from beyond twilight's tree!

Face the West and say:

Hail to the Powers of Earth!
May the sacred ones of Vanaheim guard us from beyond sunset's sacrifice!

Face the North and say:

Hail to the Powers of the Mountain!
May the wise ones of Jotunheim guard us from beyond the forest's faring!

Face the East and say:

Hail to the Powers of the Folk!
May we guard each other in the might of Midgard's circle!

Face the South and say:

Hail to the Powers of Fire!
May the ancient flame guard us from beyond the heat's hallowing!

Face the West and say:

Hail to the Powers of Craft!
May the Duergar of Nidavellir guard us from beyond the forge's flame!

Face the North and say:

Hail to the Powers of Ice!
May the eternal storms guard us from beyond the river's running!

Face the people and say:

Hail to the Ancestors who came before us,
and may they guard us from beyond the door of Death.

Warding Rite of the Four Directions
Galina Krasskova

As Northern Traditionalists, there are many Holy Powers and spirits to which we ought to properly pay heed. Among those often neglected in contemporary practice are four Duergar beings, mentioned only briefly in the surviving lore that the spirit workers would do well to honor: Austri, Sudri, Vestri, and Nordri. We really don't know very much about Them. They're only mentioned in the Voluspa and Gylfaginning, and even there, the information is scanty. We have the following gems of knowledge:

Austri (east), Sudri (south), Vestri (west) and Nordri (north) are four Duergar who support the vault of heaven, crafted from Ymir's skull, each in the direction indicated by Their name. This tells us several things; first, that They are extremely old. They were formed around that time when Odin, Vili, and Ve slaughtered Ymir and crafted the worlds from His carcass. They support the vault of the sky, and this does not specify just Midgard's sky. In other words, they support the structure of the worlds: all the worlds. They guard the quarters, and no one approaches the Tree without Their knowledge. Their job is to maintain the integrity of the upward support of the worlds.

Many traditions have a Deity whose specific job is to guard the gateways between the worlds, the crossroads of the worlds if you will. They are gatekeepers and guardians and are often hailed first in rituals. Gods like Ellegua, Exu, and Ganesha (for example) determine what comes in and what goes out. They open the doors of communication, and unlock the gates of the worlds so that energy may freely flow. They are powerful allies and help gird the worlds, all the worlds, against contamination and internal destruction. In the Northern Tradition, Loki sometimes takes on this job, but the four dwarves of the compass points fulfill it always on a cosmic level. What Loki will often do for those of us here on Midgard, Austri, Sudri, Vestri, and Nordri do at the Tree.

They contain. They maintain that which is hallowed. They contain all the power that can manifest within hallowed space and keep it from leaking and contaminating that which is "profane" space. They help to order the smooth functioning of the multiverse. They watch over the Tree and note the comings and goings of those who Work there (i.e.

rune workers). This means that They would be the appropriate guardians to call upon should one need assistance in consecrating a space as holy. To be holy is to be separate from regular being. It is to be touched by that which is Other, to be sacred, and given over to the Gods. This is our territory, the territory that we as spiritworkers and shamans are honed and trained to navigate. A consecrating ward is a means of creating a borderland wherein others, unprepared and untrained can be brought in for very carefully crafted engagement with the sacred too. While this is primarily priestcraft, there are times when others will have to do it as well, so it's good to know.

In honoring Them I was also instructed to honor the Tree; to pour out offerings directly to Yggdrasil. So, one can honor the four dwarves and the four cardinal elements if one feels the need to be particularly formal (and one should honor these dwarves anyway, over and above consecrating a space) or one can make a fire blessing. Perhaps the most traditional way of consecrating a space is to carry fire around that space, asking that the spirits of fire drive out any negative energy or beings. Fire by its very nature cleanses, devours, and transmutes. That is its nature and that is what makes it such a powerful ally in the warding process.

This ritual requires a main speaker and four others, of any gender, to represent the voices of the Four Duergar Gods. Start by going to the east and lighting a candle, preferably in the colors of spring or dawn. Place fresh or dried flowers next to it, and say the following prayer:

> Hail, you who guide the spring winds
> Rustling the leaves of the World Tree,
> Hallow and protect the beginning of this rite,
> O Austri who holds up the sky at dawn.

Austri:
> Look to the stars.
> Look to the sky.
> Always, look forward.
> You must know and see where your work will strike,
> How it will affect the wyrd.

You must know these things, not just for you
But for those who will follow you;
Not just for you, but for your children
And your children's children.
Do nothing, until you know what it is exactly that you do.
Look to the east before you begin and consider everything.

Next go to the south and light a candle, preferably in the colors of summer or noon. Place a hammer (and an anvil if you have one) next to it, and say the following prayer:

> Hail, you who guide the summer winds
> Tossing the branches of the World Tree,
> Hallow and protect the climax of this rite,
> O Sudri who holds up the sky at noon.

Sudri:

> Focus.
> Work with passion but work with focus.
> It must never yield.
> It must never waver,
> Not for a single second during the work that you do.
> Focus as though everything in your world
> Depended upon that skill.
> It does. Believe me, children, it does.

Next go to the west and light a candle, preferably in the colors of autumn or evening. Place a sheaf of grain or a bunch of dried leaves next to it, and say the following prayer:

> Hail, you who guide the autumn winds
> Circling the trunk of the World Tree,
> Hallow and protect the pauses in this rite,
> O Vestri who holds up the sky at twilight.

Vestri:

> Know what you can control,
> And what lies beyond your reach.
> Accept this. There is that which you may wield,
> And that which will flow through you to wield itself.
> Know the difference.
> Know yourself and why you do the work that you do.

> Know what you will sacrifice
> And what should never, ever be placed upon that altar.
> Know when to yield and when not to yield.
> Know and do not waver in the knowing.

Next go to the north and light a candle, preferably in the colors of winter or night. Place a piece of ice or a bare branch next to it, and say the following prayer:

> Hail, you who guide the winter winds
> Whistling around the trunk of the World Tree,
> Hallow and protect the ending of this rite,
> O Nordri who holds up the sky at midnight.

Nordri:
> Look to your roots.
> Look to your dead.
> Look to the source of your power.
> Look to the Tree and take your turn at nourishing its roots.
> If you do not do these things,
> You deserve to be swept away,
> Into the aether, into the void, into nothingness.
> This you will have done to yourself.

Then go to the middle and lift your arms, and cry out:

> Hail to Irminsul, the pole from deep below to high above,
> The living Tree that bears the Worlds,
> That holds all things in its branches.
> Hail to the Dead at the roots,
> Hail to the Sky above the leaves,
> And all that is in between.

Pour out a libation to the Tree, bowing and touching the earth or the floor as you do so. Then you are ready to begin your rite.

Divide And Conquer: Advanced Group Liturgical Design
(Or How to Honor a Dozen Gods With a Hundred People)
Linda Demissy

In this article, I'd like to go over some common ritual design problems and ways to fix them so everyone can have a better spiritual experience. The first section deals with optimizing repetitive ritual tasks such as purifications, the second is for communing with gods and wights as meaningfully as possible. Whether you're writing rituals for a small group or trying to plan for larger groups, I hope you'll find these ideas useful.

ଔ ଔ ଵ ଵ

Ever been painfully bored at a public ritual? I know I have. Rites that work beautifully for a handful of people usually don't work very well for fifty or a hundred. Yet people keep writing small group rites for larger groups because that's what they know how to do. Neo-Pagan rituals were originally designed for covens of no more than a dozen people, honoring two deities and four directions. When you have more gods or more people, you need to apply Caesar's rule of "divide and conquer" to make it work.

Before I explain it, I ask that you gather your courage. This solution uses one of the darkest and most terrifying forms of magic. Even people who read the Necronomicon as bathroom literature and laugh at Nameless Horrors typically recoil in dread at the mere mention of this word: Mathematics. With the eldritch power of basic math, you too can make your rites work with larger groups and longer lists of invited deities. I promise it won't stain your soul ... much.

Do you cringe at the mere mention of math, thinking it coldly rational and devoid of meaning? Let me remind you that until a few hundred years ago, mathematician was just another way to say magician and astrologer. Astrologers were the only ones who needed higher math, specifically geometry. The paths of planets and stars, the holy principles above that guide the path of life below, these were all studied in the language of mathematics across many religions. One for unity and two for duality, three for fertility and four for stability ... numbers have meaning.

Architects were the other ones to use math extensively. Why do you think Freemasons became a secret society? They were hiding their secret math spell formulae! Mind you, they also preferred geometry over algebra (whose popularity is entirely modern). Ancient Greek philosophers wrote a lot about sacred geometry and even formed secret societies around it. To understand geometry was to understand the gods and the cosmos. So I encourage you to give numbers another chance. When you're in a hard spot, they're the ones you can really count on.

Just think of it this way: math formulae are exactly like spell formulae. You can memorize them and apply them like recipes, or you can understand how they work and modify them to do your bidding. We'll start with simple and obvious examples and progressively make them more complex.

Part 1: Ritual is repetition

Purifying Twelve People

Things that are trivial for solitary devotions take a little bit more time when you have just a few more people. Asperging with water takes about five seconds per person (including the time it takes to walk over to the next person and say something like "may the waters purify you"). Smudging[1] one person takes me twenty-five seconds if I sing through the entire mugwort verse of the Song of the Nine Sacred Herbs[2]. If I'm doing it quickly and not doing the full verse for each person, it takes me about ten seconds to go down one side of the person and up the other. Here are some options for doing it in a group of twelve, assuming ten seconds to smudge and five seconds to asperge:

One at a time: One person does all the purifications, going around with water to each person, then doing the same with smoke. Time: Three minutes.

The spell formula is: (12 people × 15 seconds) + (12 people × 10 seconds)

Two at a time: One person purifies with water at the same time as another does it with smoke. Smudging takes two minutes (12x10s), asperging one minute (12x5s). Time: Two minutes.

Spell formula: Whichever is greater between 12x10s and 12x5s.

---

[1] or recaning if you want to use Saxon words
[2] From the Nine Sea Songs and Other Tides CD by Raven Kaldera.

Twelve at a time: Everyone purifies themselves simultaneously. You need multiple bowls, mugwort sticks and lit candles for everyone to do it at once. Time: about thirty seconds (while people fumble around for matches).

Three minutes versus thirty seconds, who cares, right? For small groups, it doesn't really matter.

Purifying a Hundred People

Now you have a hundred people, one bowl and one mugwort stick. Remembering that purifications take fifteen seconds per person, let's do the math. 100 × 15 seconds is like 25 × 1 minute (dividing 100 by 4 and multiplying 15 by 4 to count in minutes) which means purifications will take *twenty-five minutes*. Yikes!

That's completely unreasonable. What can we do to improve it? Well, we can asperge and smudge more quickly. Say we do it in ten seconds. Then 100 people × 10 seconds ... is 1000 seconds. Divide that by 60 seconds per minute, and you get about *seventeen minutes*.

That's still far too long, even if we use the *Standard Ritual Fix #1:* Chanting. Chanting is wonderful, but it shouldn't be used like duct tape to fix poorly designed rituals. After a while people get tired, bored, cranky, and their energy drops along with their enthusiasm. How about we just *run* with the stick and the bowl of water around the circle? We can certainly do that in one minute!

Wait! Stop! We aren't flipping fast food burgers here, and this *isn't* McPaganism[3]. We *could* rush through the steps, but what would be the point of that? No one will get anything out of it, which defeats the whole purpose of doing a spiritual rite. We need to thinks about it differently.

Divide and Conquer

The first step in using "divide and conquer" is to decide how long you *want* the purifications to take. That's right, it's your rite and you get to choose. I think three minutes is quite adequate. So how do we make purifications last only three minutes? By using math and delegating. First, let's figure out how much smudging one celebrant can do in three minutes, assuming it takes them ten seconds per participant. Our spell formula is:

---

[3] Unless you're Scottish of course.

1 smudger = 3 minutes divided by 10 seconds per person
= 3 × 60 seconds / 10 seconds per person
= 3 × 6 = 18 people

Our bold smudger can thus purify eighteen people in three minutes. But there's a hundred participants, so how many do we need to get everything done on time? 100 people / 18 people = 5.5 smudgers. Thus we need six smudgers and six mugwort sticks.

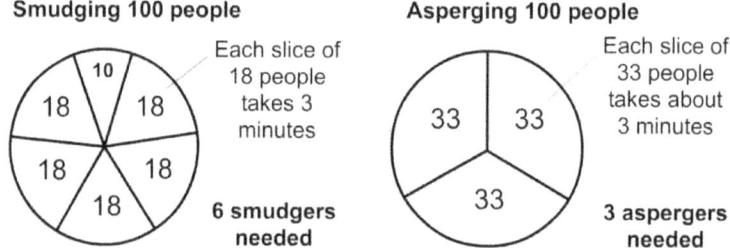

At the same time, we can have a few more assistants do the asperging.

1 asperger = 3 minutes divided by 5 seconds per person
= 3 × 60 seconds / 5 seconds per person
= 3 × 6 × 10 / 5 = 3 × 6 × 2 = 36 people.

One asperger can purify thirty-six people in three minutes. 100 / 36 = 2.8 aspergers. So you need three bowls and three people doing it. Thus to purify a hundred people in three minutes, you need a staff of nine people: 6 smudgers and 3 aspergers.

What if there's only four of you leading the rite? How long would it take? Try it out on paper. The answer (#1) is at the end of the article. *Hint: use three sticks and one bowl. Come on, you can do it! We're not summoning Cthulhu with non-Euclidian geometry. We're just doing a little division.*

The Simple Way: Assume you need one assistant per twenty people. For a hundred people, get five assistants; for two hundred, get ten.

The Trap: The first reaction of many Pagan ritual leaders when given five assistants is to assign each of them a different element or task. This is a common mistake. If you have each assistant doing a different element, you don't divide the time, you multiply it! They each have to go around to every single person and that takes seventeen minutes for a hundred people. In order to divide the time, your assistants must all be doing the same thing.

This principle can be applied to any ritual action that is repeated for each participant, such as blessing people as they enter the ritual space. Another element to watch out for is the *central mystery*, and I'm guilty of making that mistake.

Giving Options – The Central Mystery That Failed

Three women sat at the center, embodying the three Fates. Each participant was told to get blessings and advice from each of them, starting with the Fate of the past. A hundred participants, thirty seconds of advice per person, you do the math. Really, do the math, the answer (#2) is at the end of the article. If I hadn't been one of the Fates, my voice would have been hoarse from chanting for so long.

For that many people, you really can't create this kind of bottleneck. People should be asked to choose *one and only one* of the Fates to consult. That roughly divides the time by three, assuming each option is equally popular. You'll have to "sell" the idea that each option is equally useful for different reasons if you want the people to be evenly split among the Fates. Fifteen minutes spent on the rite's central mystery is reasonable. *Fifty* minutes is not, especially if you're the one who waited forty-nine minutes for everyone else to get through it. So, to summarize this part:

For purifications: reduce the time by splitting work among multiple celebrants, i.e. get more people to help you.

For the central mystery: reduce the time by splitting participants into a few groups.

Part 2: Planning For Epiphanies

Solo Rite For Six Gods

Let's say you're on your own, and decide to spend an evening honoring your six favorite gods. You start with one, light their candle, commune, recite poetry, etc. A little later, you check the clock and realize it's time for bed, but you've only gone through three of these deities. No biggie, you can do the other three tomorrow. No one is there to be disappointed that things didn't go as planned.

But perhaps you *really* wanted to honor all six that night, because they're a family group, and you don't want any of them to feel like you're giving them less importance. In that case, you'll have to manage your time and decide how long to spend on your devotional. Let's say you choose to do an hour of devotions. Basic math tells you that to honor six gods in sixty minutes, you should spend ten minutes on each. That was easy! *See, you're good at math!* What if you had two hours? How long would you then spend with each deity? *(See answer #3 at the end).*

More Gods Than You Can Shake a Stick At

If you've ever been to a rite that honors a long list of gods, you've probably noticed the problems with doing so. Doing long descriptive evocations of each deity works for up to about three or so main guests. After that, it becomes a tiresome laundry list which bores participants, dampens the energy and stifles their enthusiasm. One alternative is to keep the evocations very short, maybe one sentence, but that doesn't give anyone much time to make a real connection to the deities. You have a choice between boring and superficial, neither of which are useful for creating meaningful spiritual experiences. There's a third choice, though.

Sharing the Work of Worship

If you have twelve deities, and you'd like people to spend ten minutes communing with each of them ... just get folks into twelve smaller groups. Give a symbolic prop and a cue card to one person in each group (outlining the basic attributes, symbols and typical actions for that deity). Send each group off on their own to commune for ten minutes with their respective deity, then call them back.

Each deity thus gets sufficient time to be honored properly, a decent connection with their worshippers, and participants have enough time to make a spiritual connection with the deity they've chosen. The downside is that each participant only gets to commune with one deity.

One solution is to have people rotate between "deity stations" so they get ten minutes with each deity. For twelve deities, that will take two hours (spell formula: 12 deities × 10 minutes = 120 minutes).

Another solution is to do a form of "show and tell": Instead of just going to commune with the deity, have the participants brainstorm and prepare a performance piece designed to be one minute long which they will then share with the larger group. This way gives folks a personal understanding of their chosen deity by creating something to honor them. They also get to see a completely original performance piece made by others. The benefits are:

- Everyone gets new insight into each deity.
- The ritual organizers don't have to come up with twelve brilliant devotional pieces (and lead them) because the participants will do that on their own.
- Everybody wins, and no one gets burned out.

But what if you don't have a hundred people? How many do you need to honor a dozen gods? You need twelve. It doesn't take a group to do a performance, and in fact, it's often easier to plan something on your own than to coordinate the actions of a group. Each person picks a deity, their prop, their cue card, and goes to brainstorm by themselves for ten minutes. It works really well, and the whole ritual can be completed in about half an hour. Count three minutes for the choosing of a deity, ten minutes of brainstorming, twelve minutes of performing, and maybe five minutes of transition time.

If you have only six people, it's still doable, but they each have to prepare a performance for two deities. Some people can handle that, some can't, It really depends on who you have. If you have nine people, at least three of them should be able to do double duty like that. We've very successfully honored nine deities with six people, and ten deities with nine people.

How Many is Too Many Gods?

I personally wouldn't invite more than a dozen or so deities to a rite with this method, but if you were foolhardy enough to try, I'd suggest making groups of groups so it doesn't get too confusing. With a dozen people, you could probably do a rite for the twenty-four Futhark runes and draw them on their palms. One person would have Fehu on one hand, and Uruz on the other, do two brief performances, and then something that points out how they're similar and how they're different. Ansuz and Thurisaz also make a good pair, and so on. Yes, you have twenty-four concepts, but they get reduced to twelve pairs. It's more manageable and less confusing that way.

Putting it All Together: Six People, Six Gods

Let's take a simple case of six people honoring six gods. What are our choices?

Sequential: Everyone spends ten minutes communing together with the first deity, then the second, third, etc. Time: 6 gods × 10 minutes = 60 minutes.

Round-Robin: Set up six shrines around the ritual area, assign a person to each shrine, rotate every ten minutes. Time: 6 gods × 10 minutes = 60 minutes.

Sumbel: Using a talking stick or a drinking horn, each person in the circle spends 1 minute briefly honoring that deity however they see fit. It could be words of praise, a short story, a poem, a joke, etc. Each round is dedicated to a different deity. Time: 6 folk × 6 gods × 1 minute = 36 minutes.

In the next options, instead of everyone honoring everyone, we assign one god to each person. Let them choose their deity or let the fates and the deities decide by doing it randomly. People can pick goddess names out of a hat, colored marbles, or one of six runes in a bag (establishing which rune is for which deity beforehand), etc. If a goddess wants someone's attention, it's a good way to let her get it.

Sharing Circle: Each person picks *one* of the deities to privately meditate on and honor for ten minutes. Someone starts drumming or rings a bell to call everyone back when the time is up. Again as with the talking stick (sumbel option), there is a sharing circle where everyone recounts their personal gnosis experience for one minute. Time: 10 minutes meditating + 6 minutes sharing = 16 minutes.

Performance: As above, each person spends ten minutes alone with one of the six deities. However, the focus this time is to prepare some sort of performance for that deity. It could be a poem, song, dance, drawing, story or theatrical performance, and it should last about a minute. People come back, and take turns performing their piece. Time: 10 minutes brainstorming + 6 minutes performing = 16 minutes

The greatest advantage of the final option is that it scales up really well. If you have twelve people, they go off in pairs to prepare their one minute performance. If you have sixty people, they go off in groups of ten to prepare their one-minute group performance. No matter how many participants you have, it doesn't make the rite any longer. In option two and three, it still takes one minute per participant per deity, so with sixty people and six gods, that means 6 × 60 or 360 minutes.

Twelve Gods And A Hundred People

Let's look at how each method scales up for honoring twelve gods, depending on the number of participants.

Number of Participants:	1	12	50	100
1) Sequential 12 Gods × 10 min	120 min	120 min	120 min	120 min
2) Round-Robin 12 Gods × 10 min	120 min	120 min	120 min	120 min
3) Sumbel 12 Gods × Participants	12 min	144 min	600 min	1200 min
4) Sharing Circle 10 min + Participants	12 min	22 min	60 min	110 min
5) Performance 10 min + 12 Gods	22 min	22 min	22 min	22 min

What I'd like you to notice is how each option scales up in terms of time. In the first two cases, it's essentially a bunch of people doing solo rites in the same space. It's no better than doing it on your own. In the third case people share what they know of that deity, but they don't have time to get any new insights. The deity gets honored, but the total understanding of the group doesn't improve by much.

In the fourth case, we start applying the principle of "divide and conquer". Each person spends enough time communing to get some new insights, then they share and *everyone* gets new insights. The fifth case is similar, but you're actually creating art that makes a potent devotional offering, as well as being inspiring to others in the group. Shared insights may or may not be remembered, but dramatic performances tend to stick in the mind of viewers a lot more, providing new material to meditate on and get insights from. It's like those gum commercials: juicy, and the flavor lasts a long time.

The last two are also interesting in that they involve two kinds of trance. One is a communion trance where you're seeking inspiration or communication from the deity or spirit. The second is an artistic trance. I believe the Celtic expression of "fire in the head" applies. If you're inspired, it's an altered state. Creative frenzy is a holy state all on its own. In Norse terms, it's getting a smidgeon of the Mead of Inspiration, and you can thank Odin, Bragi or Kvasir for that. You'd be amazed at what people come up with. I know I was. There's only the small matter of everyone knowing the deities they're honoring to consider.

What's She the Goddess of Again?

Maybe your group knows everything there is to know about each goddess you plan to honor. Yeah, right. Groups will have one or more lore geeks – I mean scholars – who can quote scriptures with the best of them. The rest usually have only a vague notion beyond the short list of their favorite deities. It gets worse in large public rituals where you'll have people who are completely unfamiliar with your pantheon or who are very new to it. You need to give them tactical support in their devotional work.

That's why I suggest you make cue cards. For sequential rites, you can read them out before everyone goes to meditate on that deity. For round-robin rites you can leave one with each shrine. For sumbels you can read them before that deity's round. For sharing circles, each person will need their own cue card, since they're all meditating on different deities. If you have sixty people, you need sixty cards; ten cards per deity. For performance, you just need one cue card per deity because the group will be sharing that cue card. It's also great to make a prop for that deity which the group can use or hold onto. Using objects in that way helps create hallows for your group (sacred items associated with a deity).

A Sample Cue Card

Let me give you an example of a cue card for a performance piece in honor of ... Mr. Spock! (No, he's not a god, no matter what some Trek types say, but we'll use him as an example anyway.)

What kind of performance could you do based on this? Some people could act emotionally: hugging, laughing. Others would then comment on it being illogical to do religious devotion for an imaginary

> **Mr. Spock = Science Officer, Starship Enterprise**
> **Embodiment of Logic**
>
> Dismiss anything that has to do with emotions. Only logic matters. Judge things to be logical, or highly illogical. Show no emotions, rationalize anything you want to do for emotional reasons as being logical. Act honorably. Spock is an alien from the planet Vulcan.
> **Symbols:** Vulcan salute: form a V between the first two and next two sets of fingers. Pointy ears and green blood.
> **Actions:** Vulcan salute with the phrase "live long and prosper". Arching one eyebrow in contempt. Estimating impossible odds precisely. Giving numeric answers with lots of decimals. Pinching people at the base of the neck and shoulder to render them unconscious.

character, while the first gave passionate reasons to honor Spock. It could be a game of doing silly things to make the stoic-faced Vulcans laugh while they make comments on the illogic of it all. It could be explaining some daring plan and having the Vulcans comment on the declining and astronomically unlikely probability of success. It could be a jeering gauntlet, insulting the impassive Vulcans who walk through it. People with greater knowledge of the character could certainly propose things not detailed on the cue card. What do the viewers get from this? Perhaps an understanding that logic is only one part of a person; it cannot stand on its own without contrast with emotions and both have value.

Mystery Plays

Witnessing a mystery play is totally unlike reading about it. The whole point of a mystery is that it cannot be explained, it has to be experienced. Performers and viewers both get to experience something in this which cannot be reduced to words. It's like talking about sex. You can talk about it all you want, but it's not the same as the experience of it. Spiritual mysteries are like that and rites are attempts at sharing these mysteries.

I hope these ideas are useful to you in designing rituals. I share them in honor of Isaac Bonewits, from whom I have learned so much in terms of ritual design. May he live long and prosper in our memories.

Oh, and one more thing. Please, you know that super-dry ritual bread that makes your mouth feel like the Sahara desert? It should be shared *before* the ritual drink, especially if you expect people to chant afterward.

ॐ ॐ ॐ ॐ

Answers:

Answer 1: With four celebrants available for a hundred people, we assign 1 to asperge and 3 to smudge.

We already know one asperger can purify 36 people in 3 minutes, which is about a third of the group. That's 3 minutes for the first third, 3 minutes for the second, 3 minutes for the last, which means about 9 minutes. Our detailed spell formula is:

100 people × 5 seconds = 500 seconds

500 seconds / 60 seconds per minute = 50/6 = 25/3 = 8.3 minutes

We have 3 people doing smudging, so they each need to do a third of the group, which is 33 people.

33 people × 10 seconds = 330 seconds

330 seconds / 60 seconds per minute = 33 / 6 = 5.5 minutes.

After 5 ½ minutes, smudging will be done, but you'll need to wait the full 8.3 minutes for asperging to be done. Knowing this, you could recruit someone at the rite to help with water purifications. A second person would cut the time in half, down to 4 minutes. This is pretty reasonable, and the total time is down to 5 ½ minutes (the time it takes to smudge).

Answer 2: 2 hours is 2 × 60 minutes. No need to calculate that, it's a waste of effort. You just want to divide that by 6 gods. So 2 × 60 minutes / 6 gods.

Simplify the sixes, since 6 divided by 6 is one. You get 2 × 10 minutes / 1 = 20 minutes.

Answer 3: 100 people × 30 seconds = 100 × ½ minute = 50 minutes.

Rites of Passage

Ritual to Bless a Newborn
Raven Kaldera

All should gather either in some outside place if the weather and season permit, or inside if they do not. If possible, the mother should bring either the afterbirth or, if this has not been saved, some cloth or paper with the blood of the childbirth on it. If the child is adopted or the mother has died, this step can be skipped. However, assuming that something has been brought, a large tub of soil should be prepared if this is an interior rite. If it is held outside in a place where it is appropriate, a hole should be dug with a shovel passed hand to hand among those present. The hole in the earth, or the hole in the tub of earth and the tub itself, should be large enough to easily absorb the following:

- A small cake, baked with seeds.
- A cup of milk – cow, goat, sheep, human, it does not matter which.
- A cup of mead.
- A handful of grain.
- A small fruit.
- A sprinkling of salt.
- A spoonful of honey.
- A spoonful of vinegar.
- A handful of dried nettles.
- A handful of dried elder flowers.
- A handful of dried chamomile blossoms.
- A small polished stone, of a type to be ideally determined by divination.
- After these, a small tree sapling, shrub, perennial herb, or other plant.

To begin, the parents step forward, carrying the child. The officiant steps forward and says the following prayer:

> Hail to those who have sent this new soul into the world,
> And may all the world stand forth to greet him/her.
>
> O newcomer to the bounds of Midgard,
> May you grow a strong *huge* in a strong *lich*,

And may learning pass many-gifted into your hands.
May you always have a warm hearth to come home to,
A full cup offered to you,
A safe haven to rest your head.
May the storm pass you by,
The fire only warm you,
The tides bear you up,
And the landvaettir be a friend beneath your feet.
May your ancestral Mothers offer you courage,
May your ancestral Fathers offer you wisdom,
Or if you must forge away from your blood's path,
May your tale be one to inspire generations to come.

Hail to those who have sent this new soul into the world,
And may all the world stand forth to greet him/her.

The eldest person present steps forward and says, "In the name of the ancestors, may you be nourished," and drops the small seed-cake into the hole.

The child's mother takes the afterbirth, or bit of bloody cloth, and casts it into the hole, saying: "I brought you forth with pain and love, made of my own flesh and blood. Like the seed in the earth, you came into the light."

The child's mother then takes the cup of milk and hands it to the officiant, who anoints the child with it. The child's mother then takes it back and pours it into the hole, saying: "Child of mine, may your spirit blossom like the starry sky overhead."

The child's father steps forward with the cup of mead, and hands it to the officiant, who anoints the child with it. The child's father then takes it back and pours it into the hole, saying: "Child of mine, may your spirit bloom like the rising Sun." *(Note: If there is only one parent, that parent does both of these things. A same-sex couple can divide up the roles as they like.)*

Another stands forth, sprinkles a handful of grain into the hole, and says: "Hope of the future, may your beginnings reap a fertile harvest."

Another stands forth, drops a small fruit into the hole, and says: "Hope of the future, may your beginnings bear fruit in the fullness of time."

Another stands forth, sprinkles a little salt into the hole, and says: "Hope of the future, may you always have enough to survive, and do more than survive."

Another stands forth, drips a spoonful of honey into the hole, and says: "Hope of the future, may you have sweetness in your relationships."

Another stands forth, drips in the spoonful of vinegar, and says: "Hope of the future, may you find worthy work that captures your heart and your hands."

Another stands forth, tosses in a handful of dried nettles, and says, "Hope of the future, may you find blessings in all obstacles."

Another stands forth, tosses in a handful of dried elder flowers, and says, "Hope of the future, may you always find healing of body and soul."

Another stands forth, tosses in a handful of dried chamomile, and says, "Hope of the future, may you sleep soundly in the arms of love."

The officiant stands forth and places a small polished stone in the hole, saying: "Child who has come through the door of life, ancestor brought back to us or soul new as the dawn, we welcome you to this community. May it be a foundation stone that bears you up. May it be a keystone of your learning. May it be a stepping-stone to your future. May it be a hearthstone to come home to. May it be a runestone to remember you always."

Everyone cries "Hail (*child's name*)!" and the babe is lifted toward the sky by many hands. The tree, shrub or plant is then placed in the hole and dug in, and watered. If it is in a pot, it will be planted later on land where it can stay, and can be visited.

Seven-Year Rite
Raven Kaldera

In old folklore, children were said to have passed a special milestone of growth at the age of seven. It was thought that their minds took a leap of comprehension at this point, and also that any psychic or intuitive talents they might have would begin to show themselves. Sometimes they were given a charm of luck and protection on this birthday. This ritual is a Northern Tradition marking of a child's seventh birthday, with the blessing of Thor and Sif.

The child shall be dressed in their best clothing, and come forth before the community or religious group with their parents and/or other trusted adults. A wreath of green leaves – or, if it is winter, evergreen twigs – is crafted to fit them, and hung with small charms. These can be runes, or small pine cones, or any symbols of luck and protection. The altar is set up with cloth of blue and yellow, candles of blue and yellow, a hammer and a spindle of glittering golden thread placed together, a horn of mead, a charm on a loop of sturdy string, and a pile of lengths of brightly colored ribbons.

A man and a woman are chosen to speak for Thor and Sif. If there are godparents, or however you want to call them, this would be their role; if there are none or if they do not desire it, the godhi or gythia and whoever they choose to speak next to them will handle it. If the child is a girl, the woman speaks first. If the child is a boy, the man speaks first. We will proceed with this ritual as if it were a girl, but it can easily be switched about, using masculine pronouns and hailing Thor before Sif.

                    ଓ   ଓ   ଚ   ଚ

First, sacred space is created by however the group prefers to do that. A yellow candle is lit, and Sif's speaker holds up the spindle of golden thread to the sky, and says: "Hail to you, Sif, golden one with hair like the ripening fields. May you smile upon all of us, and hallow this space with the light of sunrise."

Next, the blue candle is lit, and Thor's speaker holds the hammer to the sky, and says, "Hail to you, Thunderer, master of storm-cloud and lightning, defender of the common people. May you smile upon all of us, and hallow this space with the breath of adventure."

Sif's speaker says, "On this day, we bring (*child's name*) before us. She has now seen seven autumns, and s/he is old enough to understanding endings as well as beginnings."

Thor's speaker says, "On this day, we bring (*child's name*) before us. She has now seen seven springs, and she is old enough to understand that every ending is a new beginning." They both anoint the child with a drop of sacred mead on her head.

This next part is spoken as is, regardless of the gender of the child. As each of the speakers take turns speaking back and forth, a ribbon is tied onto the wreath. The tying can be done by the speakers, or the parents, or the godhi and gythia, or any two who are chosen for it. This should be done where the child can see it, so that they will remember that each ribbon is a gift to them.

> In the name of Thor, Midgard's Shield,
>> may you develop a strong and healthy body.
>
> In the name of Sif, Fertile Field,
>> may you develop a strong and healthy intellect.
>
> In the name of Thor, Mjollnir's Master,
>> may you develop a strong and passionate heart.
>
> In the name of Sif, Hallowing Maiden,
>> may you develop a strong and visionary spirit.
>
> In the name of Thor, Reiner of Goats,
>> may you have courage to face hard times.
>
> In the name of Sif, Thunderer's Love,
>> may you have the wit to avoid them when possible.
>
> In the name of Thor, Deep-Minded,
>> may you learn common sense.
>
> In the name of Sif, Light of Bilskirnir,
>> may you grow a love of knowledge.
>
> In the name of Thor, Bilskirnir's Lord,
>> may you always have loving family about you.
>
> In the name of Sif, Mother of Ullr,
>> may you learn to welcome newcomers into your family.
>
> In the name of Thor, Man's Well-Wisher,
>> may you have luck to keep you out of trouble.
>
> In the name of Sif, Thor's Bride,
>> may you learn wisdom to show you where it lies.

The wreath is placed on the child's head, and both speakers say, "You are blessed!" Then the horn is lifted, and one or both of the speakers pours it out, saying, "Hail to the Thunderer and the Golden Maiden his bride! Hail to the rain that falls on the earth, and nourishes it! Hail to the earth that gives forth grain to reach for the sky! Hail to the cycle that touches us all!"

Then everyone adjourns for general merrymaking. However, if the parents want to arrange a special part for the child to thank Thor and Sif for their blessing, they can collect rainwater and some seeds of grain. The child can plant them in a pot or in a garden, and water them with the rainwater. Whether this is incorporated into the ritual or done at a later time will depend on the child in question, the situation, and the time of year.

A Note On Coming-Of-Age Rites
Raven Kaldera

There has been a lot of research in recent years about rites of passage for adolescents, and their efficacy toward actually making the teenager feel like they have undergone something important and crossed over an emotional boundary toward adulthood. In all too many modern cultures, there are either no meaningful rites of passage at all, or symbolic ones that do not seem to make a long-term psychological effect on the teenager in question. Some researchers have come down on the side of pain and endurance – that for the ritual to mean something, it must be difficult, cathartic, and leave some kind of mark, like highly physical (and often painful) rituals from certain indigenous cultures. However, the current and most surprising research shows something different. The key point to the lasting effectiveness of the rite of passage seems to have little to do with the nature or the ritual, and much more to do with an actual change of status afterwards in the eyes of the community. Without this public status change, the rite of passage comes to seem, if only unconsciously, like an empty ritual with no real meaning.

This means that a parent who wants to design a rite of passage for their adolescent needs to think long and hard about how their child's status will change after this ritual, and they also need to consult with the adolescent about that change, so that they will be on board with the concept. This change can't just be something simple like a few extra chores; it needs to be a real change in status that will be seen and respected by the community ... some sort of community, at least. Obviously, greater society will continue to regard them as a legal minor who cannot make their own decisions, and if they go to public school, their day-to-day captors will not acknowledge any changes. However, there must be some alternative in their life where this change can be recognized. For example, they may be given control over their diet (and no longer required to eat meals that they don't like), or wardrobe, or hair. If they are old enough to have a part-time job, they can be asked to contribute rent in exchange for keeping their room any way they like. Perhaps they will be allowed to sit in on family finance discussions, and help to research better ways to save around the home.

Religious community, if there is one, can be another such possibility, especially if that community is involved in the design and execution of the ritual itself. Is the adolescent mature enough to be allowed to have some adult-style authority in at least part of the religious community's decisions? If not, perhaps the rite of passage itself needs to be delayed for a year or more. Since we do not live in a culture where adolescents will breed not long after physical menarche – and thus must have the skills to support a household as soon as possible – this ritual becomes more about emotional maturity than physical development; puberty is simply the earliest point that it makes sense to begin to consider it.

The values of that particular religious community, however, need to be taken into consideration. Some Northern Tradition sects have written about how the adolescent in question should have mastered certain skills before they can be allowed to make this transitioning ritual with the community's blessing. Some of the preferred skills have included first aid training, a trade skill that they could use to support themselves, or martial training. Other communities prefer that the elders interview the youth and get an idea of their emotional maturity. Still others want recommendations by various adults, much like a job interview. Yet others just take anyone who is old enough and not mentally challenged. Each community must make its own decisions; they have a right to set standards for someone who may soon be helping to make policy for the group. The following rituals have suggested questions for the adolescents, but these can be added to as necessary.

Coming of Age Rite for a Girlchild
Raven Kaldera

When a young girl first comes to her menarche, if she is willing and comfortable with it, and if the community considers her mature enough, this ritual can be done to mark and celebrate her new physical status. Five goddesses are invoked in this rite; all are associated with rites of passage or the guardianship of young girls, either in the historical sources or in the peer-corroborated personal gnosis of modern people. Five women are chosen to perform the ritual. They should have either a relationship with or some kind of affinity of lifestyle or character with these five goddesses. The staff roles are:

- **Freya's Speaker:** Dressed in the green of spring and bedecked with flowers (real or artificial depending on season), she bears a cup of honey.
- **Gefjon's Speaker:** Dressed in yellow and light brown, she bears a spindle of handspun red woolen thread.
- **Iduna's Speaker:** Dressed in golden and apple-green, she wears a crown of apple blossom (real or artificial) and bears a cup of apple cider.
- **Skadi's Speaker:** Dressed in snowy white with white furs, she bears a bow and arrows.
- **Mordgud's Speaker:** Dressed in black, she should ideally be wearing armor and carrying a spear hung with ribbons.

A wreath of flowers is crafted for the girl, and special charms can be hung from it. The best rune for this rite is Berkana, which is medically associated with the breasts and female organs; small Berkana runes can be hung from the wreath, along with perhaps other good-fortune runes like Wunjo, Dagaz, Fehu, Gyfu, etc. An archway of some kind is set up, also decorated with flowers and dangling with charms. A light cloth of red is hung from the top of the arch, blocking the opening.

Everyone comes to a circle on one side of the archway – the girl, her family and friends, and any members of the community who are welcome. Traditionally the girl wears red, but if she cannot abide that color, the color of one of the goddesses will do.

CR CR SO SO

Mordgud's Speaker comes forth first.

Mordgud's Speaker: We welcome you here, young one, to the place of Changing. Life goes through many transitions, and this is the first great natural change that you will face. Your body is already changing, and your life will change as well. We are gathered here to acknowledge that change among your people, but first we must determine your readiness to cross this threshold. Do you believe that you are ready?

Girl: I do.

Freya's Speaker: Then I will ask you for three answers. First, tell us your good qualities. What makes you worthy?

The girl speaks after each question, so I will leave her responses out for now. The Goddess Speaker who asks the questions is who will judge them as adequate. If they are not adequate, she will ask the girl for clarification until she gets an adequate answer or determines that the girl does not have one.

Freya's Speaker: Second, what do you love in life – what is your passion? And, thirdly, what kind of a woman do you believe that you will be?

If the questions are answered adequately, Freya's Speaker goes to her with the cup of honey and places some on her tongue.

Freya's Speaker: I bless you with the honey of love! May you have much of it in your life. May the sweetness of Freya's blessing follow you through every spring.

Gefjon's Speaker: Now I will ask you my questions. First, what gifts and talents will you bring to this community? Second, how will you use your gifts and talents to make the world a better place? Third, what is the one thing that you would pursue above all other things, even if all the world threw obstacles at you, and everyone told you to turn aside?

If the questions are answered adequately, Gefjon's Speaker approaches her with the spindle and unwinds a bit of thread from it, tying it loosely around the girl's wrist.

Gefjon's Speaker: I bless the threads of your fate, and may the Nornir be easy on you! May Gefjon smooth the road of life so that it stretches out every day before you like a wild summer's adventure.

Iduna's Speaker: Now it is my turn. First, what skills do you have to support yourself, should that suddenly become necessary? Second, what skills do you intend to learn to better yourself, and where will you go to learn them? Third – and answer me honestly – do you take good care of your body, the vessel for your soul?

If the questions are answered adequately, Iduna's Speaker goes to her with the cup of cider and has her drink from it, and marks her hands with the cider.

Iduna's Speaker: I bless your working hands with the bounty of the harvest! May you reap much from the seeds that you sow, and may every autumn yield a crop of memories as fine as Iduna's apples.

Skadi's Speaker: Now it is my turn to ask three questions. First, are your boundaries firm, or do you give way in the face of pressure or intimidation? Second, can you keep from giving way even in the face of love, when you are asked to do something you know is not right? Third, how will you defend yourself physically if you are attacked?

If the questions are answered adequately, Skadi's Speaker touches her with the bow and arrows, pressing one arrow tip into her chest at the heart center.

Skadi's Speaker: I bless you with the strength to be able to withstand anything that comes. May this strength help you to endure even Skadi's harshest winter.

Mordgud's Speaker: And now you come to me. As the Speaker for a Guardian of a World-Gate, I am the one who can see you through this gate now ... but first, the questions. First: What do you fear most in life? What will you do to defeat this fear? And lastly, when you are dead, what do you hope that the folk will say of you at your funeral?

If the girl answers adequately, Mordgud's Speaker salutes her with the spear and then touches her with it, gently but firmly.

Skadi's Speaker: Then you may pass, and I bless you with guidance as you walk your road and pass many more gates. May Mordgud watch your footsteps and keep you far from the final gate, until it is truly your time.

She signals the people to walk to the other side of the archway and form their circle there, and then uses the spear to hold the curtain aside.

Skadi's Speaker: Pass from girl to woman.

The girl passes through the archway and everyone on the other side cheers, and hails her name. The wreath is placed on her head by the woman closest to her age. She is embraced, and given gifts, and the leaders of the group bless her as well. Then, if it is appropriate, she should give away some of her own belongings to those present – especially younger children who will still have use for them. After this, everyone goes to the feast-hall and celebrates. If there is to be a private time with the other women, to tell her stories of womanhood and answer her questions out of the public eye, it should happen that evening after the feast.

Rite of Passage for a Boychild
Raven Kaldera

When a young boy first comes to his physical adolescence, if he is willing and comfortable with it, and if the community considers him mature enough, this ritual can be done to mark and celebrate his new physical status. Five gods are invoked in this rite; all are associated with rites of passage or the guardianship of young boys, either in the historical sources or in the peer-corroborated personal gnosis of modern people. Five men are chosen to perform the ritual. They should have either a relationship with or some kind of affinity of lifestyle or character with these five gods. The staff roles are:

- **Frey's Speaker:** Dressed in the gold of the harvest and wearing a crown of leaves and nuts, he bears a cup of honey.
- **Thor's Speaker:** Dressed in blue and white, he carries a hammer.
- **Logi's Speaker:** Dressed in flaming red and orange, he carries a torch.
- **Ullr's Speaker:** Dressed in dark green with white furs, he bears a bow and arrows.
- **Heimdall's Speaker:** Dressed in sky-blue with a thick golden chain around his neck, he carries a spear with rainbow-colored ribbons.

A wreath of twigs and leaves is crafted for the boy, and special charms can be hung from it. The best rune for this rite is Inguz, which is medically associated with the male organs; small Inguz runes can be hung from the wreath, along with perhaps other good-fortune runes like Wunjo, Dagaz, Fehu, Gyfu, etc. An archway of some kind is set up, also decorated with leaves and dangling with charms. A light cloth of white is hung from the top of the arch, blocking the opening.

Everyone comes to a circle on one side of the archway – the boy, his family and friends, and any members of the community who are welcome. Traditionally the boy wears green, but if he cannot abide that color, the color of one of the gods will do.

ଓ ଓ ଚ ଚ

Heimdall's Speaker comes forth first.

Heimdall's Speaker: We welcome you here, young one, to the place of Changing. Life goes through many transitions, and this is the first great natural change that you will face. Your body is already changing, and your life will change as well. We are gathered here to acknowledge that change among your people, but first we must determine your readiness to cross this threshold. Do you believe that you are ready?

Boy: I do.

Thor's Speaker: Then I will ask you for three answers. First, what gifts and talents will you bring to this community?

The boy speaks after each question, so I will leave his responses out for now. The God-Speaker who asks the questions is who will judge them as adequate. If they are not adequate, he will ask the boy for clarification until he gets an adequate answer or determines that the boy does not have one.

Thor's Speaker: Second, how will you use your gifts and talents to make the world a better place? Third, what is the one thing that you would pursue above all other things, even if all the world threw obstacles at you, and everyone told you to turn aside?

If the questions are answered adequately, Thor's Speaker approaches him and touches him with the hammer.

Thor's Speaker: I bless your word and your honor, and may it remain strong! May Thor bless your life so that it rises in joy like the wild winds of springtime.

Logi's Speaker: Now it is my turn. First, what skills do you have to support yourself, should that suddenly become necessary? Second, what skills do you intend to learn to better yourself, and where will you go to learn them? Third – and answer me honestly – do you take good care of your body, the vessel for your soul?

If the questions are answered adequately, Logi's Speaker goes to him with the torch, and waves it about him, and places his hands on the handle.

Logi's Speaker: I bless your working hands with the energy of flame! May your energy never fail you, and may Logi of the Fire bless your ardor with the heat of summertime.

Frey's Speaker: It is my turn now. First, tell us your good qualities. What makes you worthy? Second, what do you love in life – what is your passion? And, thirdly, what kind of a man do you believe that you will be?

If the questions are answered adequately, Frey's Speaker goes to him with the cup of honey and places some on his tongue.

Frey's Speaker: I bless you with the honey of love! May you have much of it in your life. May the sweetness of Frey's blessing come into your hands like the harvest of every autumn.

Ullr's Speaker: Now it is my turn to ask three questions. First, are your boundaries firm, or do you give way in the face of pressure or intimidation? Second, can you keep from giving way even in the face of scorn and mockery, when you are asked to do something you know is not right? Third, how will you defend yourself physically if you are attacked?

If the questions are answered adequately, Ullr's Speaker touches him with the bow and arrows, pressing one arrow tip into his chest at the heart center.

Ullr's Speaker: I bless you with the strength to be able to withstand anything that comes. May this strength help you to endure even Ullr's harshest winter.

Heimdall's Speaker: And now you come to me. As a Speaker for the Guardian of a World-Gate, I am the one who can see you through this gate now ... but first, the questions. First: What do you fear most in life? What will you do to defeat this fear? And lastly, when you are dead, what do you hope that the folk will say of you at your funeral?

If the boy answers adequately, Heimdall's Speaker salutes him with the spear and then touches him with it, gently but firmly.

Heimdall's Speaker: Then you may pass, and I bless you with guidance as you walk your road and pass many more gates. May Heimdall watch your footsteps and keep you far from the final gate, until it is truly your time.

He signals the people to walk to the other side of the archway and form their circle there, and then uses the spear to hold the curtain aside.

Heimdall's Speaker: Pass from boy to man.

The boy passes through the archway and everyone on the other side cheers, and hails his name. The wreath is placed on his head by the man closest to his age. He is embraced, and given gifts, and the leaders of the group bless him as well. Then, if it is appropriate, he should give away some of his own belongings to those present – especially younger children who will still have use for them. After this, everyone goes to the feast-hall and celebrates. If there is to be a private time with the other men, to tell her stories of manhood and answer his questions out of the public eye, it should happen that evening after the feast.

Rite of Passage for an Ergi Child
Raven Kaldera

Some children are neither wholly male or female, either in body or in mind or both. Usually if someone is going to end up being *argr*, and they live in a family where there are not great penalties for being honest about difficult subjects, the parents will probably be aware well before puberty of their child's nature. Almost no other religious traditions have a place for an *ergi* adolescent when it comes to acknowledging them with rites of passage. In today's modern times, such adolescents are at high risk for suicide, so it is worth it in the great scheme of things to acknowledge their nature and their value to the family and community. If the adolescent is willing and the family and community are open-minded enough to honor them for who they are, this ritual can be performed for them when they come of age physically, regardless of whether their body is maturing in a male, female, or mixed way.

Five deities have been chosen to bless this rite. Two of them – Frey and Freya – are a male-female brother-sister pair. Frey was known to have ergi priests; and Freya was, among other things, a warrior maiden. Two others – Loki and Angrboda – are a married couple, but Angrboda is also a warrior woman while Loki is a shapeshifter who has taken male and female forms, and borne a child as well as sired them. The fifth stands in for Jormundgand, who is both male and female – and neither as well.

Five people are chosen to perform the ritual. They should have either a relationship with or some kind of affinity of lifestyle or character with these five deities. The staff roles are:

- **Freya's Speaker:** Dressed in the green of spring and bedecked with flowers (real or artificial depending on season), she bears a cup of honey.
- **Frey's Speaker:** Dressed in the gold of the harvest and wearing a crown of leaves and nuts, he bears a small loaf of bread.
- **Loki's Speaker:** Dressed in red, and in whatever unusual clothing seems right for the Trickster, he bears a flaming torch.
- **Angrboda's Speaker:** Dressed in leather and fur in the colors of the earth – brown, green, russet – she bears a sword.

> **Jormundgand's Speaker:** Dressed in greenish-blue and wearing serpent jewelry, s/he bears a staff tied with many colored ribbons.

A wreath woven of ivy and other twining vines is crafted for the adolescent, and special charms can be hung from it. The Futhorc rune Ior is a good one as it is associated with the hermaphroditic Midgard Serpent. Another possibility is a bind rune of Berkana and Inguz (the male and female runes), Mannaz (which can be seen as the man and woman holding hands for a wedding, thus also representing the individual as a living sacred marriage), and general good-fortune runes such as Gyfu, Fehu, Wunjo, etc. An archway of some kind is set up, also twined with vines and dangling with charms. A light cloth of blue-green is hung from the top of the arch, blocking the opening.

Everyone comes to a circle on one side of the archway – the girl, her family and friends, and any members of the community who are welcome. There is no traditional color for the *ergi* youth to wear; anything will do.

ଔ ଔ ଊ ଊ

Jormundgand's Speaker comes forth first.

Jormundgand's Speaker: We welcome you here, young one, to the place of Changing. Life goes through many transitions, and this is the first great natural change that you will face. Your body is already changing, and your life will change as well. We are gathered here to acknowledge that change among your people, but first we must determine your readiness to cross this threshold. Do you believe that you are ready?

Youth: I do.

Freya's Speaker: Then I will ask you for three answers. First, tell us your good qualities. What makes you worthy?

The youth speaks after each question, so I will leave their responses out for now. The Speaker who asks the questions is who will judge them as adequate. If they are not adequate, they will ask the youth for clarification until they get an adequate answer or determine that the youth does not have one.

Freya's Speaker: Second, what do you love in life – what is your passion? And, thirdly, no matter where your path leads, will you always honor the female within you?

If the questions are answered adequately, Freya's Speaker goes to them with the cup of honey and places some on their tongue.

Freya's Speaker: I bless you with the honey of love! May you have much of it in your life. May the sweetness of Freya's blessing follow you through every spring.

Loki's Speaker: Now I will ask you my questions. First, what gifts and talents will you bring to this community, including the ones that come from being argr? Second, how will you use your gifts and talents to make the world a better place? Third, what is the one thing that you would pursue above all other things, even if all the world threw obstacles at you, and everyone told you to turn aside?

If the questions are answered adequately, Loki's Speaker approaches them with the torch and waves the flames about their body.

Loki's Speaker: I bless you with the ability to slip past the destructive powers of fire! May Loki send you laughter even in the midst of darkness and turmoil.

Frey's Speaker: Now it is my turn. First, will you swear to take care of your body, the vessel for your soul, even if it is not what you might have wanted it to be? Second, will you swear to hold out for the ones who will love you as you are, and never compromise yourself for another out of loneliness and desperation? Third, no matter where your path leads, will you always honor the male within you?

If the questions are answered adequately, Frey's Speaker goes to them with the bread and gives them a piece to eat.

Frey's Speaker: I bless you with the nourishment of family and community, no matter where your path takes you. May you come into the fullness of your identity and reap a harvest as joyful as the perfect autumn.

Angrboda's Speaker: Now it is my turn to ask three questions. First, what skills do you have to support yourself, should that suddenly become necessary? Second, what skills do you intend to learn to better yourself, and where will you go to learn them? Third, how will you defend yourself physically if you are attacked?

If the questions are answered adequately, Angrboda's Speaker touches them with the tip of the sword, pressing it into their chest at the heart center.

Angrboda's Speaker: I bless you with the strength to be able to withstand anything that comes. May Angrboda help you to feel solid as the winter earth, and proud of your own differences.

Jormundgand's Speaker: And now you come to me. As the Speaker for the Guardian of Midgard itself, the living liminal space, I am the one who can see you through this gate now ... but first, the questions. First: What do you fear most in life? What will you do to defeat this fear? And lastly, when you are dead, what do you hope that the folk will say of you at your funeral?

If the youth answers adequately, Jormundgand's Speaker salutes them with the staff and then touches them with it, gently but firmly.

Jormundgand's Speaker: Then you may pass, and I bless you with guidance as you walk your road and pass many more gates. May Mordgud watch your footsteps and keep you far from the final gate, until it is truly your time.

The Speaker signals the people to walk to the other side of the archway and form their circle there, and then uses the spear to hold the curtain aside.

Jormundgand's Speaker: Pass from the joining of boy and girl to the joining of man and woman.

The youth passes through the archway and everyone on the other side cheers, and hails their name. The wreath is placed on their head by the last youth of any gender to come of age. They are embraced, and given gifts, and the leaders of the group bless them as well. Then, if it is appropriate, they should give away some of their own belongings to those present – especially younger children who will still have use for them. After this, everyone goes to the feast-hall and celebrates. If there is to be a private time with ergi adults, perhaps ones who have been brought here for this occasion, to tell them stories of how to survive and answer their questions out of the public eye, it should happen that evening after the feast.

Runic Handfasting Rite
Raven Kaldera

This handfasting ritual is useful when there will be a large group of people who want to participate in the ceremony, but there is no time for briefing or rehearsal. It is also a nice thing as it creates a rune set as a group wedding gift for the bride and bridegroom. The rune set should be made beforehand, preferably by the close friends of the couple, out of wood or fired clay or engraved stone. The first time this was performed, each stone was taped to an index card with the accompanying line on it; these were passed out beforehand to anyone who wanted to participate. Each person in turn stepped forward, read their card, detached the rune, and placed it in the bowl on the altar. Because there was no time for rehearsal, the officiant in charge chose to let them go in any order, rather than the traditional order. A special bag had been made for the wedding runes, and it was given to the couple afterwards to keep them in. (This ritual lists both the Old Norse Futhark runes and the Saxon/Frisian/Northumbrian Futhorc runes. You may use either.)

The altar should be set with an evergreen branch in a bowl of water, a honey cake, a horn of mead, and a wooden bowl to collect the runes in.

ଔ ଔ ଓ ଓ

To begin, the officiant shakes the evergreen branch over the couple, saying, "With this I wish your love forever green and whole." Then the officiant says, "You who have gathered here to watch these two become one! Who will speak for this man, this bridegroom?"

Some members of the bridegroom's family or friends speak up and say, "I will speak for him." They proceed to say good things about him, telling of his excellent qualities and why he will make a good husband.

The officiant says, "Who will speak for this woman, this bride?"

Some members of the bride's family or friends speak up and say, "I will speak for her." They proceed to likewise extol her virtues, and praise her as a good future wife.

The officiant says, "The union of these two will bring together two clans of kin. Will you honor their marriage, and the bridge they make between you?"

The families say, "We will!"

The officiant says, "Many of you have good wishes for this man and this woman. Stand forth now and give them the gifts that you would wish upon them." Each person with a card and a runestone stands forth one at a time and reads the card, depositing the rune into the bowl. The invocations are as follows:

- Fehu (or Feoh) is the Rune of Wealth. May you gain riches and comfort, like the farmer with many herds of cattle.
- Uruz (or Ur) is the Rune of Strength. May you be strong for each other, like the wild aurochs and his mate.
- Thurisaz (or Thorn) is the Rune of the Thorn. May you be a comfort to each other in times of pain and trial.
- Ansuz (or Aesc) is the Rune of the Divine Message. May you learn to listen to one another, which is more important even than speaking.
- Raido (or Rade) is the Rune of Travel. Although you have walked two separate paths, may you now walk one road hand in hand.
- Kaunaz (or Ken) is the Rune of Fire and Truth. May you speak only truth to each other, and never resort to deception.
- Gebu (or Gyfu) is the Rune of the Gift, of Partnership, of the crossroads where you now stand. May you always give of yourselves generously.
- Wunjo (or Wyn) is the Rune of Light. May your path be bright; may your times in the darkness be few.
- Hagalaz (or Haegl) is the Rune of Hail. Misfortune will come, for it always does; may you hold together against the forces of chaos that rain down upon you.
- Nauthiz (or Nyth) is the Rune of Need. May you find ways to fill each others' needs, yet not depend on each other so much that you cannot look elsewhere for aid.
- Isa (or Is) is the Rune of Ice. May your hearts never freeze and turn cold to each other; instead, let your love melt all ice between you.
- Jera (or Jer) is the Rune of the Harvest. May all your hard work come to fruition, and may you reap the rewards you deserve.
- Eihwaz (or Eoh) is the Rune of the Yew Stave. May you protect and defend each other from all harm.

- Perth (or Peorth) is the Rune of the Dice Cup, the Cave, the Womb, the Mystery. No matter how well you know each other, let there still be some small mystery left for the discovering.
- Algiz (or Eolx) is the Rune of the Elk. May you meet all challenges with courage and exuberance.
- Sowelu (or Sigil) is the Rune of the Sun. May you each be the Sun that brings life to each others' lives.
- Teiwaz (or Tyr) is the Rune of the Warrior. May you stand together as shieldmates, and not rend each other in mutual battle.
- Berkana (or Beorc) is the Rune of the Birch Tree, of Growth. May you each encourage your mate to make new growth in all areas of life.
- Ehwaz (or Eh) is the Rune of the Horse, of Movement. May you always find fair footing along your path, and ever have good progress.
- Mannaz (or Mann) is the Rune of Humanity. May you never forget that we are all human, and we make mistakes, and must be forgiven for them.
- Laguz (or Lagu) is the Rune of Water. May you learn to flow together, in harmony with each other.
- Inguz (or Ing) is the Rune of the Sacrificial God. May you learn when it is the right time to make sacrifices for your relationship, and when you should stand firm.
- Dagaz (or Daeg) is the Rune of Dawn. May you wake up every morning in love with the one who lies next to you.
- Othila (or Oethel) is the Rune of Heritage. May you have peace between your families, clans, and friends.
- Ear is the Rune of the Grave. May you be together even unto death.
- Ac is the Rune of Endurance. May you stand straight as an oaken stave together, and never be ashamed.
- Ior is the Rune of the Midgard Serpent that surrounds the Earth. May you be willing to go to the ends of the Earth for each other.
- Os is the Rune of the Skald. May the words that are spoken between you be magic, so that you may always be able to understand each other.
- Yr is the Rune of the Bow. May your sight be keen and sharp, and may you learn to aim in the same direction.

- ᛋ Cweorth is the Rune of the Funeral Pyre. May you be able to let go of what is necessary, without ever losing hold of each other.
- ᛋ Stan is the Rune of the Stone, the Keystone and the Touchstone. May this marriage form a strong center for both your lives.
- ᛋ Chalc is the Rune of the Chalice, the Holy Grail. Whatever quests may take you away from home, may you always remember that your thirst for love can only truly be slaked at home.
- ᛋ Gar is the Rune of the Spear, wrought from the World Tree. May you never forget your place in the Universe, amid the branches of the World Tree, where all things are part of the same cycle and circle.

Now the couple take what vows they will, exchange rings, are declared husband and wife by the officiant, kiss, and share a honeycake and the horn of mead.

Originally published in *Handfastings and Wedding Rituals: Welcoming Hera's Blessing*, by Raven Kaldera. Llewellyn Press, 2003.

Frigga Wedding Rite
Raven Kaldera

This rite is arranged around the blessings of Frigga, Norse/Germanic goddess of marriage, and her handmaidens. Boughs from a tree that is still green should be placed across the threshold; if it is not winter, they can be deciduous; if winter, use evergreen boughs. Everyone should step over the boughs in order to enter; this is considered good luck.

The altar is set with a horn of mead, and lots of room around it for all the items that will be presented. The bridegroom and bride enter from opposite sides, accompanied by family and friends. They both carry swords or long knives at their belts, but these should be easily removed. Both should wear wreaths, and have belts on which can be bound later items.

ଔ   ଔ   ଚ   ଚ

The officiant recites the following invocation:

> Gods and goddesses all I hail,
> Aesir, Vanir, Rokkr, all,
> Generous the Wights observe,
> Salute the honored ancestors;
> Bless what work is wrought this day.
> Clans and tribes and families all,
> Be with us in frith together.

Then the officiant says, "We come here on this joyful day to honor the union of _____ and _____, who wish to be married. This will be a union of souls, and of heart, and of households, and also of clans. (Turns to the bridegroom.) Do you, _____, wish to take this woman unto your heart and your hearth? (Bridegroom answers.) Do you, _____, wish to take this man unto you heart and your hearth? (Bride answers.) Then first lay aside all that might hinder your joy."

The bridegroom removes his sword or knife and lays it before the bride, and says, "Thus I dedicate this to you, to serve you always with honor."

The bride removes her sword or knife and lays it before the bridegroom, and says, "Thus I too dedicate this to you, to serve you always with honor." They take up each others' blades, and lay them before the altar.

A happily married woman comes forward with a drop-spindle, on which is hand-spun a quantity of yarn or thread. She says, "We call upon Frigga, Lady of Marriage, Spinner and Weaver of relationships, peacemaker and welcomer, Mistress of Asgard. Bind these two together as one with your magical threads of contentment." She places the spindle on the altar.

Next, thirteen more people come forward to invoke Frigga's handmaidens. These are traditionally women, but need not be; anyone can call upon a goddess. Their lines are as follows:

- We call upon Fulla, Lady of Abundance, you who make the grain bountiful upon the Earth. Bring wealth and riches to they who stand before us today. *(Places a sheaf of grain on the altar.)*
- We call upon Lofn, Lady of Reconciliation, you who intercede between warring lovers. May battles in this new household be fair and quick to be resolved. *(Places a knife on the altar.)*
- We call upon Gna, bright messenger who rides to bring good news. Spread the word of this great love to the four winds, that all may know of its glory. *(Places a feather on the altar.)*
- We call upon Gefjon, who aids the unmarried. Bless this couple as they leave your tutelage to start a new life together. *(Places a white stone on the altar.)*
- We call upon Eir, healer and physician, minister to the many wounds. Aid these two in healing each other of whatever ills have gone before. *(Places a pot of healing salve on the altar.)*
- We call upon Sjofn, peacemaking maiden. If there is anger between these two, may it fade away in the light of their love. *(Places a pink stone on the altar.)*
- We call upon Snotra, you who study discipline and understand that virtue comes from labor. Teach us what labor is required to build the finest marriage. *(Places a short-handled hoe on the altar.)*
- We call upon Huldra, lady of the herds, whose cattle meant wealth and security. Bless they who stand before you with eternal security of storehouse and pantry. *(Places a cow's horn on the altar.)*

- ꙮ We call upon Vor, prophetess who can see the future. May the future be bright and joyful for these most beloved, and may they live long in years. *(Places a silver ribbon on the altar.)*
- ꙮ We call upon Saga, lady of written knowledge. May these two love burn like that of all the lovers in the old stories, but may it follow only those tales with happy endings. *(Places a book of love stories on the altar.)*
- ꙮ We call upon Hlin, lady of consolation who mourns all that is lost, that these two may be so for each other, and may bear up with strength should one be lost. *(Places a black cloth on the altar.)*
- ꙮ We call upon Syn, who is all-fair and all-just, upon whose name contracts are sworn. May these two be honest and worthy in their dealings with each other. *(Places a coin upon the altar.)*
- ꙮ We call upon Vara, taker of oaths and promises, who sees every vow. May these two keep the oaths that are spoken today, and not forsake them. *(Places the two wedding rings upon the altar.)*

A happily married man steps forward, and says, "We call upon Odhinn, husband of Frigga, All-Father of Asgard. To be a good husband is as important as to be a good wife. No matter how urgent and important are your other duties, you should never take for granted this marriage, nor forget the toil and support of your beloved. Duties may come and go, but if well-tended, love will last forever."

Next an unmarried woman with many lovers should come forward; she should wear a fine necklace to symbolize Freya. She says, "We call upon Freya, Lady of Love. May you never run short of desire and adoration, no matter how long and weary the years. May your life be fertile in beauty and harmony, and may the walls of marriage be a safe haven and not a smothering cell." She lays a bouquet of flowers on the altar.

Next an unmarried man steps forward and says, "We call upon Frey, Lord of the Fields. May this union be fertile in love, riches, and children." *(This last can be left out if the couple cannot or do not wish to have children.)*

A strong and powerful man steps forward and says, "We call upon Thunor, Lord of Thunder. May you both protect each other from the cruel words of the ignorant, with strength and vigor!"

The officiant says, "The two of you have given up your weapons; shall you now take on the loving duties that shall replace them?"

Then the woman who invoked Frigga steps forward, and removes a ring of keys from her belt, and holds them out to the bridegroom, saying, "This keeps the house in order and unlocks all secrets. Do you wish for this woman to administer to your heart, your holdings, and your hopes?"

The bridegroom says, "I do." He takes the ring of keys and gives it to the bride, saying, "I trust you, and you alone, with all that I have and own." She fastens the keys to her belt.

The woman who invoked Frigga says, "This day you gain a treasure greater than any you have ever had. Guard her well and care for her always, for she is your good fortune."

The man who invoked Odhinn takes a small utility knife from his belt, and holds it out to the bride, saying, "Not a weapon but a tool, to remedy and repair. Do you wish for this man to administer to your heart, your holdings, and your hopes?"

The bride says, "I do." She takes the utility knife and gives it to the groom, saying, "I trust you, and you alone, with all that I have and own." He fastens the knife to his belt.

The man who invoked Odhinn says, "This day you gain a treasure greater than any you have ever had. Protect him well and care for him always, for he is your safe haven."

The officiant takes the rings from the altar and says, "The vows spoken today will be heard and hallowed by Sjofn, Syn, and Vara, and all the gods and mortals present. Speak them with all integrity and sincerity."

The bridegroom takes the bride's ring and puts it on her finger, saying, "I take thee for my wedded wife, in darkness and in light, in summer and in winter, in weakness and in strength, through all of our days in Midgard."

The bride takes the bridegroom's ring and puts it on his finger, saying, "I take thee for my wedded husband, in darkness and light, in summer and winter, in weakness and strength, through all of our days in Midgard."

The woman who invoked Frigga then retrieves her spindle from the altar, and unwinds yarn or thread from it, and says, "By the power of Frigga, Holy Spinner and Weaver, I bind thee both together as one." She winds the yarn around their hands, breaks it, and ties it off, so that their hands are loosely bound.

The officiant then says, "By all the gods and goddesses, by all the names of the ancestors, by the Ever-growing World Tree, I pronounce thee husband and wife." They kiss.

The officiant says, "Drink to each other's health, and the health of all!" and hands the horn of mead to the bride, who pours a small offering onto the ground (or, if it is inside, into a bowl to be ceremonially emptied later) and drinks. She then hands the horn to the bridegroom, who does the same. Then the horn is passed deosil around the circle, and all drink to the couple. The officiant takes the final drink and gives a toast: "Hail to the bride and the bridegroom!"

All repeat: "Hail to the bride and the bridegroom!"

Ideally at this point, the couple should be escorted with all speed to their bedchamber, where they should be partially undressed and put to bed by the members of the wedding party. The bed should be sprinkled with flower petals, or at least scented with oil, and the horn of mead should be left for them. The visitors should wish them well, leave the chamber and close the doors, and proceed to sing and make music outside, until such time as the nuptials are well and truly celebrated, and the couple comes out of the bedroom bearing the horn and no longer bound together. Then all should retire to a great feast.

Originally published in *Handfastings and Wedding Rituals: Welcoming Hera's Blessing*, by Raven Kaldera. Llewellyn Press, 2003.

Vanir Wedding Rite
Geordie Ingerson

Weddings, for the Vanic practitioner, are presided over by Frey and his bride Gerda. For a small Vanic home wedding, have on hand a small cake, a pot of honey and a cup of good homemade ale, and a bit of brass on which is inscribed a bind rune of the runes Mannaz and Gebo. Instead of flowers, the bride should carry a sheaf of grain, and both should wear wreaths of woven straw from which dangle straw ornaments. The wreaths may also bear fresh flowers for Freya, if it is desired. The wedding rings are nearby, slipped onto a branch of evergreen.

ଔ   ଔ   ଵ   ଵ

As the couple enters, a mixture of earth and grain is sprinkled beneath their feet. (This is why this rite is best done outside, but if it must be done inside due to the weather, a cloth may be laid down and then gathered up after, and the grains and earth returned to Nerthus outside.) The one who speaks for the Gods begins with this blessing:

> Hail, O Gods of Vanaheim's shores,
> Who look down on us on this joyous day.
> Hail to Frey, eternal bridegroom,
> Hail to Gerda, eternal bride,
> Hail to Freya, Bringer of Love,
> Hail to Njord, consort of the Earth,
> Hail to Nerthus, lover of the Sea.
> Hail to the spirits of field and wood,
> And to the ancestors whose families
> Are about to bind together in joy.
> Hail to those who stand before us,
> And to all who gather around.

The one who speaks for the Gods then asks the couple these three questions, which each must answer in the affirmative:

> Lord Frey gave up his sword for his beloved. Are you ready to give up your defences in the name of love?

Lady Gerda left her father's home, surrounded by protecting flame, to be with her beloved. Are you ready to give up your safe solitary space in the name of Love?

Lord Frey and Lady Gerda wed in spite of all voices against them. Are you willing to defend your marriage to all who frown?

If the answers are received readily in the affirmative, the one who speaks for the Gods should ask them to say whatever vows they would say, or which they have decided upon. After the vows are spoken, the rings are taken from the branch and each places a ring on the other's finger. Then the bread is broken between them, and this is said as they feed each other:

> As the Earth yields up its gifts to us with our gratitude,
> So you will nourish each other with equal gratitude.

The pot of honey is given to them, and they feed each other a fingerful of it, while this is said:

> As the bee sacrifices its sweetness for us, with our gratitude,
> So you will be a source of sweetness for each other,
> With equal gratitude.

The cup of ale is given to them, and they share the drink while this is said:

> You are two, but you will share one cup,
> One life, one heart in two bodies,
> Even as Lord Frey and Lady Gerda
> Share one life in many different worlds.

The evergreen branch is waved over them, with a cry of: "Erce! Erce! Erce! Be thou wed, and be thou blessed!" and they must kiss. Then there is much feasting.

Originally published in *Ingvi's Blessing: Prayers and Charms for Field and Farm*, by Geordie Ingerson. Asphodel Press, 2011.

Handparting Rite
Geordie Ingerson

In this ritual, we call upon Njord and his sometime bride Skadi, the frost-giantess and goddess of winter and hunting. The two of them tried to marry, but could not agree whether to live by the shore or in the snow-covered mountains. Both hated the other's chosen home and longed for their own, and finally decided to part ways amicably. While it is always sad when a couple must part, one hopes for the ideal of an amicable relationship where each blesses the other's future and wants only happiness for them. This rite can be done by one who loves them both, or by one of the two themselves (in which case just change the pronouns from "them" to "us").

ଔ ଔ ଓ ଓ

For this work, tie a blue string to an item symbolizing one of the partners, and a white string to an item symbolizing the other. Tie the two ends together in a loose knot. Keep a small dish of honey and a pair of scissors at hand, and say:

> Father Njord, sail them on separate journeys
> And soothe their hearts until they can be friends again.
> Skadi, Frost-Maiden, cool their anger
> And split them cleanly from what they have made.
> By the song of sea-birds, may they be healed!
> By the whirling blizzard, may they be healed!
> By the turning of the year, may they turn again
> And be family, if not lovers, and eternal friends.

Take the scissors and cut the string through the knot, so that it falls apart. Make sure that no piece of the other is left tied to each end, but do not cut away more than is absolutely necessary. Dip the two ends in honey, untie them from their objects, and coiled them up separately. Bury them in two different places on the same land, for example by the front and back doors of the house.

Originally published in *Ingvi's Blessing: Prayers and Charms for Field and Farm*, by Geordie Ingerson. Asphodel Press, 2011.

Vanir Ritual for the Joining of Families
Geordie Ingerson

When two marry who have already grown families from prior marriages or relationships, there is often a great deal of adjustment while two separate groups struggle to become a household and family with people they have not grown up with. To help make two families one, bring everyone together around the kitchen table with a candle, a horn of fresh milk, a loaf of bread and some butter, a bowl of salt, and a bowl of water. Each of the activities listed in the rite can be done by a single person, or by different people.

ଅ ଅ ଓ ଓ

First the gods are called in this way:

> Sacred family, Blessed Vanir,
> Help us to become as close as you,
> And as joyous, and as loving.
> Hail to you, Gods of the Earth!

The salt is passed around the table and everyone tastes it, while someone says:

> Nerthus, Mother of Vanaheim, give us patience
> To hold on when all is bitter and hard.
> Give us firm footing for our family
> Like the Earth beneath our feet.

The salt is poured into the dish of water and someone says:

> Goodfather Njord, give us far vision
> To be objective in the face of fears.
> Make us loyal to this new clan we create
> and let that loyalty be paid back a hundredfold.

The candle is lighted and someone says:

> Freya, Spring Maiden, bright light of Vanaheim,
> Help us to see each other with the eyes of love.
> Bring laughter to our family gatherings
> That is at the expense of no one.

The bread is sliced and spread with butter, and each takes a slice and then shares it with the next person, so that each gets part of their slice and part of someone else's. Another speaker says:

> Frey, Lord of the herd that huddles together,
> Teach us to share our warmth with each other.
> Teach us when it is needful to make sacrifices
> For the good of the others at this table.

The horn of milk is passed around so that all may drink, and someone says:

> Gerda, bride of Frey, who married into the Vanir
> And took your husband also into your own family,
> Teach us how to be a bridge between different houses
> And to welcome the stranger in, and make them kin.
> Teach us to give the milk of human kindness
> To all our new brothers, sisters, parents and children.

Then everyone should sit and share a meal together. When the meal is finished, the last of the milk, the salt water, and the bread and butter are taken outside to be poured or placed as an offering. When all have returned, the candle is blown out and the rite is over.

Originally published in *Ingvi's Blessing: Prayers and Charms for Field and Farm*, by Geordie Ingerson. Asphodel Press, 2011.

A Note On Funerals
Raven Kaldera

When we first began this book, we intended to provide sample rituals for all the different rites of passage in a person's life, from womb to tomb. However, funerals are difficult to write a generic ritual for. In Elizabeth Vongvisith's Northern Tradition prayer book *Be Thou My Hearth And Shield*, five different prayers for a funeral are provided. If something needs to be formally recited, one of those would probably suffice.

Funerals are deeply personal rituals. Some err on the side of what the deceased would have wanted, while others err toward what will comfort the survivors. Making that decision, and then figuring out what will work best for that specific person or group of people, is a very delicate decision that takes a lot of thought and consideration. Elaborate boilerplate rites aren't going to do the trick. In addition, funerals are the one ritual where people are least likely to be in an emotional state for doing staged rites. Ritual staff and even clergy may break down and weep in the middle of whatever they are supposed to be doing, and forgetting lines will be at an all-time high. Even the most beautiful ritual can still be an added stressor at this time, so it's best to keep things simple.

What, then, are the elements of a Northern Tradition funeral? Most people think about the burning Viking ship on the water, filled with grave goods and a corpse. Not only is this physically impossible for most people, it's not necessarily appropriate – originally, only warriors who died in battle got that kind of funeral. Some people will want to be cremated, and some will want to be put into the earth. Some will donate their bodies to science, and it may take months for the (always cremated) remains to be returned to the family, so there may not even be a body present. Funerals and memorial ceremonies (and these days the lines are vague as to which is which) must be flexible for all the various inconveniences that Death visits upon us.

However, the giving of gifts as grave goods, symbolic or otherwise, is a traditional rite that can be adapted to modern times. At one such funeral I attended, the deceased had donated his body as a research subject for the disease that killed him, so his family bought a three-foot-long Viking ship and encouraged people to fill it with gifts. These included tiny paper and wooden versions of things he had enjoyed in life, bits of his favorite food and drink, letters and wishes written to him, and occasionally bits hair or clothing. The ship was placed ceremoniously on a fire and burned, and people sang as it went up. At another funeral where the deceased was buried in the earth, a box was decorated and filled with similar grave goods, and placed on top of the coffin after it went down.

In ancient Anglo-Saxon funerals, there was traditionally a dirge sung by a female relative or friend, and then twelve people on horseback rode singing around the funeral pyre. (The sagas only describe the funerals of great warriors who died in battle; other folk weren't deemed worthy of sagas.) Since soloists with appropriate dirges are few, and horses aren't generally allowed into gravesites, the singing could be done by a group of twelve selected people walking around the grave or altar or even the whole room. If everyone falls in behind them, this can serve as a transition to the next phase of the ritual.

After the main part of the funeral in each of these cases, people adjourned to a sitting area where they passed a horn and told stories about the deceased, and what they remembered most about them. This creates a different atmosphere from the more traditional custom of saying something solemn about how good the person was, and is more mutual than a drunken, maudlin wake. In a way, the storytelling circle is the most Northern Tradition part of the rite, regardless of whether it can be proved to have actually been done. Having people sit in a circle (or a series of concentric circles) instead of a Christian-church-like lectern and "pews", and having them share actual stories that will be added as memory-pictures to the minds of everyone there, is a powerful group bonding. Everyone leaves with more memories than they entered with, and their last thoughts are not simply about the act of disposing of a body. It also ritually begins the transition of the deceased's place in the community from just-alive member to honored ancestor.

It may be a good idea if those who were not the closest and most beloved of the deceased are the ones to go first with their stories. They are less likely to choke on torrential emotion, and more likely to be able to keep their contributions positive and focused. This sets the scene for more people to be willing to speak up. While at traditional funerals the most bereaved are pressured to go first, the storytelling ritual allows them to gather their wits and decide if they want to share stories. They should not be pressured to speak up if they choose to remain silent; there can be a great comfort in simply sitting and listening to others talk about the contribution of your beloved lost one to their lives. Usually, though, the memories of others will remind them of some memory of their own that begs to be shared.

After this – prayer, grave goods to fire or earth, storytelling – there is usually an adjournment to feasting in honor of the deceased. Whether the feasting is a raucous and joyful event, or a quiet time for mourners to offer individual consolations, will depend on the chief mourners and their wishes. Ideally, those wishes should be made clear to whoever is handling the details of the funeral and reception/feast. While everyone will make their own decisions on the spur of the moment, we heartily recommend that the closest family members not be in charge of the party. If they can choose someone trustworthy and competent who is not grieving as hard as they are, and simply give their wishes as to how the funeral should be done, it is a great burden off of them. (Some people, of course, cope with grief through working and thus may want to run things themselves.) If nothing else, such preparations as making food for the feasting and cleaning the venue before and after can be a wonderful way for people who are grieving only a little, but who want to show their respect for the deceased, to help out.

Seasonal Rites

Candlemas Creation Rite
Raven Kaldera

This ritual is dedicated to the oldest living being in the Nine Worlds, Surt the Lord of Muspellheim. It is to be done at night during the dark time of the year, when all is cold and frozen. We tend to use it for Imbolc, but it can also be used at Yule or any other winter ritual. Many candles are placed around the room, including four large ones in the four directions, and an altar in the center of the room is draped in red with a hibachi or other small firepot on it. Very strong liquor – the sort that will easily catch on fire – should be available for a libation. The officiant holds a candle in a holder, and a wand or large knife decorated with glittering ribbons in flaming colors – red, orange, gold, etc.

ଔ ଔ ଓ ଓ

The room is placed in darkness, and the officiant begins by saying:

> Welcome to the darkness that we name Ginnungagap, the cosmic void before there was light and heat in the Universe of the World Tree. Below us in the darkness is stone and ice, but nothing moves or breathes. Then the darkness was split but Surt, Lord of Fire, who cut his way into Ginnungagap with his flaming sword.

The officiant lights their candle, and waves the wand close enough to it that people can see the flash of glitter. Then the officiant goes to the four directions and lights a candle in each one, starting in the South, and saying the following four invocations:

> Hail, Fires of the South, home of Fire,
> Bright Sun and heat that devours,
> Bring the light of Flame to the darkness.

> Hail, Fires of the West, Fire of the Hearth,
> Flame beneath the bubbling cauldron,
> Melt the ice and free the waters to rise.

> Hail, Fires of the North, Fire beneath the Earth,
> Volcano that cracks the cold stone,
> Thaw the mountains that hide the first signs of life.

Hail, Fires of the East, Fire in the Sky,
Send the warm winds across the face of the land,
Awaken the first souls in the shadow.

The officiant then turns to the people and says:

> This is the story of creation in our cosmology: the meeting of Fire and Ice. Surt touched his sword to the most barren of rocky lands and it burst into flame, and became Muspellheim, the Land of Fire. The darkness was lit for the first time with the red glow of that world, and its heat began to melt the ice that gripped the realm next to it – Niflheim, the Land of Ice. Surt's flames turned it into a land of mists and icy waters, and once its mountains had thawed, Ymir – the first ancestor of the frost-giants – was revealed. His children, and Surt's, would one day mingle their bloodlines and create many races throughout the Nine Worlds. Hail Surt the Black, who sparked life in the Universe!

The people reply, "Hail Surt!" and the officiant lights the firepot on the altar. Then the officiant says:

> However, first Surt drew forth his other half from the fire of creation, and she came dancing. Her name was Sinmora, the Lady of Fire, and with him she bore all the first fire-spirits of Muspellheim. Here we gift them both!

The officiant pours strong spirits into the firepot, and says:

Hail Sinmora, Mother of Muspellheim,
Bright dancer in the wasteland,
Creativity of a woman's heart,
Teach us to make our hopes manifest
In a shower of sparks!
Hail Sinmora!

All reply, "Hail Sinmora!" The officiant waves the fire wand, and then says:

> Fire is creativity, the bright spark that kindles the flame. Come forward, each of you, and find a flame.

> Whisper to it what creative power you would have, and ask it to nest inside of you and help you to find that power.

The people come forth, one by one, and whisper their desires into the candle flames. If a flame accidentally goes out, it is a signal that this desire was not possible, and the person should find another candle and name something else. (It is probably wise to have significantly more candles than people.) Then the officiant says:

> The other side of creative fire is anger. Go back to your candle and whisper the name of that which makes you the most angry, that which you fear will crack your self-control. Then blow out the candle and we will leave in darkness and silence again – but we will be grateful for the light and warmth that we will walk into. Never shall we take that light and heat for granted again!

The people go to their candles and whisper their secret rages, and blow the candles out one by one. In the meantime, the officiant galdrs the runes Kenaz and Cweorth, until the final candle is blown out, and then stops short. There is a moment of silence in the darkness, and then a slow procession is led out of the area, and the rite is over.

Oimelc Candle Rite
Raven Kaldera

This ritual is very simple, and goes with the Candlemas Hymn whose sheet music is below. Thirty-three candles are set out, plus an extra taper to light them, which is lit beforehand as part of the opening of the circle. Each candle is carved with a rune of the Futhorc system. The song is sung, solo if necessary but ideally by a group, and each time the people sing the word "One," a candle is lit. The final candle should be large, green, and sitting in the middle to represent the World Tree, carved with Gar (the rune of Odin's spear, which is also a kenning for the Tree).

When the song is done and all the candles are lit, we generally ask folks to take them outside one by one and place them in a fireproof area. We suggest that each person take the candle carved with a rune that corresponds to something they desire or are currently struggling with in their lives. Since we live in New England and there's usually snow out, we sink them in a snowbank and they burn down and go out safely. (It's also very beautiful to see, the glowing spots of flame in the snow.) If there's no snow, one could use a concrete sidewalk, asphalt driveway, or just a patch of bare dirt. The candles are left to burn down in the night.

Candlemas Hymn
Raven Kaldera

Charming of the Plough Ritual
Geordie Ingerson

The Charming of the Plough is a celebration marking the beginning of the English agricultural year, generally held on the first full moon in February. For a small household version of this rite, bring the plough (or cultivator) and any agricultural tools out and lay them out on the earth.

ଔ ଔ ଓ ଓ

First the spirit of the land is honoured by pouring out a cup of milk onto the ground and reciting this blessing:

> Hail to the Land-Vaettir and may they be blessed,
> And may we never forget their generosity
> In allowing us to share the beauty of their home.

Light a candle and pass the flame all around the plough and the tools. Say the following prayer to Nerthus:

> Erce, Erce, Erce, we honour you forever,
> Abundant mother, body beneath our feet,
> You who open the earth to us, blessed Nerthus,
> Look kindly and grant us a new year of plenty
> And may our pantry and cupboards be filled.
> Bless this plough that comes to embrace you,
> And give forth your bounty once again.

Smudge a bit of honey onto the plough and all the tools, saying:

> Freya, Spring Maiden, come to us soon
> And open the earth for us to enter,
> And may the green shoots dance upwards
> In every fair footprint you make.

Sprinkle a handful of grain and a cup of beer onto the tools, saying:

> Frey, Lord of the Fields, follow your sister
> And bring us the gold after the green,
> We praise you and your family with high praise
> And may peace and good seasons follow us.

Bow to the Earth and return the plough and tools to their sheds.

Originally published in *Ingvi's Blessing: Prayers and Charms for Field and Farm*, by Geordie Ingerson. Asphodel Press, 2011.

Ostara Rite
Geordie Ingerson

Ostara is the celebration of spring on the equinox, usually March 21st or 22nd. It is dedicated to Freya in her guise as the spring maiden, and we like to celebrate it with the usual practice of blowing eggs hollow, dyeing and decorating them, and then hanging them outside on a large bush that will flower later in the year. Usually they are decorated with symbols of wishes, and it is considered good luck if they blow off and crumble before the following Ostara. Two eggs, one gold and one green, are decorated with spring flowers for Freya. All but these two eggs are hung on the bush before the rite begins.

If possible, whoever speaks this rite should be a woman, and should wear a gown of light green. If cowslips or primroses are blooming by this time, they should be picked into a bouquet. The ideal drink for this holiday would be homemade cowslip wine, but if that cannot be had, a horn of mead will do as well.

ଦ ଦ ଚ ଚ

All process to the gardens, and no matter the cold, the woman should stand barefoot in a bed of unplanted soil for at least a minute, and say:

> Hail Freya, Spring Maiden!
> You come with the wild winds
> And the buds of green,
> Spreading like a wave across the land.
> You awaken the roots
> And breathe the blossoms into life.
> Earth blooms in your footsteps,
> And may we follow you to bloom as well!

After she is done speaking, she steps off the garden bed (and may don shoes, if it is cold enough). Everyone takes up sticks and twigs and lays down the runes of Dagaz (for awakening), Jera (for the year-cycle), Berkana (for growth), Gebo (for the gifts of Earth), Fehu (for Freya), and Sowelu (to bring the Sun down to Earth). The two eggs are laid in the mud-footprints that have been left in the soil. All pass the horn of mead or cowslip wine and hail Freya, and pour out the last of it onto the garden. As the libation is poured, the woman says: "Vanadis, take this sweetness and awaken the Earth to beauty and fertility in all things."

Then the rite is over, and all return to the house for feasting. The egg mixture from the blown eggs should be made into food such as cake or quiche or other egg dishes and served with new greens.

Originally published in *Ingvi's Blessing: Prayers and Charms for Field and Farm*, by Geordie Ingerson. Asphodel Press, 2011.

Northern Tradition Beltane Rite
Ari

While traditionally a Maypole ritual involves splitting the audience by gender, and having the men handle the pole while the women dig the hole, I have chosen to divide things differently. Instead of being divided by gender, the people are divided by deity. The four deities honored on this day are Frey, Freyja, Thor, and Sif. Bunches of ribbons are given out in four colors that represent the springtime colors of these Gods – green for Frey, pink for Freyja, light blue for Thor, and yellow for Sif. People of any gender decide which deity's "team" they wish to be on for the day, and then tie an appropriately colored ribbon around their head or arm or belt. It is not necessary to be a regular devotee of one of those deities in order to honor them on this day.

ଓ   ଓ   ଛ   ଛ

A Maypole is prepared, with a wreath of flowers and an even number of ribbons, attached to a ribbon at the top which will be tied around the top of the Maypole. Words of happiness and good luck can be painted onto the Maypole; this can be a group activity, as can binding flowers and ribbons onto the wreath. A hole is dug in the earth, and stones brought to set around it. Ideally the Maypole should be prepared by the Frey team, the wreath of flowers by the Freyja team, the hole dug by the Sif team, while the Thor team takes charge of the ribbons and ties them to the "tying" ribbon.

Everyone gathers around the hole in the ground, bringing a small loaf of bread, a cup of milk, a cup of rainwater, and a cup of honey. One person from the Frey team says, "Hail, Spirit of the Land beneath us! Take our offering on this Beltane morning, and may you give forth nourishment and wealth to us for the rest of the year. Hail Frey, Lord of the Great Staff! Bless us with love and ecstasy." The bread is laid in the hole.

One person from the Freya team says, "Hail, Spirit of the Land beneath us! Take our offering on this Beltane morning, and may you give forth fertility and beauty to us for the rest of the year. Hail Freya, Maiden of the Spring! Bless us with love and pleasure." The honey is poured into the hole.

One person from the Thor team says, "Hail, Spirit of the Sky above us! Come down to the Earth and take your offering, and rain vitality down upon us for the rest of the year. Hail Thor, Lord of the Spring Cloudburst! Bless us with love and energy." The rainwater is poured into the hole.

One person from the Sif team says, "Hail, spirit of the Sky above us! Come down to Earth and take your offering, and let all good things flow to us for the rest of the year. Hail Sif, Bride of the Thunderer! Bless us with love and fidelity." The milk is poured into the hole.

Then the Frey team hoists the Maypole onto their shoulders. The Thor team ties the ribbons to the end of it, the Freya team ties the floral wreath atop them, and the Frey team approaches the hole. The Sif team guides the end into the hole and all hands push the pole to a standing position and block it in with stones. One person from the Thor team and one from the Sif team come up to the pole together and dance around it, blessing all those who desire to be only with one beloved. Then one person from the Frey team and one person from the Freya team go around the circle, inviting anyone to come up and kiss them for luck, and send those kisses to the Gods themselves, thus blessing those who would spread their love.

The Maypole is danced, and then people go their own ways to make love in the trees, or be with the group, or feast, or whatever they will.

Litha Rite for Frey and Freya
Gudrun of Mimirsbrunnr

This ritual can be adapted for a solitary worshiper, a couple, or a group. When I perform this ritual, I use a horn and a necklace of large chunks of amber, and a bottle of mead.

ଔ ଔ ଓ ଓ

Stand outside in full sunlight and place the items on a cloth of green and gold. Pour the mead into the horn and speak the following invocation:

> *Vanaguð, ágetasti af asum, folkum stýrir,*
> We hail you, mighty Frey and wise,
> The green that we greedily devour,
> The gift to our craving bellies.
> You are the gift of high summer,
> Green as the grass we lie in,
> Golden as the light on the leaves.

Hold up the string of amber so that you can see the sunlight through it, and speak the following invocation:

> *Vanadis, fegjafa, fagr-ferðugr,*
> We hail you, fair Freyja and wise,
> The blossom that yields to fruit,
> The fruit that bursts in our mouths.
> You are the gift of high summer,
> Green as the grass we lie in,
> Golden as the light on the leaves.

Sprinkle a bit of the mead in all directions, and speak this invocation:

> Hail to the Vaettir of the land
> That cradles my footsteps and traces my path.
> I come to ask for blessings, for wealth
> Of growth, of light, of all things come to fruition.

Pour out the mead onto the grass, and speak the following invocation:

> Bless this land, O Sacred Twins,

> Brother, sister, children of Earth,
> Givers of fertility of tree and flower,
> Of animal and human, of all life.
> As I offer you the honey's kiss
> I see you, Golden God and Goddess,
> Double blessing sprung from one womb
> One fair day in great Vana-land,
> Come together as one light, one sun
> Brought down to earth and earthly power!
> Gift this land with blessed growth,
> May blossoms rush to luscious fruit,
> May leaves and stems grow lush and tall,
> May seeds hang ripe in clusters heavy,
> May roots swell beneath the turned earth.
> May no disease or blight find us
> In our safe harbor of earthen goodness.
> Come together, Sacred Twins,
> Tvifaldleikr, Gullbjartr,
> Entwine your bodies and your hearts
> With all the holy land around.

As these words are spoken, twine the string of amber about the horn, which is now empty and point-upward. When it is tightly twined, set the horn down where you have poured out the mead, bow to the horn and amber, close your eyes in respect, and back away. Let the energy of the Sacred Twins work through what you have left in the grass. At the end of the day, when the rays of the sun are dying away, come and retrieve the horn and amber and separate them, and silently thank Brother and Sister together.

Originally published in *Honey, Grain, and Gold: A Devotional for Frey*, by Joshua Tenpenny. Asphodel Press, 2010.

Northern Tradition Lammas Rite
Raven Kaldera

This Lammas ritual celebrates the various Nordic Gods and Goddesses of agriculture. An altar is laid in the center of a feast table, draped in golden cloth and set with figures of livestock, with a great sheaf of wheat in the middle. Somewhere on the altar should be a wooden bowl of dried barleycorns. Around the edges of the altar, place seven goblets and seven bottles or pitchers, holding beer, milk, whisky, rum, apple cider, cold herb tea of some red color, and mead. Around this a great feast should be set, with a number of special dishes for the Gods. Other food can also be laid out, but the necessary ritual dishes are as follows:

- One large loaf of bread, made to look like a wheatsheaf, for Frey. (For specific instructions in how to make one, look in Joshua Tenpenny's devotional to Frey, *Honey, Grain, and Gold*.)
- A dish of roots – scarlet beets, golden carrots, parsnips, etc. surrounded by fresh green herbs.
- Some dessert of baked apples – pie, cake, tart, raisin-stuffed, etc.
- A honey-cake with berries in or on it.
- Baked or roasted ocean fish of some sort.
- Beef and green vegetables together on a platter, with a sickle around the edge.
- A leg of goat meat, served on some cooked grain.
- One empty platter.

This rite is written for one officiant, but the parts can easily be split up among many people. Four items are placed in the four directions: a digging-stick in the south, a winnowing-basket in the west, a basket of black compost in the north, and a scythe in the east.

The officiant goes first to the south and lifts the digging-stick to the sky, and says:

> We honor you, Ancestors,
> Fathers and mothers who went before us,
> Brothers and sisters who worked the Earth.
> On this day of sacrifice
> We honor the sacrifice

> Of those who toiled under the hot sun
> To plow the earth and open Her body
> That your descendants might live to know Her grace.

Then the officiant crosses the circle to the north and lifts the basket of compost to the sky, and says:

> We honor you, Ancestors,
> Mothers and fathers who went before us,
> Sisters and brothers who worked the Earth.
> On this day of sacrifice
> We honor the sacrifice
> Of those who fed and watered the soil
> With peat of bogs and droppings of the animals
> That your descendants might live to know Her grace.

Then the officiant crosses the circle to the east and lifts the scythe to the sky, and says:

> We honor you, Ancestors,
> Fathers and mothers who went before us,
> Brothers and sisters who worked the Earth.
> On this day of sacrifice
> We honor the sacrifice
> Of those who cut down the waving heads of grain
> That stood so high and proud in the Sun
> That your descendants might live to know Her grace.

Then the officiant crosses the circle to the west and lifts the winnowing basket to the sky, and says:

> We honor you, Ancestors,
> Mothers and fathers who went before us,
> Sisters and brothers who worked the Earth.
> On this day of sacrifice
> We honor the sacrifice
> Of those who winnowed seed from chaff,
> Who ground your nourishment on the turning wheel,
> That your descendants might live to know Her grace.

The officiant then goes to the altar and brings forth the empty platter. This is for the food given as offerings to the Gods. As each dish is brought forth, a serving of it is placed on the empty platter, and a cup is filled with drink. First, Frey the Harvest King is called, and the wheatsheaf loaf is brought forth. The officiant breaks off a piece of it, lays it on the platter, and speaks the following invocation, with all the people echoing each line (call-and-response):

> Hail to Ingvi Frey, the Harvest King!
> Hail to the Sacrificed One
> Who dies that we might live!
> Hail to the Golden God of the Grain,
> Hail to the horned head that lays down its life,
> Hail to the sheaf bound in sacrifice,
> Hail to the flesh that is bread, the blood spilled like wine.

A cup of is filled with beer, then poured out on the Earth, then filled again and set back by the altar. Next, Gerda the bride of Frey is called, and the tray of roots and herbs is brought forth. The officiant dishes out a portion onto the platter, and speaks the following call-and-response invocation:

> Hail to Gerda, bride of Frey!
> Hail to the Lady of the Walled Garden
> Whose roots we dig in the autumn eve!
> Hail to the mistress of savory herbs,
> Hail to the goddess who hangs the elderberries!
> Hail to the guardian of the wild tubers,
> Hail to the bride who welcomes him home.

A cup is filled with cold herb tea, then poured out on the Earth, filled again and set back by the altar. Next Iduna the orchard-goddess is called, and the tray of apple dessert is brought forth. The officiant dishes out a portion onto the platter, and speaks the following call-and-response invocation:

> Hail to Iduna, Orchard's Blessing,
> Goddess who hangs the fruit on the tall trees,
> Whose gifts we seek as the summer wanes!
> Hail to the giver of health and joy,
> Hail to the hands that work and toil,
> Hail to the gardener of Asgard,
> Hail to the Goddess who purifies our flesh.

A cup is filled with cider, then poured out on the Earth, then filled again and set back by the altar. Next Freya the sister of Frey is called, and the tray with honey-cake and fruit is brought forth. The officiant dishes out a portion onto the platter, and speaks the following call-and-response invocation:

> Hail to Freya, Lady of Love!
> Sweet are your fruits that lie upon the Earth,
> Gleaming like jewels in their lace of leaves!
> Sweet is the honey that pours like gold,
> That gleams like amber in the honeyed Sun.
> Hail to the Lady whose sweetness we crave,
> Hail to the Spring Maiden whose gifts grace the fall.

A cup is filled with mead, then poured out on the Earth, then filled again and set back by the altar. Next Njord the Ship-King is called, and the tray with the fish is brought forth. The officiant dishes out a portion onto the platter, and speaks the following call-and-response invocation:

> Hail to Njord, Lord of Ships!
> Hail to the Fisher-God who fills the nets
> And sweeps his flocks into our hands and bellies.
> Hail to his silver cattle in the ocean's field,
> Hail to his small sheep crouching in their shells,
> Hail to his corn waving black in the waves,
> Hail to the God whose bounty keeps us whole.

A cup is filled with rum, then poured out on the Earth, then filled again and set back by the altar. Next Nerthus the Earth Mother is called, and the tray with beef and vegetables is brought forth. The officiant dishes out a portion onto the platter, and speaks the following call-and-response invocation:

> Hail to Nerthus, Mother of Green,
> Mother also to Freya and Frey,
> Lady who brings the milk to the teat,
> Lady who brings the shoot through the soil.
> Hail to the goddess who swings the sickle,
> Hail to she for whom the sacrifice bares its throat,
> Hail to the Goddess of the devouring Earth.

A cup is filled with milk, then poured out on the Earth, then filled again and set back by the altar. Next Thor the thunder god is called, and the tray with the goat meat is brought forth. The officiant dishes out a portion onto the platter, and speaks the following call-and-response invocation:

> Hail to Thor, Lord of Thunder!
> Hail to the God who brings the rain,
> Who waters the crops with his summer storms!
> Hail to the patron of the common man,
> Hail to the working-man's guardian and guide,
> Hail to the chariot pulled by goats,
> Hail to the high one who looks after the farmer.

A cup is filled with whisky, then poured out on the Earth, then filled again and set back by the altar. The tray of food for the Gods is placed back before the altar, and the officiant says:

> By sap and blood, by juice and sweat,
> We honor the Gods and Ancestors who taught us to grow.
> By sickle and scythe, by basket and net,
> We gather their legacies in from the fields.
> By generous Earth beneath our feet,
> May we all be grateful for what is given.
> Jera, Jera, Jera!
> Inguz, Inguz, Inguz!
> Hail to the Gods of the Harvest Home!

All present repeat, "Hail to the Gods of the Harvest Home!" and the rite is over. The rest of the food is eaten as a feast, and at the end of the feasting the cups are again emptied onto the earth, and the platter placed out overnight so that the Earth will send her children to devour it.

Equinox Ritual for Idun
Shannon Graves

The goddess Idun, mistress of apples and the orchard, is usually honoured by our group either on the spring equinox, during the apple blossom season, or on the fall equinox when the apple harvest is in full swing. The spring ritual tends to be much more informal, so I share the autumn one with you here.

First a very large apple pastry must be baked, and cut into squares. Into this tart, along with apples and sugar and spices and cornstarch and whatever else the bakers prefer, go four rounded glass "gems", of the sort without the iridescent coating. One is apple-green, one is apple-yellow, one is apple-red, and one is apple-blossom pink. All present are warned about the glass gems, so that no one is incautious and breaks a tooth.

One perfect yellow apple should be set aside, with a knife close to hand. Jugs of cider both hard and soft, and plenty of cups, should be brought forth. We do use a horn at this ritual, but we do not pass it in a traditional way; instead it is filled with the first pressing of cider and set aside on a piece of turf. It goes without saying that this ritual takes place in an orchard, or at least under an apple tree.

ଓ ଓ ଔ ଔ

The godhi, or whoever is running the rite, stands forth and says:

> Now is the time when day and night stand even,
> When earth and sky are even,
> When growth and death are even.
> Now is the time when the trees give up their blessings
> And we praise them, for they sustained our forefathers.
> Here, in this place of the Apple Spirit,
> We honour the Lady who knows the Apple
> And who balances work and inspiration.

The godhi takes up the horn, and holds it to the sky, saying:

> Today, while we love the fruits of the trees, we do not understand how important it was to our forefathers. Everywhere in the world, there is always a god of the fruits that grow on tree and vine, because trees can often grow where grain cannot. Every culture that took food from

plants had a sacred tree that sustained them – the grape, the olive, the cornelian, the fig. For the Northmen, it was the apple – sweet harvest of the autumn that kept one well. While they did not know about vitamins, they knew that apples made for health. In our country, we were drinking cider long before the Romans arrived; we taught them the art of pressing apples where wine grapes would not grow. Idun is our fruit-tree goddess. She loves the plums, the pears, the apricots, but the apples are her favourite, and today they are ours as well. Hail Idun! We return to you what you have given to us, and may you gift us well again next year!

The godhi pours out the horn onto the roots of the nearest apple tree, and all cry out, "Hail Idun!" Then the godhi recites this prayer:

> Hail Idun, orchard-keeper of the Gods!
> Lady of the blossoms white and rose,
> Lady of the gilded fruit that grows,
> Lady of green leaves that gently frame
> The red-cheeked bounty growing in your name,
> Lady of the apple-green and gold,
> Surrounded by the harvest that you hold
> Of all the sacred trees that gave us life,
> Bless us, laughing maiden, skald's sweet wife.
> Bless us with the wisdom of the earth,
> The star of seeds that speaks of all rebirth.

At this point the godhi takes up the knife and cuts the yellow apple in half, sideways, so that the five-pointed star of seeds is visible. (This manoeuvre may need to be practiced first on other apples, in order to get it right the first time during ritual.) He holds it up and cries out, "Behold the mystery!" Then the apples pieces are laid at the roots of the tree as well.

The pie or tart is brought forth, and sliced, and pieces are given out with the words "Taste of Idun's generosity!" Whoever gets the glass stones has received Idun's special blessing, and the godhi will interpret them. The pink piece indicates that a new beginning will blossom over the next year. The green piece means that you must work hard to get anything done, and laziness will make it all go sour. The red piece indicates passion and excitement, and the yellow piece indicates prosperity.

The rite ends with everyone consuming cups of cider both hard and soft, and quietly pouring out their personal offerings to Idun.

Winternights Ritual
Ari

For this rite, five separate altars are set up, one in each direction and one in the center.

- The eastern altar is decorated with a blue cloth and covered in swords, spears, and other weapons, and a horn of mead.
- The southern altar is covered with a white cloth and is also covered with weapons, but these should be chosen for their beauty and decoration. A golden cup of white wine is also placed there.
- The western altar is covered with a sea-green cloth and holds shells, salt water, fish, pictures or models of sunken ships, and a bottle of rum.
- The northern altar is covered with a black cloth and holds skulls, gravestones, black stones, and a great silver cup of red wine.
- The central altar is covered with a patchwork cloth or old tablecloth, and it bears photos or written names of the Dead, many cups and a variety of bottles of liquor, a pot of tea, and a pot of coffee.
- Five bouquets of flowers are carried into the room: red roses, orange roses, yellow roses, white roses, and one bouquet that is many different kinds of flowers. Ideally, everyone present should have contributed at least one flower to the fifth bouquet.

ൽ   ൽ   ഌ   ഌ

The officiant calls everyone together, and says, "Hail to you all on this night which is the harbinger of Winter." A dedicant of Odin, Thor, or Tyr goes to the eastern altar and says:

> Hail to you, O Dead of Valhalla,
> Fallen warriors of many wars
> Gathered under the wing of Odin,
> Harvested by his Valkyries
> And brought to your final reward.
> Bless us, O ancestors, with your strength.
> We give you scarlet as your blood
> In honor of your sacrifices.

The bouquet of red roses is laid on the altar.

> Bless us, Odin, with courage to fight

Even when the battle seems too much for us.
Hail Odin, Gungnir's Master!
Hail, Tyr, Lord of Swords!
Hail Thor, Lightning Strike!

The horn of mead is taken from the altar, and a libation poured for the Dead. Then it is passed around, and everyone present repeats back the last three lines and hails these three gods, drinking or pouring more libation. Then a dedicant of Freya goes to the southern altar and says:

Hail to you, O Dead of Sessrumnir,
Women warriors chosen by the Vanadis,
Queer warriors chosen by the Vanadis,
The handsomest men on the battlefield
Who caught the eye of the Vanadis!
Bless us, O ancestors, with your diversity
And your strength in the face of obstacles.
We give you the color of the rising Sun
In honor of your glory.

The bouquet of orange roses is laid upon the altar.

Bless us, Freya, with the will to go on
Even when the road seems too much for us.
Hail Freya, Warrior Goddess!

The cup of white wine is taken from the altar and a libation is poured for the dead. The cup is passed around and everyone repeats "Hail Freya!" They may drink, or pour out more libation. Then a dedicant of the Sea Gods – Aegir, Ran, and their daughters – goes to the western altar and says:

Hail to you, O Dead of Aegirheim,
Sailors lost at sea in storms
Or overboard in nautical battles,
Submarines vanishing into the depths,
Landbound folk washed out to sea
By the breakers, the storms, the great waves.
Bless us, O ancestors, with your bravery,
And your ability to dare the danger.

> We give you gold like the coins we give to Ran
> In honor of the risks you took for us.

The bouquet of yellow roses is laid upon the altar.

> Bless us, Aegir and Ran, and all your daughters,
> With the knowledge of when to surrender.
> Hail Aegir! Hail Ran! Hail to their daughters!

The bottle of rum is taken from the altar and a libation is poured for the dead. The remaining rum is poured into a cup which is passed around, and everyone repeats the last lines, hailing the Sea Gods. Then a dedicant of Hela goes to the northern altar and says:

> Hail to you, O Dead of Helheim,
> All who died the straw death of old age
> Or disease, or fell in some ordinary way,
> And walked the Hel Road, and were gathered
> Into the arms of the Dark Queen.
> Bless us, O ancestors, with your persistence,
> Your ability to work day after day
> And make not one great sacrifice,
> But a thousand small ones
> That we might someday stand here together.
> We give you the white of eternal peace
> That you have earned, to honor your toil.

The bouquet of white roses is laid upon the altar.

> Bless us. Hela, Mother of Bones,
> With the sure knowledge that Death is also a beginning.
> Hail Hela!

The cup of red wine is taken from the altar and a libation is poured for the dead. Then it is passed around and everyone repeats "Hail Hela!" and drinks or pours more libation. Then the officiant goes to the central altar and says:

> Hail to you, our Disir,
> Mothers and grandmothers who watch our lineage,
> Who gave up the promise of a blind rebirth
> To watch with open eyes the paths
> Of all your many descendants,

> To guard the lines and see us blindly stumble
> Upon disaster, upon joy, upon love, upon fame, upon sorrow.
> Some of us souls that you knew in your time,
> Some of us new souls that you welcome to the family.
> We bring you the multitudes of our living bodies
> To honor you for all you have done for our unknowing lives.

The final bouquet of flowers is laid upon the altar.

> Bless us, O Disir, with your protection
> And your guidance in times of trouble,
> For trouble you have seen, and survived it.
> Hail to the Disir!

Everyone cries, "Hail to the Disir!" The bottles of liquor are opened, and the cups are filled with coffee, tea, and liquor for the disir of people's family lines. These are not passed around; instead, everyone processes away to feast in honor of the Disir and the Gods who guard the Dead, and the rite is ended.

Mother Night Ritual
Raven Kaldera

This rite was celebrated on the evening before Yule, standing in a snow-covered garden. Large pillar candles were lit for each goddess, and placed in the snowbank, and allowed to burn down until they went out. The opposite snowbank received the libations and food. We processed to the garden carrying the lit pillar candles and the offerings. Different people had requested the hailing of the various Mothers, so a different voice called out each one, placed their candle, and poured out or placed the offering. The officiant speaks first and last.

ങ ങ ഇ ഇ

Officiant:

> Tonight we celebrate those who brought forth life,
> Who opened themselves to be the doorway for new souls,
> Who opened themselves to bring back the ancestors,
> Who opened themselves to bring each of us into the world,
> And we begin with the Mothers of the Gods themselves.

Participants, individually:

> Hail Urda, Mother of Beginnings!
> Grant us wisdom of the deepest well.

Light a dark purple candle and pour out a mug of cow's milk.

> Hail Frigga, All-Mother of the Heights!
> Grant us the blessing of the offered cup and the open hand.

Light a blue candle and pour out a horn of mead.

> Hail Bestla, Mother of Power!
> Grant us the manifestation of our great plans.

Light a white candle and lay three small cakes as an offering.

> Hail Gefjon, Mother of Bulls!
> Grant us resourcefulness in the face of limits.

Light a buff-colored candle and pour out a bottle of ale.

> Hail Sif, Mother of Truth!
> Grant us the ability to ask for what we want.

Light a yellow candle and pour out some white wine.

> Hail Jarnsaxa, Mother of Might!
> Grant us strength and perseverance through the storm.

Light a silver candle and pour out a cup of goat's milk.

> Hail Grid, Mother of Vengeance!
> Grant us aid on our most uncertain journeys.

Light a grey candle and lay out some cooked meat as an offering.

> Hail Jord, Earth Mother!
> Grant us an easy birth for every child of body, mind, and heart.

Light a green candle and lay down some home-grown vegetables as an offering.

> Hail Aurboda, Mother of Stillness!
> Grant us protection as within a wall of flame.

Light a rust-colored candle and pour out a cup of medicinal herb tea.

> Hail Gunnlod, Mother of Eloquence!
> Grant us song that reverberates through the soul.

Light a deep blue candle and pour out a small bottle of mead.

> Hail Ran, Mother of the Waves!
> Grant us knowledge of the tides of life.

Light a sea-green candle and sprinkle sea salt as an offering.

> Hail Nerthus, Mother of Fertility!
> Grant us rich soil for our dreams to grow.

Light a brown candle and lay a loaf of bread down as an offering.

> Hail Freya, Mother of Jewels!
> Grant us blossoming in its own time.

Light a golden candle and pour out a cup of honey.

> Hail Sinmora, Mother of Fire!
> Grant us creativity in all its forms.

Light a red candle and pour out a ginger beer.

> Hail Laufey, Mother of Chaos!
> Grant us serenity to see us through the madness.

Light a green candle and lay out a tree fruit as an offering.

> Hail Loki, Mother of Sleipnir!
> Grant us nurturing from unexpected sources.

Light a red candle and pour out some terrible cheap spicy liquor.

> Hail Angrboda, Mother of Monsters!
> Grant us love in spite of our flaws.

Light an orange candle and pour out a bottle of Jack Daniels.

> Hail Sigyn, Mourning Mother!
> Grant us endurance in our darkest hours.

Light a pink candle and pour out clear spring water from a small metal bowl.

Officiant: Hail to the Mothers of the Gods!

All: Hail!

All process back inside, where a feast is waiting. Before eating, however, the officiant gathers everyone in front of the food. Cups of hot mulled cider are passed around with a "Waes hael!" for toasting.

Officiant: Hail to the Disir who guard our family lines!

All: Hail!

Blutmonath Journey to Helheim
Raven Kaldera

This ritual was actually written not for a Northern Tradition group so much as a group of eclectic Neo-Pagans; it was meant to be a "mystery play" rite to teach them about one of the mythic places in our cosmology. Rituals like this – using Northern mythology but geared toward less experienced people – can be a great bridge-builder between Nordic and non-Nordic Pagans. There is, of course, no reason why it could not be used as a celebratory rite for a Northern Tradition group as well. We've chosen to place this in the Seasonal Rituals section because it can be used as a late fall rite. While Samhain itself is a Celtic holiday, it heralded the start of Blutmonath, or Blood Month (November), in the Anglo-Saxon calendar. This is an excellent Blutmonath rite, although it can theoretically be held at other times as well.

In Norse/Germanic mythology, there were a number of places that people could go when they died. Some went to ancestral mounds or "villages"; some went to the homes of their patron deities to serve them. Drowned souls went for a time to be entertained in the hall of the Sea gods before being sent on to the Land of the Dead. Odin, chief of the Aesir or sky gods, chose specific brave warriors to come to his hall, Valhalla, and join his personal militia. Freya the Goddess of Love also chose battlefield souls and took them to her hall. However, the vast majority of people would end up in Helheim, the Land of the Dead. Its Lady was Hela, who looked after her many charges with quiet conscientiousness.

The geography of Helheim was fairly well laid out, or at least the parts of it where living people were allowed to go. To get there, one walked the Hel Road and passed various obstacles. Helheim had many gates, but each one had a guardian, as much to keep the living out as to keep the Dead inside. Once inside, nothing got past Hela, who knew all that happened within her realm.

This ritual includes an actual feast that will be enjoyed, to whatever extent, by the participants. The actual point of the feast will be to share the food with the Dead by allowing them to experience tasting food and drink through the bodies and minds of the living. This will be explained beforehand, and people who are uncomfortable with the thought of allowing the Dead to commune with them physically to that extent can do something else as their offering – sing, or pray, or stand quietly. Bringing gifts to the Dead is the main point of this ritual, and this should be impressed onto the crowd. Ideally, and announcement should have been made beforehand for people to bring donations of food, drink, gifts, etc. to be given to the Dead. Musical instruments for donations of song and music can also be brought along.

Staff positions for the ritual are as follows:

- **Greeter:** The greeter gathers the people at the opening area and explains the important facts of the ritual to them. They guide them as far as Mordgud's tower, and after the Hel Gate Groa takes over their guiding. The Greeter carries a bag of clear glass marbles or glass lumps.
- **Mordgud:** This giantess-goddess is the sacred gate-guardian of Helheim. She is a large sturdy woman dressed in black armor (real or costume) and carries a spear hung with black and white ribbons. Whoever plays her must swear not to leave her post for the length of the ritual, even though she will spend most of it alone; this does mean that she will miss the feast of the Dead, but part of Mordgud's power is her steadfastness.
- **Garm:** The great Hound of Helheim; he is Hela's guardsman. He is dressed as a man-sized hound with great claws and teeth; his costume should be terrifying rather than cartoonish.
- **Groa:** A deceased giantess and sorceress, she is the party's spirit-guide throughout Helheim. Like all the giantess parts, she is not a small woman. She wears a robe covered in runic symbols and carries a staff; her robe, staff, hair, and anything else can be dripping with bones, beads, feathers, etc. Her face is made up to look like that of a corpse.
- **Ganglati:** Hela's handmaiden. She should be a very large hefty woman, dressed in various rags, beads, and pieces of fur. She carries a pitcher of water and a red cloth. She is sarcastic and grouchy, although she can be mollified with courtesy. However, a bad attitude in the party members merely makes her own worse.
- **Suffering Souls of Nastrond:** You can have as many of these as you like. If you don't have enough people, use a recording of people screaming.

- **Nidhogg the Dragon:** This can be one person, but should ideally be two or more in Chinese-dragon form. Nidhogg is a large blue-and-white wingless dragon, European-style, but long and twining. The dragon's head should have an open mouth with many teeth, and the person behind it should be able to reach through and pull things into it, as Nidhogg chews on corpses.
- **Baldur:** The God of Light, he is dressed in Norse costume of white and gold with long blond hair, and is very handsome. His skin can be made up to glitter subtly. There is a red stain over his heart. He smiles a lot, sometimes sadly.
- **Nanna:** Baldur's wife, she is ordinary-looking, shy, dressed in ancient Norse garb.
- **Hela:** The Goddess of Death and Queen of the Underworld, Hela is thin and bony. She is traditionally shown as half beautiful woman and half rotting corpse or skeleton. This can be done with theatrical makeup – either dividing the face down the middle with makeup, or attaching half a skull mask to the face with skin adhesive. One side of the body can be painted to look like rotting flesh, or a black suit and glove with skeleton bones on it can be worn. She wears a simple long gown that is black on her living side, and grey with many rents and tears (to show the rot or bones) on her dead side. Hela moves slowly, speaks quietly but with calm presence, and only offers her dead hand to the living. She will offer her living hand to Groa, but to no one in the party.

The stations for the ritual are as follows:
- **Gathering Area:** This is where the greeter meets people, and gives the opening explanation. This can be decorated with gravestones, or for a more authentic feel a mound of dirt can be set up with a pile of stones for a cairn on top. The food and drink that will be taken into the underworld is collected here. If the ritual staff is donating food, it should be parceled out to people to carry. The beginning to the Hel Road should be marked with some kind of archway, decorated with ribbons of black, white, and grey, and bones or skulls or other sigils of Death. The rune of Hela and Helheim is Ear, from the Anglo-Saxon Futhorc runes, and it can be displayed in various places. The Hel Road is symbolized by a

bind rune of Ear and Raido (the rune of the Road), which can be set up on a stick like a road sign.

- **Hel Road:** The path between the Gathering Area and Mordgud's Tower is decorated with "ghosts" hanging from posts or trees, or on wires so that they can be pulled along by a string (perhaps by the Greeter). These are lightweight hanging figures made of old clothes (perhaps torn and bloodied) or skeletons with white draperies, or whatever the decorating crew feels will work. At the end of the Hel Road is a "river", which can be a blue cloth laid across the path with a large tub of water on each side. A narrow "bridge" of contrasting cloth is laid down over it, delineating the path, and false "knives" made of tinfoil are standing edge up along the first half of it.

- **Mordgud's Tower:** This can be a circle of staves, flags, or some other structure that represents the tower. It is beyond and to one side of the bridge. Mordgud waits here. She has a small cup of lampblack with which to mark people's foreheads.

- **Helgrind:** This is the Gate to Helheim. Just beyond Mordgud's Tower is another archway, this one simply draped in matte black cloth. Garm waits, crouched in front of it, and Groa waits a little way beyond.

- **Nastrond:** The Beach of Helheim is piled with corpses. These can be stacked "bloody" severed mannequin pieces, or any other sort of artificial bodies. Nidhogg is here, perched on the pile of corpses, devouring them.

- **Nastrond Hall:** This is a place of torture, or rather, self-torture. It can be represented by an archway with two double doors, or a small building or separate room if you like. If there are not enough ritual staff members, you can have closed doors with a recording of people screaming behind it. If you want to show the inside of Nastrond, acquire rubber snakes and hang them from the "ceiling", perhaps ropes strung across the area if there is no ceiling. Nastrond Hall was said to be hung with poisonous serpents dripping painful venom on everyone within; a hung vessel can drip some kind of green slime (thin gelatin works well) onto the screaming, tortured people lying below. The screamers should be realistic rather than melodramatic. They need not interact with the rituallers, and indeed should ignore them.

- **The Island of the Ancestors:** This area is delineated by a long blue cloth encircling an area, or perhaps a series of pots or trays of water. This "moat" can have the writhing faces of the Dead in it, if you desire. The island in the center has a mound (which can be a mound of anything sturdy, including a large box draped in canvas and then covered with stones and dirt) with a flat spot on top, large enough for a person to climb up and sit. A "treasure box" sits next to the mound, alongside a large stationary drum.
- **Baldur's Place:** Two flags of white and gold with Wunjo runes on them flank this area. It can be simple, with a chair for Nanna to sit in, and a few lit candles of white and gold for Baldur.
- **Elvidnir:** The castle of Hela has a "door" archway, and beyond it are feast tables flanked by two rows of poles with banners. The banners on one side are crisp and new, if colored in with somewhat morbid symbols – ravens, skulls, bats, her rune, etc. The banners on the other side have symbols of beauty on them, but they are ragged, stained, torn, and look very old. The tables are set with candles, dishes, food and drink. Ganglati stands at the door with a basin of water, a ewer, and a red towel. More basins, ewers, and towels sit to the side. Hela stands behind a cloth hanging at the back, unseen. If the ritual is outside and a bonfire can be made, Elvidnir should be next to the bonfire.

The rituallers begin at the Gathering Place. The Greeter waits until they have collected, and then speaks to them.

Greeter: Tonight we journey into the Underworld of the Germanic peoples, the Norse and Germans and Anglo-Saxons. While there were many places for the Dead to go in that cosmology, most who passed went to Helheim, the Land of the Dead, ruled by Hela the Goddess of Death. Helheim lies at the very bottom of the World Tree, beneath its roots. To get there, we will have to cross the great river Gjöll, and the Bridge of Knives. Then we must pass the Guardians of Helheim, who will decide whether to let us pass or not.

Why do we go to the Land of the Dead tonight? We go for an honorable reason. We go to bring food and drink and music to the Dead, to give them joy and cheer and the memories of being alive – the best memories, not the painful ones. We will do this in many ways. First, we will feast them with food and drink – many of you have donated some, and we thank you for that. Second, those who can sing or play music should do so, that the Dead might be entertained. In addition, some of you may choose to eat and drink for the Dead, allowing them to taste the food through your bodies.

To do this, simply approach the table and sit, and declare to the Dead that they have permission to use your flesh to experience the feast, but only on the condition that they take nothing else, and leave you when you are done. Be warned that you may not feel, afterward, as if you have eaten or drunk – they may take it all from you, or they may not. If you are not comfortable with doing this, do not feel that you must – instead, sing, or dance for them, or simply sit and pray. We will be having a feast for the living later, after we have returned from Helheim.

Also, remember to act with respect to the Dead and their keepers, and the Lady who has been gracious enough to allow us to enter her land. Now we walk the Hel Road, where thousands of our ancestors have walked before us, and we walk with the Dead who died today, and are traveling to their new home.

The Greeter turns and leads the way through the arch, moving in a slow and stately manner. If there are "ghosts" hanging from lines, they may pull the strings attached to them in order to make the ghosts flank the rituallers for a few steps. As they approach the bridge, the Greeter stops everyone.

Greeter: We stand before the icy river Gjöll, before the Bridge of Knives. Gjöll is so cold that even to touch it will freeze you – it is one of the oldest rivers here, dating from the age when all was frozen. In order to cross the bridge, we must make an offering. Think of something that you must change, for it is harmful to the world. Take this ice from me, and name it for that act, and fling it into Gjöll as a sacrifice.

The Greeter hands out the pieces of clear glass, and each person names their unwanted act and flings it away into the river.

Greeter: Now who will be the brave one to walk across the Bridge of Knives? If you close your eyes, take a breath, and start walking, you will find that the bridge yields to you.

The bravest person will start forward with their eyes closed, and the tinfoil knives will crumple beneath their feet. Everyone follows across. At the other side, Mordgud blocks the way with her spear.

Mordgud: I am Mordgud, the Guardian of the Helgrind, Hel's Gate. It is my charge to protect the Dead, and to guide them on the final steps to their new home ... and to keep foolish mortals out of our realm. Why have you come?

The Greeter should let others speak; only if they cannot answer Mordgud satisfactorily should the Greeter interrupt and explain their mission.

> Well, that is all right then. If you come only to give, and not to take away, you may enter. But whatever you do, don't fall asleep here ... you might not wake up again. Oh, and watch out for Garm.

She steps aside. If people ask, "Who is Garm?" she just smiles. As they move toward the gate, Garm leaps up and comes at them, growling. The Greeter calls out, "Do not move! Remain still!" Garm moves through the crowd, sniffing everyone, then returns to the Greeter, who gives him a piece of meat. He retires to the side, then, chewing his meal, and the group passes through the archway. On the other side of the archway stands Groa.

Groa: Welcome to the Deathrealms. I am Groa, and long ago I walked the world of the living, a giantess and sorceress. I died many centuries ago in a terrible battle, and now I dwell here. My mistress has sent me to guide you, and show you a few of the mysteries of this place.

She turns and beckons, and the rituallers follow. At this point I feel a need to add that if you are doing this ritual with an extremely large group, you may wish to add two other Dead souls to Groa's station, and split the party into three groups. Then each group can go on to one of the next three stations, and keep rotating until they have each seen all three. However, for a single group, the first station is ideally Nastrond. Here, the Dragon is curled on the pile of corpses, chewing on them. She leaps up as they approach, and comes toward them with an undulating motion, hissing.

Nidhogg: Sssss ... What have we here? Visitors to the Strand of Corpses? These are the Dead who pile up beneath the Earth, who must be transformed ... by me. Yessss, children, I am the ones who turns rot into Earth. Remember that everything you walk on was once rot. Remember that everything you eat had to grow in what was rotted down. This is the bottom of the World Tree, and here we deal with what was thrown away. What do you throw away, children, that you could do otherwise with? Do you believe that there is such a place as "away"?

Everyone answers Nidhogg, as best as they can. She is somewhat hostile with her questions, sticking her muzzle in people's faces and insisting that they speak of what they have thrown away, and how it could have been recycled better. Ideally, she extracts promises from them as to how they can better deal with their refuse, and learn that there is no such place as "away". Then she sends them on with Groa to the Hall of Nastrond. Here people are lying on the ground writhing in pain, screaming, with "venom" dripping on them from the serpents above.

Groa: Yes, their suffering is terrible. But notice ... there is no locked door on this hall. No one keeps them here. They stay here for their own reasons, because they believe they need to suffer for one reason or another. You will not be able to convince them otherwise, believe me. When they have decided that they no longer need to suffer, they will come out and be at peace. But if you wish, you can pray for them.

She encourages everyone to kneel by the door, and pray for not only the souls inside, but all the people they know who are locked into a cycle of pain and suffering from which they do not know how to extract themselves. Then she takes the party to the next station, which is the Island of the Ancestors. She leads them across the "water", telling them that they can walk across it, and then to the Island. Here she climbs up and sits on the mound.

Groa: This is the Island of the Ancestors, where they come to you in order to tell you their wisdom. You must climb up on the mound of the Dead and sit for a moment, and silence yourself, and wait for the space of thirty heartbeats. Either they will give you a message, meant only for you, or they will not. While you sit, the other will beat out thirty heartbeats for you. Then you will come down and relinquish your place to another, and take a treasure from the box of the Ancestors' wisdom.

Some person or persons are chosen to beat the drum slowly, like a heartbeat. Each person in turn climbs up onto the mound, sits silently, and then comes down. Groa holds the box in such a way that they cannot see into it, and they reach in blindly and choose something from it. These can be sayings written on paper, or small charms, or pictures of some long-gone person or place or thing, or whatever is decided by those who run the ritual.

When everyone has done this, Groa leads the group to Baldur's station. He is standing facing away from them, and Nanna is sitting on a chair a bit behind him. As they come toward him, he turns and gives them a brilliant smile.

Baldur: Do you know who I am? *(Whether they can name him or not, he continues:)* I am the light incarnate that was plunged into darkness, and now I light the dark places. I am living proof that even within the darkest places there is still a light, whether you can see it or not. I await the end of the world, when I will be released again to light the upper world.

Nanna rises and comes toward them.

Nanna: Do you know who I am? *(Whether they can name her or not, she continues:)* I am love so strong that it does not fear death. I am the courage to walk with love even through the flame and blizzard and drowning wave and devouring earth. I wait in the darkness with Light, and you will find me here as well, when you are cast into the darkness at any time in your life.

Baldur: Don't be afraid. I will not test you, or shock you. I am just here to bless you, if you want my blessing. If you want to be able to see that small point of light in the darkness, I can show you the way. Who would be blessed?

If any wish to come forth to receive his blessing, they do so. They should kneel before him, and he will place his hands gently on their head, and say, "You are blessed. Never be lost in the dark again."

Nanna: How strong is your love? Would you know love as strong as mine, both in the eyes of the one who would follow you to Hel, and in your own heart to give it back? Would you find that love when you are caught in dark places, whether from human hearts or from the Gods? Then come and take my blessing as well, and may it bear you up in the face of all the hardship that life can inflict on you and your loved ones.

If any wish to receive her blessing, they do so. She embraces them, one by one, and says, "You are blessed. Never be without love in the dark again."

Baldur: Do not forget us. Even though we are dead, we are still Gods. The Dead are not powerless; remember this.

Nanna: Remember us! Find us in darkness. We are Light and Love.

Then Groa leads the party to the final station, which is Elvidnir, Hela's palace. If there have been multiple parties making the rounds of the stations, this is the point where they all come together. Ganglati stands in the gateway to meet them.

Ganglati: Welcome to Elvidnir, the palace of my Lady, Hela the Queen of the Dead. Here is where the Dead are feasted, and where you will do your duty to them. But first, you must be purified. Kneel, each in your turn, and I will wash you clean of your old resentments, the old anger that has rotted within you. Give it a decent burial here. Let it fall into the earth of Hela's land, and be done with. Then enter into the place of the Ancestors clean of these old things.

Ganglati cleanses the hands of the first person, but does not let them in. Instead, she speaks to them, loudly.

Ganglati: What, would you have me serve everyone here, and with no aid? If you are truly cleansed, take the water and cleanse another. Give the blessing that you received. Service is honorable, fool! Serve your friends and fellow travelers.

It is likely that they will acquiesce, but if they refuse for any reason other than extreme physical disability, Ganglati is free to turn foul and curse them out. However, ideally all the next few people will take a set of implements and begin purifying, until all the sets of implements are in people's hands. Then they should wash the hands of one or several more, and then pass on the basin and ewer and towel to another. It is important that it be done this way, not only for speed and the ability to handle many at once, but also because one of Ganglati's lessons is willing service. Thus the work should be passed on to the people rather than all done by a row of attendants. The staff members who play Nidhogg, Baldur, Nanna, and any other dead folk may remove their costumes and join the crowds as mortals wishing to honor their Dead. Mordgud, however, must hold her post. Garm may come with them, but as Garm, and he must lay down beside Hela's throne for the remainder of the rite. When everyone is cleansed, Groa comes to Ganglati.

Groa: Old friend, let us all go in together.

They turn and lead everyone into the hall together. People are lined up on the doorway side of the feast table(s), but they should be prevented from standing on the far side of the farthest table, for this is where Hela will stand.

Groa: Welcome to the feast hall of the Dead. You cannot see them, but they are all around you now. They welcome you, for you are all the future that they worked and struggled for. Every one of us must pass this gate, and although the Dead may go to many places, it is likely that nearly all of you have at least one ancestor here, watching you, smiling, happy that you are alive for them to see. Hail to the Dead!

All: Hail to the Dead!

Ganglati: We hail also Hela, the Queen of this realm, who cares for every one of the Dead like a mother. Your ancestors here have passed through Her love, and live in it still. Hail Hela!

All: Hail Hela!

Hela steps forth from behind the curtain, and comes slowly up to the table. She reaches out the right "human" hand, and Groa kisses it.

Hela: For my beloved Dead, and all of them are beloved to me, no matter who they were in life.

Then Hela reaches out the left "skeletal" hand, and one of the party who has been briefed beforehand kisses it.

Hela: For the living, for they are beloved to me as well. So many of you will one day pass my gates, after all. I wish to see you come to me strong in spirit and not defeated, but if you come broken I will heal you and love you anyhow. But now, will you feed my Dead? I feed them every night, but tonight I ask your aid in doing so.

The people come forth with their offerings and place them on the tables. If they wish to speak the names of beloved Dead, they should do so now. Those who choose to do so may eat and drink some of the offerings, and allow the Dead to taste them through their bodies. Groa should remind them to save some for Mordgud, who must stay at her post. While this happens, Hela is seated on the throne, and speaks up when it has all been done.

Hela: You have received the blessing of the Light and the Love in the darkness. Would you now take the blessing of the

Darkness itself, that you might never walk in fear into its embrace? Would you learn to lay down your fear of Death itself? Then come to me for a blessing.

Those who wish the blessing can come forth and kneel, and kiss Hela's skeletal hand, and be told some thing that only they can hear. When all who would come forth have done so, Hela speaks.

Hela: Go forth from here now, and feast among the living, but do not forget my children here, whose children you are.

Groa leads everyone out, and back to the bridge. There she turns them back over to Mordgud.

Mordgud: Have you feasted the Dead? Good!

The party then gives her the offerings they have saved.

Mordgud: Well! You have learned something of courtesy in our cold land. Go in peace, then ... until I see you again.

They cross the bridge, and the rite is over.

Originally published in *Sacred Masque: Ensemble Rituals for Pagan Groups*, by Raven Kaldera, Asphodel Press, 2012.

Sun Wheel Rite for Yule
Raven Kaldera

This is a Neo-Pagan rite that has been adapted for the Northern Tradition, honoring the Wheel of the Year, to be performed at Yule when the Sun is at its lowest point.

We made a Sun Wheel by lashing pieces of wood to a yard-wide metal hoop bought in a craft store, so as to form an eight-spoked wheel, and we covered the unsightly metal by wrapping it with colored yarn. More yarn was tied to the ends of the spokes and knotted together, about four feet up from the center of the wheel. A flat candle holder was affixed to the center. The first time that we did the rite that this one is based on, the wheel acquired its eight sacred dangly objects. After that, we would bind (with more colored yarn) evergreen boughs onto it.

We always lit a short fat red candle in the center, where the strings were farthest away, but sometimes we put candles on the edges as well. When it was covered in fresh evergreens, we would cut oranges in half and hollow out the inside (throwing the orange bits into the Yule punch), and nestle the half-orange-peel cups in among the boughs holding votive candles. We never had a problem with the candles burning the fresh greenery or the wettish orange peels (if carefully arranged and watched), but if you try this, be very careful that no candle flames are near enough to the supporting strings to burn through them, or the whole thing will come down in a flaming mess.

This rite uses at least nine people, so it's a good one for an inside ritual where you've got a lot of folks who want to participate. Each person was dressed in the appropriate colors. Our sun symbol was trashpicked, someone's thrown-away art project, a base with a big gilded metal spiral and a candle holder on top. One could just as easily be made from a toy horse and cart and a wooden disk, all sprayed gold.

☙ ☙ ❧ ❧

Eight people gather around the sun wheel, decorated and hanging from the ceiling. The ninth – the Sunna officiant – is clothed in colors of glittering flame and carries the sun symbol. The Sunna officiant lights the candle in the center of the sun wheel and says:

> Hail to the Sun who walks the way
> Of dusty dawn, of golden glow,

Of glint of growing, turning Day.
Hail to the cycle and the flow.

    Welcome to our hearth and home and tribe.

    This is the darkest day of the year, the longest night, when the Sun is swallowed up and dies. In ancient times, the Sun was brought back to life with fire and light on the Solstice.

    Let us imagine, now, those dark and ancient times. Go back six thousand years to a cold place. You are clad in clothing of rough wool and fur, and you speak a language unlike ours, yet with some words that will someday be passed on to us. Your people have lived in this cold place for so long that you remember the glaciers melting, the Ice Age receding. It is part of your creation myths.

    Imagine that you are standing in a clearing in the woods, the scent of pine all around you, just before dawn. It is freezing cold, and for days uncounted you have huddled inside next to a fire, with the sky too dark to work or even to see outside. Yet on this morning your eyes are fixed on a single standing stone, or perhaps a pole driven into the earth, which will prove the rebirth of the Sun which gives all life.

    Imagine that you watch the Sun rise, seeing it come up in its appointed place as it always does, and a hush of wonder falls over your tribe, crowded around you. It is the promise of the new year, the promise that the days will get longer, and eventually warmer, and the spring will come. You rejoice. You cheer. You weep with joy. You beat on drums and shout. You call this day Yeohwla, which means simply, the Winter Solstice.

    Someday strangers will come, driving wagons, great numbers of them. They will settle next to you, and intermarry with you, and teach of things like wheels and horses, and you will give them the words "wife", and "child", and teach them the mysteries of "Yeohwla", which their descendants – and yours – will pass on as Yule. You will teach the mysteries of Hope and Rebirth, of fire and light that resurrects the year. And they will stand in that cold place and learn to praise the coming of the Sun, and so will their children's children. And so do we.

Take flame now, flame from the wheel of the Sun, and carry it close to you, for fire is precious. It means warmth and light and cooked food. Be careful with it, neither letting it spread nor go out. Each of you light a candle and hold it close.

Everyone comes forth with small candles and lights them from the wheel's flame. The Sunna officiant lights the Sun symbol. Then the first of the eight callers steps forth, dressed all in white and gold. The Sunna officiant moves to stand behind them, holding up the Sun symbol so that it can be seen above their head, and says:

> Hail to the sleeping Sun Maiden who awakes!
> Hail to her first steps, like one newborn,
> As she feels the change, the shift,
> The turn from downward to upward!
> On this the shortest day of all,
> Odin leads the Wild Hunt in shrieking furor,
> Bonfires burn and voices are upraised in song,
> And Sunna blinks her sky-bright eyes
> And blesses us on the frosty Yule morning.

The first caller ties a straw pinecone to the end of one wheel spoke. The second caller steps forward, dressed all in red and gold, and says:

> Hail to the Sun over the snowfields!
> Hail to her light over the frozen land
> As the lambs are born and the ewe's milk flows.
> Frau Holle shakes the snow from her pillows
> Like clouds of feathers in the sky,
> We hail the Disir of our ancestors,
> The women who survived to watch in wisdom,
> And Sunna lights the darkened sky
> And blesses us on this frozen Oimelc morning.

The second caller ties a snowflake to the end of one wheel spoke. The third caller steps forward, dressed all in blue and gold, and says:

> Hail to the Sun in the time of Spring!
> Dawn's own moment, the in-breath of perfect air,

> The time of wind and rain, fierce storms
> And freshest of wet mornings. Hail Ostara
> As she dances through the greening fields, hail Freya
> With flowers blooming in her footsteps.
> Hail Thor who brings the rain and washes clean,
> And Sunna lights the equinox sky
> And blesses us on this wet Ostara morning.

The third caller ties a colored egg to the end of one wheel spoke. The fourth caller steps forward, dressed all in green and gold, and says:

> Hail to the Sun in the time of Greening!
> The trees spread their leaves, the flowers bloom,
> The pole rises to touch the sky!
> For deep in the darkness Odin the Wanderer
> Who hung three nights in the embrace of the Tree
> Has won the runes and broken free, and we rejoice!
> Walburga walks the woods, the Hunt can never catch her,
> And Sunna lights the green-leaved sky
> And blesses us on this fair Walpurgisnacht morning.

The fourth caller ties a bunch of colored ribbons to the end of one wheel spoke. The fifth caller steps forward, dressed all in yellow and gold, and says:

> Hail to the Sun on her most perfect day!
> We are torn between great joy and great sorrow
> For the Sun is golden overhead, and abundant are the fruits
> Of the earth, and yet Baldur's blood soaks
> Into that earth as well. It is the first sudden funeral
> Of the year, and we dance for sorrow and for joy.
> The first golden king walks the Hel Road,
> And Sunna reigns over the tear-blue sky
> And blesses us on this bright Litha morning.

The fifth caller ties a tiny golden sun to the end of one wheel spoke. The sixth caller steps forward, dressed all in amber and gold, and says:

> Hail to the Sun over the fields of grain!
> On this day Frey, the second golden king,
> Walks willingly to his doom. As the sickle cuts,

> As the grain falls, as the harvest is begun,
> The people are fed, and the Sun's bounty is collected.
> Hail to Frey and his willing sacrifice, no sudden thing
> But measured, open, gentle-handed like Death
> And Sunna lights the summer sky
> And blesses us on this golden Lammas morning.

The sixth caller ties a tiny wheatsheaf to the end of one wheel spoke. The seventh caller steps forward, dressed all in orange and gold, and says:

> Hail to the Sun over the Harvest Fair!
> We have worked and toiled on Jord's fertile breast
> And we reap the abundance that we deserve, or at least
> That we have been lucky enough to get this year.
> Hail to the scythe, the winnowing basket, the honey in the hive,
> The grain and beer, the milk that flows and the flesh
> That is sacrificed that we might live and thrive,
> And Sunna lights the autumn sky
> And blesses us on this cool Harvest morning.

The seventh caller ties a straw horn to the end of one wheel spoke. The eighth caller steps forward, dressed all in black and gold, and says:

> Hail to the Sun on Winter's Gate!
> The leaves fall like a carpet before Sunna's fading path
> And the barrows of the Ancestors call us, looming
> Like dark shadows through the bare black trees.
> Darkness is setting in, but we do not fear,
> For all things turn again unto the light, as Sunna
> Herself has taught us, in her dancing round of the year.
> And Sunna lights the clouded sky
> And blesses us this Winternight morning.

The eighth caller ties a skull to the end of one wheel spoke. The Sunna officiant steps forth and says:

> Hail to the Ancestors who lived that we might live,
> Who watched the Sun's round and praised her mightily.
> Hail Sunna! Bless us all with your bright gaze
> And bring the light of contentment
> With all things that flux and change

And yet always come around
Into our questing hearts.

All: Hail Sunna!

A horn of mead is passed, and folk speak of some great difficulty that troubled them, but that they have now come to terms with, and how they came to understanding on a day-to-day basis. This is the sort of thing which Sunna excels at – aiding those who would learn how to cope daily with something hard that will not pass, and teaching them never to let it dim their light. The candles are not put out until everyone has left the room, unless they become a fire hazard.

Originally published in *Day Star and Whirling Wheel*, by Galina Krasskova, Asphodel Press, 2012.

Rituals for Gods

Rite of the Tides
Seawalker

How to do a rite to the Ocean-King
And his family, they ask me? First, the sea.
Perhaps it could be done around a bowl
Filled with shells, sea salt, water from the tap
And perhaps not. The Gods are who they are,
And sometimes it is not fair, their demands.
Perhaps they feel that if you truly value them
A trip to the shore would be worth the price, even
If it were a thousand miles. But first, the sea.

Walk through the sand in procession, carrying
The sacred artifacts. If you are but one, walk still
As if a dozen followed you. Each footstep placed
Deliberate, pressing the sand or pebbles underfoot.
Up to the edge, where the water touches your toes
But no further. Then you sing. What? It does not matter,
It is the singing that counts. Then you call their names
One by one, and with each one walk one step further
Into the water. Invocations are good, have you a tongue
Of silver, but the names alone will do.

For Aegir first, the Ocean-King, new beer
Brewed in someone's kitchen, their finest made.
No corporate bottle and chemicals, only hops
And grain and yeast, and other wholesome flavors.
Pour it into the tide and let the ocean take it.

For Ran, his queen, there can be only gold.
Some jewelry, perhaps – rings she loves,
And better still it be the memory of some lost love
Bitterly soaked in tears. She will cleanse it
With the salt of a thousand waves. But gold, only gold.

The Nine, if you have nothing else
You can offer them blood, and they will accept it.

But were you to give gifts, Kolga will take a piece
Of dry ice, frozen gas to bubble and swear in the
Waves. Or perhaps some clear water or wine frozen into
A cunning shape. Duva, pearls. Single, or on a strand,
But pearls win her favor. Hronn, something sharp
Of stone or shell, something you cringe to throw in
For imagining some child's foot pierced tomorrow,
As they wade unheeding through the ebb and flow,
But still, it is her wish. Hevring, only tears will do.
Shed them with feeling – there will be something
In your life that deserves them, some grief.
Bylgja, a die cast, or the figure of a horse,
Or perhaps a sea horse dried and curled. Bara
Will take no gift from you save a chunk of land
Thrown into the water. Dig it with your hands
And return it to the sea from whence it all came.
Unn, a string of tiny shells, the more the better.
Himinglava, a glass crystal, with the sun
Caught in its shine before it hits the water.
And Blodughadda, there is only blood for her.
Blood her last, so that if all nine wish a drop
Of your red life, you may give it,
As you have fingers enough and one to spare.

Then sing again, waist-deep now in water,
And stay to hear their wisdom, or go,
Singing as you walk, as if a dozen
Processioners followed you, as if eleven
Pairs of eyes followed you,
Which in fact they do.

Originally published in *Full Fathom Five*, by Galina Krasskova. Asphodel Press, 2007.

Rite of the Nine Mermaids
Linda Demissy, Lokabrenna Kindred

This group rite is meant to honor and commune with the nine Mermaids, but can also include their mother Ran and father Aegir, as well as Njord the Ship-God. It can be done with two to a hundred people, preferably near a body of water – the sea, a lake, or a river that drains into the sea. It *might* work with a stagnant pond, indoor or outdoor pool, but the further removed it is from connecting to the sea, the more difficult the connection seems to becomes. It's best done whenever local water is warm enough to flow to the sea, or at any time if you are by the seashore. My kindred does it around August 1st.

Ideally, one should have spent time doing devotions to the nine Mermaids before leading this rite to have some kind of connection with them. Doing so by the sea is ideal, but I discovered that singing Blodughadda's Song[1] near a river can open a connection to the sea and to the Nine Sisters, provided she likes you. I was driving over the Champlain Bridge[2] at the time, and she demanded I return the next day to make offering. Not one to argue with a goddess, I did so, whereupon she announced that what is offered to one must be offered to all nine. That led to a very interesting summer of weekly trips to the river shore to meet all of the Sisters, and since I'd offered her a fruit and nine drops of my blood, that is what I had to offer to each of them. Of all the fruits I tried, lemon and lime were most appreciated. All that seafood, and no lemon juice to go with it! Bara also liked granola bars (I baked her a giant one after she enjoyed a small commercial one), and I'm told Blodughadda enjoys blood red berries such as raspberries.

For this group rite (and my home altar), I prepared a set of "sea hallows" with twelve stainless steel wine cups from the camping supplies department. The three extras were for Ran, who demanded my presence at the river during a thunderstorm, as well as Aegir and Njord, as I expected to eventually meet them. I designed crests on cardstock and glued them to the cups with Outdoor Modge Podge™. Links to my experiences and crest images can be found on the online

---

[1] From the *Nine Sea Songs and Other Tides* CD, by Raven Kaldera.
[2] I live on the island of Montreal in the middle of the St-Lawrence Seaway, a great river leading to the sea.

Nine Sisters's Shrine[3], and you are most welcome to use them. You could also use a variety of different cups and tape their names on to make temporary hallows.

Altar Setup and Preparing the Space

The altar for the rite consists of nine to twelve cups set upon an altar or cloth (twelve if you are also honoring Ran, Aegir and Njord). Each of the cups contains a folded cue card detailing their basic attributes and symbolic actions. There are also two vessels of water to asperge with for purification and consecration. One is filled with safe drinkable water and the other with "dangerous" water collected from a natural source, which may or may not be safe to drink. A big jug of drinkable water should also be near the altar and available; let people know they can drink from it. Bring a watch so you can allot ten minutes to brainstorming. You'll also need a drum and someone who can play it. Where do you put the altar?

Altar in the center: This gives everyone a better view of the altar and cups. It works best in small groups where everyone is close to the altar.

Altar on the edge of the circle: The altar should be placed in the direction closest to the water, so that people see the water when they're looking at the altar and celebrants. If you're in a building or far from water, just pick whichever direction is closest to the sea or a body of water. You can point that out to people during the rite. Here in Montreal I would say: *"Now we face the St-Laurence river, which leads the sea."* This layout makes it easier to be heard when addressing the people, because there's no one behind you when your back is to the altar. When addressing the sea spirits, go across to the other side of the circle, facing the altar. Again, most of the people will be in front of you and able to hear you.

Before the rite, you can have people go around with garbage bags to pick up litter as an offering to the spirits of water and shore.

ශ ශ ෨ ෨

---

[3] http://www.northernpaganism.org/shrines/ninesisters/

Check-in

Example: *"Where is your head at? How are you feeling? And what do you hope to get out of this ritual? I'll start with what I'm feeling and hope to get from this: I'm excited about doing this ritual and I want to see how well people can connect to the Mermaids through this rite."*

For a large group, ask that it be just one word (or very few words) for how they're feeling, and another for what they want. It's useful for the main celebrant (priestess or priest) to know if people are tired, sleepy, worried or enthusiastic so they can adjust the rite. Example for a large group: *"I'll start with what I'm feeling and hope to get from this: 'Curious', and 'meet the Mermaids'."*

If people are sleepy, don't have them sit and meditate for a long time with their eyes closed; they'll fall asleep. You might want to add something that makes them get up, move around and breathe during the rite so they can wake up a bit, i.e. *"Let's do the wave!"* If they're tense, having them shake their body out can help, *"Before the meditative calm comes the storm. Let's dance the storm, shake your body like a great sea storm and let the drums roar like the pounding wind!"* If they're feeling clueless, spend more time on the pre-ritual briefing and answer questions. If the group is small and doesn't know each other well, people can share a bit more, and perhaps talk about where they're coming from. This shouldn't take more than ten minutes for a small group, and five minutes for a large group.

It's generally a good idea to do a check-in before rituals (something I stole from the Reclaiming Tradition), but it's especially important to let people express their emotions for *this* rite. After all, these deities help deal with difficult emotions, and you can't do that if you don't express them. Right?

It's also important that people have a personal goal. If you come to a ritual or perform a devotion without a personal goal, chances are you won't get what you need from it. You'll wait for the ritual leaders or the gods to give you a goal, which they often won't, or you'll simply miss out on the blessings received because you weren't looking for them. If you know what you're looking for, you have a better chance of finding it. Pick a goal, any goal. Don't let me see it. Put it back in the deck.

Horn and Banner 117

Pre-Ritual Briefing

Give a verbal outline of the ritual so people know what to expect and what will be expected of them. Teach them the chants if they're expected to sing, as well as any call and responses.

Example:

> The goal of this rite is for us to have a personal experience of each of the nine Mermaids, the daughters of Aegir and Ran. Aegir is the god of the sea, and host of great feasts for the gods of Asgard. His daughters all embody more or less difficult emotions, and for the central part of the rite, you'll get to choose which one you want to work with. When you've chosen, you'll go off with those who want to honor that same Mermaid and spend ten minutes brainstorming. Notice that there's a cue card in each cup to help you out. The goal is to prepare a one-minute performance that represents what your Mermaid is all about. It could be dance, poetry, theatre, singing, knitting, a personal relevant story, or whatever else you want.
>
> When the sound of drum calls you back, each group will take a turn performing. We'll all get to experience each of the Mermaids, either by honoring her directly, or by watching.
>
> You have the choice of working with the Mermaid of Rivers, Blood, and Sacrifice; of Whirlpools, Fear, and Faith; of Sorrow, Suffering, and Grieving Loss; of Fog, Mystery, being Lost and Found; of Tides, Time, and Memory; of Ice, Cold, and Loneliness; of Fair Weather and Joy; of Breakers, Obsession, and Motivation; of Joyful Aggression, Erosion, and Patience.
>
> The rite will start with grounding and centering, hallowing and purifications, then singing Blodughadda's song to ask her to invite her sisters. You'll choose your Mermaid cup, go off for ten minutes, come back, do your performance, and then we'll go to the water for personal prayers, so you can ask for the blessing you want, from any of the Mermaids, and decide what you're willing to sacrifice in your life to have that blessing. We'll come back

for a final grounding and centering, and then thank the goddesses. Any questions?

Meditation

We are centering in our hearts and grounding in the sea. People can sit or stand for this. Drum "Down With Water" during the centering, grounding and synchronizing meditation. The rhythm is: *Dum–dadada– – – – – –*. The feeling is a sinking one, as water sinks down into the ground. It's played slowly with a long pause. The drumming lasts three beats and the silence lasts five beats. This means you play *Dum-dadada*, then count to five silently, then play the pattern again, count to five, etc.

Down With Water Rhythm:

1	&	2	&	3	&	4	&	5	&	6	&	7	&	8
Dum	-	da	da	da		-		-		-		-		-

Meditation:

We are made of the sea, *salt water*, our body is three quarters, *salt water*, our blood is mostly, *salt water*. Our center, our heart's blood is, *salt water*, and you can feel your breathing with the *salt water*, and feel inside yourself that *salt water*, to find one drop of your heart's blood, *salt water*, feel that drop, shaped like a tear, *salt water*, pulsing with life, *salt water*, your life, glowing red and alive, *salt water*, and imagine that all around it, your body is just, *salt water*, salt water flowing to the ground, *salt water*, seeping into the ground, *salt water*, with that drop of your heart's blood, *salt water*, traveling inside the ground, *salt water*, reaching the river, *salt water*, flowing down with the river, *salt water*, with your heart's blood, *salt water*, flowing down into the sea, *salt water*, becoming part of the sea, *salt water*, is sea water.

Salt water, which is where all life comes from, *salt water*, separating itself into a shape, *salt water*, climbing back onto the shore, *salt water*, returning to our circle, *salt water*, what all of us share in common, *salt water*, back to our hearts, *salt water*, our blood and our life, *salt water* (pause), *salt water* (pause), *salt water* (pause). We are made of the sea, and we are here to learn the ways of the sea.

It's best to have someone else drumming while you lead the meditation, which is meant to be spoken with a rhythm punctuated by "salt water". I suggest you sway as you speak, and you may ask people to repeat "salt water." You may also switch to saying "sea water" for the second paragraph of the meditation.

Hallowing
a) Purifications: Asperging

One celebrant holds a vessel of safe drinking water and the other of untested water from a natural source (lake, river, etc.)[4] They go around the circle in opposite directions offering "Do you want the blessing of safe waters?" or "Do you want the blessing of dangerous waters?" and sprinkle water on those who agree. You could have safe waters go clockwise and dangerous counterclockwise. You could have them asperge the ritual area outside the circle of people first, then the people, then the area inside the circle to make a triple circle of water, if you wish. For a large group, you should have one such pair of helpers per thirty people attending, to keep the pace of the rite.

b) Sacred Space: Honoring The Waters

Near the seashore:

> Spirits of the Sea, we honor you and ask that you join us at your shores. May you be blessed and may your waters flow ever more clear and clean.

Near a river or lake:

> River/Lake Spirit, we honor you and ask that you allow the Sea Spirits to join us at your shores. May you be blessed and may your waters flow ever more clear and clean.

If you're not by the sea, it is only polite to first sing or pray to your closest river or lake spirit for permission to bring sea spirits to its shores.

---

[4] We had fun using a water pistol filled with river water to shoot out the blessings of the dangerous waters. The safe tap water was sprinkled with a pine cone from a bowl shaped chalice.

Make an offering if you can, one that won't pollute the river (I've used glass marbles). Cleaning up the shores before the rite is the best offering, and you should make sure that the river or lake spirit is agreeable *before* you invite everyone to your rite. This also applies to seashore rites.

c) Opening the Ways: Blodughadda's Song

Face the water. Feel your pulse and start drumming your own heartbeat. Keep drumming and sing Blodughadda's Song to bring the sea to you, to merge the water before you with the waters of the sea. Blodughadda rules the relationship between rivers and sea, which is why we call on her to help. If you can't sing her song, you can simply speak the words[5] or make your own invocation. When you feel her presence, welcome her and thank her for coming.

As I mentioned, it's a good idea to do private devotions in the days or weeks before leading this rite. Blodughadda is an excellent choice for this if you live near a river. Another would be Unn, who connects us to the tides of the sea through rhythm and drumming. She gave me inspiration for the two rhythms used in this rite.

The point of *opening the ways* is to make it easier for the gods to reach us, and for us to notice them. How do you expect them to arrive? If you expect them to emerge from the river, then face that direction. If you have a seat of honor for them, focus on noticing their arrival there. If you look nowhere in particular, you're telling them that they should arrive as some diffuse presence in the ritual area. This is fine if that's your goal. Is it?

Generally, rites try to bridge the gap between the ritual space and wherever that deity lives. By creating common ground, it makes it easier for them to come and easier for us to perceive them. If their home is fiery, you light a bonfire, candles, or hang flame colored cloth. If it's watery, you try to do it near a body of water, or at least have a large bowl of water or cauldron. These become your focus for them to step through into our world. It's also a way of making them feel welcome.

---

[5] The words to Blodughadda's song can be found on the *Nine Sea Songs and Other Tides* CD, or *The Jotunbok*, both by Raven Kaldera.

Choice

You'll need to go over who the Mermaids are and what they do again before the drumming starts. Folks started thinking about their options during the pre-ritual briefing and have likely kept thinking about it until now.

For large groups, you can pick up each cup, talk about that Mermaid (or read the cue card out loud), then put the cup down on the ground further out from the altar to form a bigger circle of cups. This will help people remember where each cup they're interested in is located, and avoid everyone crowding around the altar to reach their chosen cup. If your circle of cups is large enough, people will be able to gather around their chosen cup.

After describing each Mermaid again, pray for inspiration:

> Ran, mother of the sea, we are here to honor your family. Mother of terror, Mother of storms, inspire us to know the storms that rage within our hearts, to find the sea within our blood, and to honor you and your daughters well today.

Start drumming "Up With Water" while people choose their Mermaid.

The rhythm is: **dadadadada Dum Dum Dum**. The beats are hard, fast and loud, and there is no pause before restarting the sequence. The beat is on a 6 count. It's used to raise the energy level of the group.

Up With Water Rhythm:

1	&	2	&	3	&	4	&	5	&	6	&
da	da	da	da	da		Dum		Dum		Dum	

Brainstorm

Once everyone has chosen their Mermaid, stop the drumming.

> Each of you, now go with your cup to find your own space. You have ten minutes to create your performance, and you will have one minute to perform it. Return when the drum calls you back.

Invocations & Offerings

Wait ten minutes. Drum "Up With Water" again to announces call them back.

You can ask for volunteers, or call them in whatever order you like. Before they perform, I do a brief invocation along the lines of "Duva, Mermaid of Islands and Fog, Mystery and Wayfinding, join us now and share with us your mysteries!" Then step back to let Duva's chosen perform. The invocation serves to call Duva as much as it helps remind everyone who we're honoring and what she's about. After the performance, and any applause there might be, call out "Hail Duva!" and encourage the group to repeat. If you have enough jingles for everyone these would be great to use instead of applause.

Blessing

Invite people to step into the water (or at least dip a hand in it) and commune silently, meditating on what blessings they might like from the Mermaids, and what they're willing to give up to have it. If inside, a cauldron or wading pool might be used.

We have witnessed the mysteries of the Mermaids, the powers of the sea. We have honored them with our performances and hope they are pleased. Take a moment to feel that. Do you feel a connection? Are they pleased?" Pause long enough for people to start nodding or smiling. "Now we may ask them for blessings, and you can once again choose any of them to pray to, whether you honored her directly or not. What do you need in your life? Do you need to deal with sorrow, grieve a loss and find your strength? That's Hevring's blessing. Do you need to learn to be more quiet and mysterious like Duva, or more persistent like Bara? Do you need to be bolder in taking what you want like Ran? To have more fun and focus in your work like Bylgja? Some relief from your darkness with Himinglava, or face your fears with Hronn? Do you need your temper cooled by Kolga's ice or to deal better with loneliness? Or do you need help with math or rhythm from Unn?

I invite you to think of what blessing you need most ... and what you're willing to give up to have it. Nothing comes without a price. To be bold, you must give up thinking of yourself as a victim of circumstances. To complete your projects, you must give up some of your distractions. Did you ever give up something you really liked so you'd have more time for something more important? You don't have time to do everything, choices must be made. *(Insert a personal example here.)* Think of this as you step toward the waters, touch the water and as you hold that water in your hand, tell them what you are sacrificing, and what blessing you wish to have. Imagine them hearing you, and then listen to what they have to say to you in your imagination. This is how the gods speak to us. We will call you back with the fast drumming to end the rite.

Start drumming "Down With Water" while everyone goes to pray.

Grounding Meditation

Drum "Up With Water" to call back everyone after five to ten minutes. Drum "Down With Water" when the meditation starts, but slowly make it faster. Keep the *same tempo,* but go from five beats of silence down to four, three, two, one, and then none. This means the pattern goes from a total of eight counts (which I count by saying in my head "Dum dadada, four, five, six, seven, eight") down to just three counts. If this makes no sense to you, don't worry. Just start with a long pause between beats and gradually shorten the pause until it's a continuous *Dum-dadada.*

This part is to help people center themselves after the experience, unmerge from the sea and from the energy of the group, and ground out excess energy in the sky with their breath. We started the rite by grounding in the sea, and merging with it. Now we take the reverse path, affirming that we have returned with their blessings, to use them in our lives.

> Now take the time to breathe deeply from your belly and feel your breath. Put your hand on your belly, and breathe deeply nine times. *(Pause. Then move your other hand over your heart.)* Find that drop of blood inside your heart, feel it, and feel the pulse of the sea in your chest, the waves that flow inside you. *(Pause for about nine heartbeats.)*
>
> Your life, your blood, came from the sea, but we are no longer part of the sea. We are now the people of the land, we live in our sealed skins, over the land, as part of the sky. It is no longer water that caresses our skins, it is wind. It is no longer water we breathe, it is air. It is air and wind that fills us with life. It is the air between us that keeps us apart. The blessings and learning that you need, keep inside you. What you do not need, breathe it out. Let

it become part of the sky over the land and sea, and know that you can stand between the land, sky and sea, to travel from one to the other at need, and that the gods and goddesses are never so far that they cannot hear your heart beating for them.

Feasting

If appropriate, you can follow up the rite with the sharing of food and drink, giving people time to talk about their experiences and ground themselves with food. If you wish to hold a sumbel, I would suggest at least a half hour break so people can collect themselves.

ଓ ଓ ଓ ଓ

Mermaid Rite Cue Cards

Blodughadda: Mermaid of Rivers, Blood, Sacrifice, Relationships

Sacrifices made into water, messages dropped in water, she carries them to the sea. Rivers feed the sea, they are like blood vessels connected to the heart. Wears a necklace of shark teeth, is fiercely protective of her sisters.
Symbols: Sharks, Heart, Blood drops.
Actions: Feeding, Distributing, Biting, Eating, Hunting.

Hronn: Mermaid of Whirlpools, Fear and Faith

Pulls you down under water, to drown in your fears, takes away your words, your breath, your friends. To fight the whirlpool is agony and death, to let it take you down, to have faith & come out the other side free of your fears is true freedom.
Symbols: Eels, Spirals, things that are Ugly or Scary.
Actions: Being Scary, Naming Fears.

Hevring: Mermaid of Surface Currents, Sorrow, Suffering and Grieving Loss

Cries for all wrongs, grieves for all who suffer. Suffering is a great teacher, if we let it. We love, and we sorrow at the loss of love. To not grieve would be to deny what we love, to abandon all that we value. Yet we are strongest when we have nothing left to lose, when everything is stripped away but our core.
Symbols: Fishes, Jellyfish, Tear drops, Rain, Wailing sounds, Disheveled hair & clothes.
Actions: Wailing, Crying, Pulling at your hair and clothing, Falling down.

Duva: Mermaid of Islands, Fog, Mystery and Wayfinding

She loves to lead people astray, but she can also help them find their way. She approves of women using their feminine charms to get what they want. Loves her treasures, and does not share except with her sisters. Likes to be begged, cajoled, flattered, likes being mysterious, coy, revealing secrets reluctantly.

Symbols: Invertebrates (Oysters, Octopus...), Pearls, Secrets, Hidden Treasures, Fog, the Lost and Found, Siren's Song, the Safe Shore in the Storm.

Actions: Seducing, Luring people away, Hiding something, Finding something.

Unn: Mermaid of Tides, Rhythms and Memory.

Unn marks time with the tides, she is moved by the Moon, whom she loves. It's said she sings numbers to him (the Moon god Mani), and he sings them back.

She knows how to move back in time and see what has been. Friendly, pretty.

Symbols: Seagulls (Seabirds), Drums, the Moon, Numbers, Mathematics.

Actions: Drumming, Dancing, Singing, Counting, Remembering.

Kolga:
Mermaid of Cold Waters, Ice and Loneliness

You are alone. In the end, we are always alone inside the prison of our skin, a sea contained, congealed, trapped. She teaches how to cool down our body, slow our metabolism, be cold, still, without shivering. She shows how to use loneliness, stillness, silence, to find ourselves in the quiet.

Symbols: Icebergs, Ice, Snowflake, Icicles, Frost.
Actions: Silence, Stillness, Blindness, Foetal Position, Shivering.

Himinglava:
Mermaid of Fair Weather and Joy

She teaches to enjoy ourselves in the moment, to appreciate small passing joys, and not try to hold onto them. Joy isn't something that we get because we deserve it, we just all get it. Then it passes, only to return when we least expect it. We can't live in perpetual happiness, it would lose its value.

Symbols: Sun, Clear Blue Sky, Sunny Beaches, Dolphins.
Actions: Smiling, Laughing, Clapping, Dancing, Jumping, Coming & Leaving.

Bylgja: Mermaid of Sea Foam Crests, Obsession and Motivation

You are only as alive as your passion. That focus moves you, and you move the world. She teaches the use of obsession to get things done, of passion, of letting yourself be swept away by the moment in all its intensity and reveling in it.

Symbols: Seals, Otters, Sea Horse, Sea Foam Crests, Tidal Waves.

Actions: Playing Games, Gambling, Running, Jumping, Shouting, Laughing.

Bara: Mermaid of Waves and Erosion, Joyful Aggression and Patience

Each wave grinds away at the shore, at the cliff, to return all the land under the sea. She teaches to find excitement in adversity, in making slow progress, in being patiently unwavering in your task, taking delight in the fight, using aggression as a positive force for change without getting angry as such.

Symbols: Whales, Giant Waves, a wooden Club.

Actions: Bashing things joyfully, Persistence, Breaking things down.

Ran: Mother of the Sea and Storms, Greed and Fishing For Souls

The Mother whose love is deadly, greedy for treasures, thief of ships and sailors, seducer of the greedy, taking what she wants from whoever she wants. "Mother Dearest" is by far the scariest of the Mermaids. Can help you ensnare those you want, but you become lawful prey for others. How much do you take for your needs, and how much do you leave to renew the population?

Symbols: Sea Vegetation, Fishing Net, Long Black Hair which is All Seaweed, Grasping Claws, Treasure Chests, Gold and Coins.

Actions: Fishing, Casting a Net and Drawing in Fish, Pulling People Under, Loving to Death, Clawing.

Aegir: Father of the Sea, Giver of the Sea's Riches, God of Hospitality

As Ran takes, Aegir gives, offering food, brewing the best ale to entertain the gods of Asgard among others. Given the Cauldron of Plenty, from Tyr's Jotun father Hymir, so he would never run out of food for guests. Are they taking advantage of his generosity, or is he a shrewd man who benefits from the alliance? How much do you give, and how much do you keep for your needs?

Symbol: Fishing Spear, Hymir's Cauldron of Plenty, Ale Cups, the Open Sea.

Actions: Fishing, Offering Food & Drink, Brewing Ale, Cooking, Making Alliances.

Njord: God of Ships and Harbors, Protector of Sailors and Travelers

Njord gave up his freedom to bring peace to his people. Mediator between land and sea, people and water, diplomat & peacemaker, the Good Father cares for children in difficult situations. In stormy seas and troubling times, he is the lighthouse that shows the way, the captain who guides to safety those under his care, the father who comforts the scared.

Symbols: Anchors, Lighthouses, Footprints in Sand, Ships, Rivers, Sea, Harbors, Captain's Hat.

Actions: Sailing, Fishing, Trading, Finding Land, Navigating Storms.

Solitary Ritual to Angrboda
Raven Kaldera

This ritual honors Angrboda, the first wife of Loki and the mother of Hela, Fenris, and Jormundgand. It can be performed whenever there is a hard task ahead of you, especially one that you fear, or that is risky, or that you know will be exceptionally painful, but must be accomplished. The rite will strengthen your will and resolve, and help you to do what must be done. You will need to be outside in a wild place; the Lady of the Iron Wood is not to be summoned in comfortable buildings. If the weather is bad, so much the better, so long as you can get a torch lit. You will need:

- A torch of some kind and the means to light it and stand it up
- A cup of hard liquor (I've always given her Jack Daniels)
- A bowl of raw meat cut into chunks
- A sterile needle and a bit of natural-fiber cloth
- Incense of agrimony (her sacred herb) which can be crumbled and burned on charcoal or bound into a stick while green and dried, then burned like a recaning stick.

Begin by turning to the south and lighting the torch, and say:

> Hail to the Hag of the Iron Wood!
> I hail you as the First Lady of Loki Laufeysson,
> Sorceress to his Magician,
> Wife to his wildness,
> Chieftess who took the trickster as your consort
> And bore him Gods for children!
> You who lay down with fire and feared not,
> Give me courage to face what is ahead,
> Give me mettle to walk through fire
> And make it dance with me,
> Instead of devouring me.

Stand the torch in the center of the circle, and then take the cup of liquor and walk to face the west. Hold up the cup and say:

> Hail to the Warrior-Chieftess of the Iron Wood!
> I hail you as the Mother of the Great Serpent,
> The mother who lost her children

> And did not weep, but planned and plotted
> And gained your revenge, even at great cost!
> Mother of Boundaries, Mother of Liminality,
> Give me the ability to defend my own space
> And not be invaded by those who would thieve away
> My self-worth, my peace, and my effectiveness.
> You who held your tears until the work was done,
> Teach me to do the same!

Pour out the cup of liquor for her, and then take up the bowl of raw meat, go to the north, and say:

> Hail to the Wolf-Goddess of the Iron Wood!
> I hail you as the Mother of chained Fenris,
> The she-wolf who bore the God of Destruction!
> Mother of Monsters who loves all her children
> No matter how terrible their visages may be,
> Who encourages them to be strong and free,
> Help me to face the unlovely parts of my soul
> Which hold me back and keep me from acting,
> And show me how to overcome them
> So that I may stand rooted, strong as your oak,
> Strong as the wildness within you.

Toss the raw meat to the ground, and leave it for the forest creatures. Light the incense and go to stand in the east, and say:

> Hail to the Wisewoman of Jotunheim's east!
> I hail you as the Mother of Hela, Queen of the Dead,
> Dark womb who gave life to death
> And taught your daughter to care for her legions!
> Great Angrboda, giantess and goddess,
> You who taught Death Herself, I pray you
> Teach me as well, and give me will
> As inexorable as the looming grave.
> Teach me to endure what must be endured,
> To breathe in and act, to breath out and let go,
> To make my way through the forest of danger
> That lies ahead on my path.

Wave the smoke around yourself and breathe it in, then put it out and scatter the burned agrimony. Go back to the torch in the center, and take the needle and prick your finger, saying:

> O Angrboda, Wolf-Mother, take this as my pledge
> That I will praise your name
> If you will help me walk this road.

Let a drop or two of blood fall on the cloth, and then hold the cloth in the flame of the torch to burn it. Once it is burned, douse the torch and leave without looking back. As soon as possible, without delay, you should face the thing that is so difficult for you. The Hag of the Iron Wood has no patience with weaklings, and helps only those who truly wish to be strong.

Solitary Rite for Baldur and Nanna
Ingeborg

This ritual is to be done in the dark house before sunrise on a day when there will be fair weather. It is to be done when there is despair in your heart, and you feel that you cannot go on, that your sun will never rise. Make an altar inside your home and place upon it one large candle, a good-sized mirror covered with a cloth, matches or a lighter, a cup of water and a teabag of chamomile tea, and a small bottle of oil of heliotrope. While heliotrope is not a plant of northern Europe – it came north from the Mediterranean in medieval times – I have claimed it as Nanna's plant, because its face follows the light.

☙ ☙ ❧ ❧

Cover all windows and cracks in doors, making the room as pitch black as possible. Find your way to the altar and sit in front of it, and say:

> In darkness I fall
> With no light inside me.
> Light is dead, and Baldur is fallen,
> And he walked the Hel Road,
> And never returned.

> In darkness I fall
> With no light around me.
> Light is dead and Baldur is fallen,
> And Hermod went to Hel
> And returned without him.

> In darkness I fall
> With no light inside me.
> Light is dead and Baldur is fallen,
> And all were to weep for him,
> And some refused.

> In darkness I fall
> With no light around me.
> Light is dead and Baldur is fallen,
> And Nanna followed him down,
> And never returned.

Find the matches or lighter, and light the candle, saying: "I light the pyre." Then sit for a moment and watch the candle, and say, "The light has not vanished, it still dwells in the depths, and I can part the veil and see His glow." Repeat this to yourself, over and over, while looking at the candle and visualizing seeing Baldur as a single bright spot in the darkness of the Underworld. When you can visualize this, say:

> Hail Baldur, Odin's brightest son,
> Golden One of Asgard,
> Bless me, O light in darkness.
> Help me to find my own light
> Within the darkness that rises around me.

Take the oil of heliotrope, and anoint your forehead with it, and say:

> Hail Nanna, child of dwarves and Valkyries,
> You who came up out of the darkness
> And followed love and light back down,
> Following with perfect faithfulness,
> Show me the way down to the depths
> Where the light still glows,
> And give me unyielding faith
> Like your own unyielding faith.

Anoint your heart chakra with it, and say:

> There is Light in the darkest place,
> And there is Love that shows the way.

Stay in the darkness, meditating on the flame, until you know that the Sun has come up. Then get up and go outside into the sunlight, and go for a walk or just generally be in the sunlight for a while. Try to keep your mind off of negative things, if only for that small piece of time. Try to look for things to enjoy and beauty to appreciate. Remember the promise of Baldur and Nanna, and they will help you to find a way.

Bragi's Ritual for Public Speaking
Raven Kaldera

If you must speak in public about an important subject, and you are concerned about your ability to do it eloquently and confidently, ask for Bragi's blessing. On the morning of the event, find some lonely place and bring with you some mead and a small squeeze-tube of some condiment. What sort it is depends on the hoped-for result of your speech. If you wish to woo people into happiness with sweet words, then some kind of syrup is best. If you want to heat them up, something spicy will work. If you want to inspire them, perhaps something fresh and minty will do. Whatever you choose, it should be entirely edible, as you will be swallowing it.

ଔ ଔ ଓ ଓ

Face the East and say:

> Hail to the Skald of Skalds!
> Lend me your gift, O fair-speaker,
> Lend me your confidence, O Poet,
> Lend me your tongue, O talented one,
> That I might do good in the world.

Take the condiment bottle and stick out your tongue as far as it will go. Draw the rune Os on it with the stream of condiment. (You might want to practice doing this beforehand, first on a surface where you can see, then on your tongue.) The bottom of the rune should be on the tip of your tongue. Take a deep breath and, with your mouth still open, exhale it in a single, clear, sustained note. Then take a swig of the mead and wash the condiment down into your belly, ingesting Bragi's rune.

Face west and pour out the mead for Bragi, saying a praise-song or praise-poem for him. (If you don't have any, check his online shrine at: http://www.northernpaganism.org/shrines/bragi/welcome.html.) Then go confidently to your speaking engagement, knowing that Bragi will aid you in your work.

Sacred Well Rite for Eir
Suki Moyne

This ritual, if done inside and not at a natural spring or outside well, requires a large bowl filled with water from a spring or well. It's all right if it's a standard Artesian well for a house – so long as the water came up from the ground as directly as possible. It also requires pieces of red and green cloth with Eir's bind rune drawn on them – Eihwaz and Raido, on top of each other – and small stones of many colors, and red thread.

ஐ ஐ ஐ ஐ

First an invocation to Eir is spoken:

> Hail to the Healer of the Holy Well,
> To Asgard's woman of soothing hands,
> Whose touch knits wounds
> And salves the marks of fire.
> Friend of Menglad on her high mountain,
> Friend of Frigg on her high throne,
> Friend of the fallen warrior who asks
> For mending and surcease from pain.
> May blood be stanched, may flesh be whole,
> May you look with generous eyes upon us.

Then each person is told to take one of the pieces of cloth, and think of a healing that they would ask for themselves, or for someone else. If it is a healing of an acute condition that needs to be treated immediately, they should take a red cloth. If it is a healing of a long-term illness that needs to be remediated, they should take a green cloth. Then they should reach into the bowl of stones and ask Eir to place the right one in their hand. The stone should be wrapped up in the cloth and tied with the red thread.

When this is done, the wrapped stones are dropped, one by one at a slow pace, into the bowl of water, while this invocation is spoken:

> Holy Well of the Goddess Eir
> Whose name means Healer
> Whose being is Mending,
> Wash us with your waters

And wash our loved ones as well.
May all be made whole,
May all be made healthy,
May all be made well.

Everyone echoes, "May all be made well," and then the bowl of water is taken to a sunlit place and left for at least an hour. Then it should be taken to a natural area and the water poured out on the ground, and the wrapped stones buried in the earth. It is all right if it takes a few hours to get it there. Just don't let it spill.

freyr: A Man To Man Rite
Dokkulfr

Even before I knew I was a Yngling, I knew I was Vaningi. I don't know when He first made His presence felt, only that among all the Northern Gods, He and His sister went right to my heart. Maybe They chose me because I was Wiccan then; They are, after all, an archetypal Lord and Lady pair ... but only They know for sure. Even then, the Northern tradition pulled at me.

My initiating priest's patron was Thor. I knew some of the Runes, and Loki had made His presence known in a major way ... but as I look back, I'm quite amused by Frey's choice in me. My mother had terrible taste in men. So as I dealt with these "excuses" for men, I began to formulate an opinion on masculinity, and not a fond one ... which is ironic, as I am bisexual. But it wasn't until later, seeking the true love and acceptance of my own masculinity, that I began to realize that Ingvi held a standard that I could, and would, be proud to uphold.

Ingvi-Freyr exemplifies what I believe masculinity should look like: Love, Frith, Sacrifice, Beauty, Passion. The following is a rite acknowledging, accepting, and committing to the example our Lord set for us.

You will need:

- A piece of deer antler
- A bowl of mead or water with honey mixed into it
- A bowl of grain (oats, barley, or a mix of any)
- The runes Jera and Ingwaz carved on a *taufr* (talisman)
- A bunch of coltsfoot and fern fronds bound with green and gold cord, string or yarn. (Optionally, a large phallus may be substituted for the coltsfoot/fern asperger.)
- A green, gold or white candle, cherry-scented if you can find it.
- Incense (I personally use "Elfin Forest" by *Scents of Midnite*, but any evergreen, pine, cedar, lemon balm, cherry, etc. would be fine.)
- A small bowl of honey
- An offering bowl
- Something made of gold

Note: Please attempt to ensure that, whenever possible, organic and chemical-free products are used.

This rite can be done any time of year, but Winternights feels right to me, allowing you to see your "harvest" in nine months. It could be incorporated as part of a Freyr's blot.

☙ ☙ ❧ ❧

Facing west, I hold aloft the deer's antler and use it to trace an Earth/Solar shield-cross. I use the following pattern: Trace a line from right to left, then curve up a quarter-circle. Then draw the line down, creating a sort of "flipped" Thor's Hammer, or a curved numeral four. Following that, complete a sunwise circle around the figure, forming the shield.[1]

Holding the antler aloft at a 45 degree angle in front of me, I say: *"Horni Vestri, Helga vé Petta ok hald vorþ!"*[2] I proceed North, East, and South *(Norþri, Austri, Suþri)* using the same formula, exchanging West *(Vestri)* for the next direction, and so on.

Upon completion of the hallowing of the space, I face West and say: *"Eg Kalla viðhinn afl frá eftir Freyr!"*[3] I pause to feel His presence and His power. Then, having connected with Him, I proceed to my altar and retrieve the mead or honeyed water and my asperger. Starting in the West, I sprinkle my vé with the mead or honeyed water, seeing the golden drops nourishing the land and its vaettir. When I finish "feeding" the space, I light the candle and incense.

I then move the offering bowl (I use one inside; outdoors I offer to the earth itself) close to the front, setting the honey-bowl left, the grain right, and the gold above. I recite a short ode of praise to Him:

Ode To Ingvi-Freyr

> I hail thee, Golden God, Lord of my soul and kin.
> Verðandi Goð, Lord of the Fields, my light within.
>
> Ingvi-Freyr, my heart sings each day,
> The taste of Your name on my lips,
> The touch of Your love, it's funny how You fill me.

---

[1] I call this my "Brisinga-Rûn hallowing", inspired by p. 52-53 of *Witchdom of the True*, by Edred Thorsson.
[2] "Horn I hold West, hallow and keep this space holy!"
[3] Literally, "I call upon the power of Freyr." My own arrangement of Icelandic, which may be grammatically off.

I call to Elf-Home, your abode,
As I walk with You along the road.
Walk along my side.
Show me the way to honor and frith,
My only wish for Your example to shine within me.

Masculine like no other, a level to inspire!
Always generous, never callous,
Sacrificing sword and steed for those You love,
God with erect phallus!

Father of my line, Yngling am I,
My blood calls to You,
You who sired my Ancestors.

Gift me with power, lead me to honor and right,
Come and fill me as I follow Your light.

After completing the praise-ode portion of the rite, I grab the *taufr* and hold it in my hand. Focusing on Ingvi-Freyr and mentally recounting the examples I wish to embody, I close my eyes and speak to Him. By now I can usually feel His presence. I say:

> Freyr! My Lord! Example of Love, Sacrifice, and Frith! I call to You! Strengthen my will to love and sacrifice like You. Give me the strength to fight without steel, teach me dignity, compassion, and manners befitting royalty. Show me the way to reap the riches of my soul's harvest. Show me the way of stewardship for all life and love. Teach me to sow for the future. Grant me virility like You and Gullinbursti possess. Teach me discretion and honor to accompany it!
>
> I see to what ends Your example grows, and as I offer You this grain *(here place some grain in the bowl or offering place)* may I harvest the qualities of gentle masculinity. As I offer this honey *(pour some honey)* may my words and deeds be kind and sweet to those I love. As I offer this gold *(place gold in offering dish/place)* may I hold those I cherish as precious as You and Your example.

I ask that you imbue this *taufr* with the qualities You embody. Grant me the privilege of Your divine ecstasy.

Focus on His essence as it imbues the *taufr*.

After I feel His essence infusing it, I place the *taufr* on my person in order to take the energy with me wherever I go. I then go to the altar and retrieve the mead bowl. Holding it high, I say: "My thanks to You, my Lord, for your presence. My life is left brighter for You bring me Right Order." I pour half of the mead into the offering bowl, then I take a drink, then I thank the Vaettir, pouring the rest out to them.

I walk to the West, and say: "I thank all the Gods of Vanaheim and all those allied with Freyr." Facing the center, I say: "I thank all the Vaettir, spirits and energies gathered here; wend your way as you will. I release the shield wall and any force trapped by my rite." And it is over.

Bibliography

Gundarsson, Kvedulf. *Our Troth V.1.* BookSurge Publishing, 2006.

Gundarsson, Kvedulf. *Teutonic Religion.* Thoth Publications, 2008.

Gundarsson, Kvedulf. *Teutonic Magic.* Thoth Publications, 2008.

Krasskova, Galina, and Raven Kaldera. *Northern Tradition for the Solitary Practitioner.* New Page Press, Franklin Lakes, NJ, 2009

Thorsson, Edred. *Nine Doors of Midgard.* Runa-Raven Press, 2003.

Thorsson, Edred. *Witchdom of the True.* Runa-Raven Press, Smithville, TX, 1999.

Four Directions Rite for Freya
Gudrun of Mimirsbrunnr

This ritual was created for a Pagan gathering, to educate a group of people who knew nothing about Norse work about the Goddess Freya, and her different aspects. Everyone sat in a circle, and I had laid the altar to the Vanadis in the center. Laid around it were four handmade cloaks which I had created as ritual vestments for her workings. There were also four wreaths, and four other items that went with each of them. (I wore only a simple white shift, which would go with any of the cloaks.)

In the North lay a cloak that was a patchwork of spring green and different fabrics printed with spring flowers. Its lining was a brilliant green satin. The wreath was silk flowers in spring colors, with many dangling ribbons. Next to it lay a basket of flower seeds.

In the East lay a cloak of gold – the color of honey, of amber – with jewels sewn onto it, and a lining of a rich rose color. The wreath glittered with gold and amber-colored beads, and there was a basket of strawberries (which were fortunately more or less in season at that point; if they are not, you might want to try some other fruit).

In the South lay a cloak of snowy white with a hood of artificial brown "hawk feathers", cascading down the back like wings, and a scarlet lining. The wreath was also of brown feathers. Next to it lay a sword.

In the West lay a cloak of dusky purple, embroidered all over with bind runes and magical sigils. The wreath next to it was of odd-looking curly weeds covered in glitter, and there lay my staff, which is actually like a carved cane. (Burial finds have shown that the seidkona's "staff" is actually what we would today consider a cane.)

ଔ ଔ ଡ ଡ

I begin by lighting a stick of dried mugwort and carrying it all around the circle, blessing each person with it. Then I begin in the North. I put on the cloak and wreath in the North and pick up the basket of seeds, saying:

> Let me tell you about Freya, the Goddess of the Vanir.
> The Vanir are a tribe of Gods whose job is agriculture –
> the creation of food. They aren't the only food-producing

Gods, but they are the experts! Freya is the Daughter Goddess among them, the daughter of Earth Mother Nerthus and Ship-Father Njord, and the sister of Frey the God of grain. Even though she has two small daughters herself, every Spring she comes up as the Maiden, bringing the cold Earth to life. This is Freya's first face.

I walk around the circle, scattering the seeds. Then I walk around a second time, giving a few seeds to each person present, saying:

As she walks on the new Spring earth, the sleeping seeds in the ground awake, and new green springs up in her footsteps. All the Vanir are Gods of fertility, and Freya is no different. As the Spring Maiden, she is the Queen of the flowers, the blossoms that blaze from each stem of green. Take these seeds with you, and plant them, and when she arises and blossoms, praise her name! Hail to you, Earthly Maiden! May you bless us with the blossoming of new beginnings.

I go to the North part of the altar and carefully lay out the flowered cloak and wreath, and lay down the basket. Then I go to the East part and don the golden cloak and wreath, and pick up the basket of strawberries, saying:

The second face of Freya is as the Goddess of Love. She is no virgin, but the one who opens her arms to many – men, women, young and old, beautiful and ugly. She chooses, yes, but she chooses not by our standards but by hers, and her standards are unknowable. She is beauty – glowing, living, sparkling beauty, with the brightness of the Summer Solstice. She is the suddenness of love that you did not expect, blowing you off your feet like the wild Spring wind, filling you with new possibilities. Taste her sweetness!

I walk around the circle, giving fruit to each person present, saying:

Once four dwarven brothers, great smiths and craftsmen, made the most beautiful necklace in the world, a thing of spun gold and amber and jewels. Freya saw it, and asked for it herself. The dwarves asked a price of her favors for four nights, one night for each of them. Freya agreed, because she knew that her great beauty and skill at love was a fair price for their great skill, and for the most beautiful necklace in the world. She knew that she was worth that, and it was no insult in either direction. And though the other Gods looked askance at her, to this day Brisingamen, the most beautiful necklace in the world, lies around the neck of Freya. Hail, golden Lady! May we learn to open our hearts to others – and more importantly, may we know our own worth when we do it!

I go to the East part of the altar and carefully lay out the golden cloak and wreath, and lay down the basket. Then I go to the South part and don the falcon and wreath, and pick up the sword, saying:

> The third face of Freya is as the Warrior. Long ago when Freya came to Asgard as a hostage after the war between the Gods of Earth and Sky, she made a bargain with Odin who chooses the slain warriors to take with him. Freya bargained to be allowed to choose one-third of the slain, and to be the first to choose – and she won! She especially loves woman warriors, and particularly handsome men. She flies over the battlefield in her cloak of falcon feathers, which give her the form of a fleet falcon, spying on the bloodiness below, among the watching Valkyries.

I walk around the circle with the sword, pointing it at people whom Freya might take, if they died in battle, saying:

> As a Love Goddess who also knows how to wield a sword, she shows us that Love is not passive and helpless. Love is strong and passionate. Love knows how to fight to protect dear ones. Love knows how to make hard choices. Love knows how to fight to protect one's own boundaries, that the garden may stay healthy and not be overrun with weeds. Love is when you have each other's back. Hail to the Warrior who sees the best, and knows to take it! May

you bless us with the courage to love ourselves as well as others.

I go to the South part of the altar and carefully lay out the falcon cloak and wreath, and lay down the sword. Then I go to the West part and don the sigil cloak and herb wreath, and pick up the staff, saying:

> The fourth face of Freya is that of the mistress of Seidr, the magical arts. She is the mysterious sorceress who can tell the future in the smoke, who can make a charm of love or vengeance, who can call the fish to the bay and the deer to the hunter's arrow-tip. She is the music in the spell's incantation, the circle dance around the fire with the wishes flung forth. She is the patron of hedge-witches, fortunetellers, and farm-wives who charm their cows into better milking. Would you know your future? Touch the staff of the seidkona, and perhaps a word will flash into your mind. If it does, speak it aloud or be silent, as you will.

I walk around the circle holding out my staff, so that each person can touch it, saying:

> This is your gift from Freya – a tiny window onto the future. Hail to the Lady of Magic, you who are the love-spell and the love-song, who can look into the future and speak it to all those gathered. Hail, Lady, who draws back the dark veil and lets the golden light shine through! Be with us in all four of your brilliant faces! Hail the Vanadis!

All shout, "Hail the Vanadis!" and the rite is ended.

Forseti Ritual, in Two Parts
Seawalker

Forseti is the god of justice and public judgment. He carries an axe, and may be associated with the hawk. This two-part rite is for a situation where an individual in authority has been chosen lawfully by a community, or is rightfully allowed due to their position in that community, to sit in public judgment over another individual within that community whose actions have caused the need for such a judgment by the community's publicly stated laws.

There are a few points to make note of in the last statement. The first is "community". Forseti is a god of the declared community, not of gossip and personal problems amongst a group of friends. Is this an actual formal community of people who have already declared themselves in this way – a kindred, a grove, a guild, a tribe, a church, a legal organization? Does the community have a name? It should, because that name will be used in the ritual. A loose gang of people who all know each other is not the same as a formal community.

The second point is that the individual who performs this ritual must have been publicly chosen to do this work by the entire community. Self-appointed judges are not within Forseti's scope. If the community has not formally recognized them – which means that the community has to have a system of approving such a role – then you should be calling on another deity, perhaps Frey in his role as God of Frith. Does the role have a title? It should, because that title will be spoken in the ritual.

Third, the individual who is being judged against must also be a member in good standing in the community, and wish to remain that way. (If the judgment is between two people, both should be looking for a way to coexist in the same community peacefully.) Forseti is specifically a God of intracommunity disputes, between members of the same group. In ancient times, when there was conflict between members of two different groups with no higher overarching authority, it was usually solved through a duel – and in that case, Tyr was called upon. If the individual to be judged has already left the group, there is no point. Similarly, Forseti will not come for someone making random judgments at outsiders that they dislike.

This rite has a private part and a public part. Both are important and neither should be omitted. The private part is so that the judge can commune privately with the force of the God of Justice, and have a place to speak out their doubts, or their hopes. The public part shows the witnesses that the judge is also subject to a higher power, and acknowledges this, and asks plainly for the help of the Gods. It's important that the spiritual "chain of command", as it were, be visible to the people. It helps reinforce that the judge is not merely acting from their own opinions and ego.

ଔ ଔ ଓ ଓ

Part I:

The judge sets up an altar with a purple cloth, a purple candle in a jar, a hawk feather or the figure of a hawk, and an axe. They kneel or sit before the altar and say: "Hail Forseti, Giver of Law, Speaker for Right Action, fair in judgment in all ways. I come before you to ask for your wisdom as I face this task."

The judge picks up the hawk feather or hawk figurine and touches it to their forehead, and says, "Grant me eyes of keenness that see all points of view, and miss nothing."

Then the judge picks up the axe and places it gently[1] against their forehead. The judge says, "May my mind be as sharp as this blade, and guide my hand to judgment that cuts cleanly in every direction."

Then the candle is lit, and the judge says, "Son of Baldur the God of Light, bring light into the place of judgment, and may the shadows of confusion be dispelled."

Part II:

The axe and the hawk feather or figurine should be wrapped in the purple cloth and borne to the place of judgment. Ideally, the candle should be taken to the place of judgment still lit, carried by the judge. This is why it is good to have it in a jar. If there is driving involved, the judge should be driven by someone else, while still carefully holding

---

[1] We are assuming that people are adults here and can do such a thing without hurting themselves. In the event that the axe slips and injures in some way, one should assume that it is a grave omen from Forseti about the fitness of the judge, and they should make arrangements to step down immediately.

the lit candle. If it goes out accidentally, it can be relit, but continual failure to stay lit may be an omen.

At the place of judgment, the purple cloth can be unrolled and the candle placed on it. The judge should take the axe and walk around the edges of the space, saying, "I hallow this place in Forseti's name; in the name of Justice, in the name of Frith, in the name of Right Doing." The axe is placed back on the cloth, with a repeat of "Hail Forseti, Giver of Law, Speaker for Right Action, fair in judgment in all ways. I come before you to ask for your wisdom as I face this task."

The judge then turns to face the people, and says, "I am not a God. My judgment is not as the Gods'. But anyone may call on the Gods for aid, and so I do call upon the Son of Light, the Lord of Justice, the sharp blade of discernment, for aid in my judgment. Forseti, guide me; help me to find what is best for my community in the long term, and help me to follow that road. Hail Forseti!"

All answer, "Hail Forseti!" and the judgment begins.

A Blót to Frigga
Mist, Gyðja of Kenaz Kindred, Canada

This ritual is from the collection of Kenaz Kindred. Our rites are written to celebrate the season, the gods, the wights and the ancestors. For the most part, we use multiple speakers in ritual, to help carry the load of the wonderful (yet sometimes daunting) invocations. We gather our inspiration from many places – not just from any lore, but many poems, sagas and other sources that have spoken to us. All of the pieces borrowed or adapted for our rituals are used with permission. A list of our sources is provided at the end of the ritual. Uncredited pieces are written by Larisa C. Pole (Mist), Gyðja of Kenaz Kindred.

This is a ritual that I wrote and performed at Kitchener-Waterloo Pagan Pride Day. I often have an assistant come with me to public performances to help do the English translations. If the word "assistant" appears in one of our rituals, it is a volunteer from the kindred who offered to help that day. You can replace this word with whatever is appropriate for you or your group.

ଔ   ଔ   ଊ   ଊ

First, the Gyðja comes forth and speaks:

> For those of you that have never been to an Ásatrú ritual, I would like to welcome all of you and thank you for honouring us with your presence. We would like to note that Ásatrú rituals honour the gods and goddess of the Northern Pantheon. If you don't know one, that is okay; at this ritual we will welcome you to lift the horn to any god or goddess that you follow, or just to the gods in general.

Gyðja: Fé, Vit, Friðr, Grið, Heill.[1]

Assistant: Wealth, Wisdom, Harmony, Security and Health[2]

At this point, we perform the Hammer Rite[3]. The Gyðja and her assistant walk to the four quarters and perform this rite; alternately, some other ritual of creating sacred space could be used.

---

[1] Pronounced *"Fay, Veet, Freeth, Greeth, Hayl."*
[2] Borrowed from the Esoteric Theological Seminary.

Gyðja: I hallow and make holy to the service of Odin and Frigga, and all the gods of the Æsir and Vanir and Jötnar, this harrow and stead, banishing all influences unholy or impure. May our minds, in this hallowed place, likewise be hallowed as is our will, to the just service of the gods and goddess of the Northern Tradition.[4]

If you like, the next part can be a call and response.

> Hail to the álfar, all ringed round us,
> The fathers of the folk.
> Hail to the dísir, all ringed round us,
> The mothers of our might.
> Hail to our kin, in the hidden lands,
> Hail the ancestors on this holy day
> The children of earth call out to the Æsir and Vanir.
> Hear us, eldest and brightest.
> To all you shining and deep ones,
> Wisest and mightiest, cunning and fair,
> Loving and comforting,
> Gods and goddesses, we offer you welcome.
> To the gods and goddesses of this place,
> Ancient and powerful, known to us or unknown,
> Gods of this place, we offer you welcome.
> To all the deities of those here gathered,
> You whom we worship,
> You who bless our lives, our patrons and matrons,
> We offer you welcome.
> So, high ones, we call to you as our elders,
> In reverence and love, to join in our magic.
> Come to our fire, Æsir and Vanir;
> Meet us at the boundary.

---

[3] The Hammer Rite was created by Edred Thorsson. Rather than reprinting it here, we encourage people to find it themselves — it is available in his book *Futhark: A Handbook of Rune Magic*, and one web search will give you dozens of places where it is available on the internet. The rite essentially calls the quarters, first in Old Norse and then in modern English, calling upon the four dwarves of the sacred directions.

[4] Adapted from the *Hammerstead Blot Book*.

Guide and ward us as we walk the elder ways.[5]

Five people come forth to honor Odin, Frigga, the land-wights, Frey, Thor, and Sif.

First Caller:
>Odin, master of runes,
>Wrist for us, good fate,
>From your rune pouch,
>Deal us great fortune, luck and weal,
>Show us what must be,
>Help us to know what lies ahead,
>Blow us, favourable winds,
>That will guide us to promising shores.

Second Caller:
>**An Invitation For Frigga:**
>Hail to you also, fair lady,
>Wife of Odin, great mother of many gods,
>All-Mother, grace us with your bounty and beauty,
>Instill in us the graciousness of hospitality,
>The fierceness of familial love,
>The warmth of the kindred,
>The strength of the warrior.
>Through your hands, cunningly craft us good health,
>Strong families and a strong community.
>Weave us together with your distaff, wind us as one,
>See us through the hard times, and good,
>Blessing each day with your warm embrace.
>Show us, Frigga, to be silent, strong and forgiving.
>Teach us patience and understanding in all things,
>For our way of life is in your hands,
>And through you may it be well lived!
>Hail, Frigga! Hail the Queen of Asgard!

Third Caller:
>To the wights of the land,
>Here we honour you,

---

[5] Borrowed from "Odin's Rune Rite" in the *Hammerstead Blot Book*.

The land which feeds us and is your domain.
Your watchful eyes protect our homes,
Your protective power imbues our fields,
Ancestors of our families that watches us still,
Protect and guard over our harvest,
And watch over the families of our kin and kindred.
Hail the Wights of the Land!

Fourth Caller:

Frey, God of bounty,
Your strength and might is felt in the green lush fields
And in the yellow hues of autumn.
Your power is felt in the rune of Ing,
Which reminds us of the turning tides,
The changing seasons, the rewards of our labours.
Frey, smile upon us and grant us great bounty,
Let the larders spill forth with your great reward,
And let all praise the great king of fertility,
Hail Frey! Lord of Peace and Plenty!

Fifth Caller:

Thor and Sif,
Husband and wife,
The hammer and the grain,
Be with us once again as we prepare to plant our livelihood.
Shine on those gathered,
Bring the sunshine back to us
And warm our seeds so that they grow strong and healthy.
Bring your strength to our table,
Bring your warmth to our hearts,
See us through the last of the harsh winter
That has beaten us down,
Restore our bodies,
So that we can bring this coming crop to fruition
In your names.
With our love and devotion,
May it grow strong and tall!

Hail Thor! Hail Sif![6]

Gyðja: For the followers of Ásatrú, the blót represents a form of sacrifice – not of blood, but of our efforts and devotion to our gods. Soon, now, the focus of most Ásatrú rituals will be on preparation for the Wild Hunt, a night of abandon, and looking forward to the festival of Yule which lasts for twelve nights. Today at this festival, the focus is on that of our community – the community of Pagans and Heathens coming together in a united effort to show others that we are not few, but many, and still alive. The blood of our ancestors runs through our veins, and our hearts beat as one, united in the efforts to hold up our community that is built through the efforts of each of us. Individually we represent a variety of paths, but together our strength is clearly present. I would ask you now to join hands with one another.

This part can also be a call and response if you like, or else shouted by the Gyðja.

> Let us open our hearts
> And open our mouths
> And shout!
> Let us send a message!
> Let us shake the World Tree,
> From the heights of Álfheim
> To the depths of Svartalfheim,
> From the fields of Vanaheim
> To the benches of Helheim,
> From the peaks of Jotunheim
> To the pit of Niflheim,
> From the halls of Asgarð
> To the gates of Muspellheim,
> From the north pole
> To the south pole of Midgarð!
> Let all the worlds know
> That we are Heathens,

---

[6] Borrowed from Kol of Kenaz Kindred.

We are trú,
And we are back!⁷

Gyðja: In Ásatrú, Frigga represents our connection to one another. As the queen of the gods and a mother figure to all, she is the essential mother. As the great teacher and nurturer, she shows us patience, and understanding.

She is known for her great knowledge of all things, but keeps all things secret. She has the ear of the All-Father Odin, and never uses her power for anything deceptive, but instead remains a vigil of womanly power among the gods. To me, she has shown a great deal of perspective and strength. She shows that women can be both mother and warrior, both lover and protector, that women are a force in the universe. In her lessons, however tough, she shows that as a woman, we must learn how to know what is right for the family and often place our own priorities aside for the greater good of our communities.

She has shown me that one's personal wants are not important, but that the act of selfless giving is that of true sacrifice and one that is honoured and remembered throughout the generations. She shows what is necessary and in her harshness can teach this lesson in ways that cause great pain. But, through this harsh road, there is an overwhelming sense of ultimate gain, by having strong community and family ties we learn what is truly of value, our sense of belonging and togetherness.

At this time we would ask that all of you join us in giving a special offering to Frigga by coming forth and tossing some sage onto the burning charcoal.

The caller who gave the Frigga Invocation steps forth.

An Offering to Frigga!
Lady of Asgard,
You who hears the secrets of the All-Father,
You who holds his heart in your hands,

---

⁷ Poem "Shout" by Gary Penzler, accessed via *Odin's Gift* online.

In you we seek what we need,
And you provide, greatly.
Let us remember your gifts,
And honour you with well-wrought work.
From our hands and our hearts,
May we aid each other in times of need.
Through you, Frigga, we can learn much,
And in you are mysteries that we seek to understand.
Wind us in your distaff, dole us fair and just fate,
Through you, Frigga we ask, that this life,
Be full of love, light, and needed strength.
Great Mother, accept our offering,
Not of blood, but of our efforts and devotion,
Our love and desire to honour you.
Hail Frigga! Hail Frigga! Hail Frigga!

Gyðja: This blót today is to honour the goddess Frigga, and to honour the spirit of community – to recognize that we as Pagans and Heathens are a strong community bound together with one common voice, a voice that rises above the ashes of oppression, and fights for independence through a faith that is built on a foundation of self-discovery and of deep and profound truth.

In Ásatrú we often use runes to hallow or strengthen the horn. The horn is a sacred vessel that is considered to be a direct connection with the gods and humans. It is through this liquid that we can acquire great wisdom. We would ask that when the horn goes around, if you do not wish to take a drink, just raise it slightly and pass it on to the next person. If you see it running low, please raise your hand so that we may refill it.

We will carve over this horn the rune of Mannaz, the rune of mankind, of our community and our connection to each other, may this rune provide us with the ability to remember our ties to one another, keeping our community in our hearts no matter where we choose to travel.

To the gods of the Æsir, Vanir and Jotnar,

> To the goddess Frigga,
> And to the gods of those gathered in this place,
> As in ancient times we raise this horn,
> And offer you sacrifice!
> Not of blood, for enough of it is shed,
> Nor as an appeasement for we stand in good stead with you,
> But rather of the sacrifice of our human efforts,
> Our struggles, and our devotion.
> May it aid us, gods and humankind alike,
> In our fight against those
> Who would wage war against Ásgarð,
> Or seek to bring gray slavery to Miðgarð.
> Accept our sacrifice, not as from slaves,
> For we have no master,
> But as a sign of our communion
> And kinship with you and with each other.
> Mighty gods all, accept this offering.[8]

The horn is carried around the circle and each person drinks. As they do so, the horn carrier says:

> I give you the blessings of the Æsir, Vanir and Jotun and especially the goddess Frigga.[9]

Gyðja: We will now close the ceremony with the very common ritual of Sumbel. Sumbel is a three-round event in which liquid from the horn is consumed after each round. If you do not wish to speak during Sumbel, please just raise the horn and pass it to the next person. If you notice that the horn is getting empty, please raise your hand and we will refill it.

The first round is to the Gods; this can be to any god or goddess, and if you don't have one then just raise your glass to whatever you wish to celebrate.

The second round is to the Ancestors; this round celebrates our ancestors, heroes, family members or anyone that has come before us.

---

[8] Adapted from "Freya's Blot" in the *Hammerstead Blot Book*.
[9] Borrowed from "Freya's Blot" in the *Hammerstead Blot Book*.

The third open round is for you. Say whatever you want; it can be a love song, sonnet, poem, or some personal accomplishment, anything you wish to say. But be warned, if you make a promise of any kind, you are promising it to the Well of Wyrd, which is binding. So be sure that you promise something that you actually have full intention of keeping.

The horn is passed in three rounds, and the people speak.

Gyðja: Thank you very much for coming to our blot! We will be around for the remainder of the day at our Community Booth if anyone has any questions or wishes to find out more about our kindred. Thank you again, and have a great time at the rest of Pagan Pride. Hail to all!

Sources

- Esoteric Theological Seminary: http://northernway.org/asaprayers.html
- Hammerstead Blot Book: http://home.earthlink.net/~jordsvin/Blots/Index.htm
- Odin's Gift: http://www.odins-gift.com/

Frigga Blót
Mist, Gyðja of Kenaz Kindred, Canada

This ritual is designed for mid-to-late winter. You will need a horn of mead for offering.

ಜ ಜ ಬಿ ಬಿ

At the beginning of the rite, the Gyðja speaks:

Gyðja: Fé, Vit, Friðr, Grið, Heill. [1]

Assistant: Wealth, Wisdom, Harmony, Security and Health[2]

At this point, we perform the Hammer Rite[3]. The Gyðja and her assistant walk to the four quarters and perform this rite; alternately, some other ritual of creating sacred space could be used.

Gyðja: I hallow and make holy to the service of Odin and Frigga, the gods of the Æsir and Vanir and Jötunn this harrow and stead, may the might of our all-mother and father be with us this day, as we honour the goddess of the folk, home and hearth.

This day we honour one who was for many years left to the women of the tribe to honour. Her name was spoken in whispers at every birth, called upon when the family needed help and aid. From the lips of ancient women her name was uttered, from the hands of women her offerings laid out, her memory never lost. The ritual we do today is to honour this mighty goddess who is known to us as Frigga, wife of Odin, the All-Mother of both gods and humans. In her honour we conduct this rite.

For those of you who are new to Heathenry, we thought we would explain each part of the ritual as we go, so you have some idea as to what is going on. The first offering we pour is for the *blót* or sacrificial part of the ritual. This initial offering is for all the gods on the

---

[1] Pronounced *"Fay, Veet, Freeth, Greeth, Hayl."*
[2] Borrowed from the Esoteric Theological Seminary, used with permission. http://northernway.org/asaprayers.html
[3] The Hammer Rite was created by Edred Thorsson, and is available in his book *Futhark: A Handbook of Rune Magic*.

Heathen Path. We ask that your mind be focused on them, the gods of the ancient Northmen, as we pour this offering to them.

The Gyðja lifts the horn of mead, and draws the rune Perthro with her finger over the opening.

> We hallow this horn with the symbol of Perthro,
> The symbol of Frigga, as Mistress of Wyrd,
> Mother of the folk, and keeper of mysteries.
> We dedicate this sacrifice to:
> Oðinn Old Wanderer, Allfather of the folk!
> Loki Long-Fettered, bringer of treasures!
> Thórr Thunder-Hammer, protector of Midgarð!
> Freyr Field-Blesser, rider of the boar!
> Freyja Falcon-Cloak, weeping bride!
> Frigga Frith-Seeker, wise to fates!
> Njorðr Noatun-Master, wealth-giver!
> Nerthus Nether-Earth, peace-maker!
> Balder Bearer-of-Rings, guest in Hel's hall!
> Nanna Never-Lonely, grief-stricken!
> Heimdall Horn-Blower, guardian of the bridge!
> Ægir Ale-Brewer, ship-wrecker!
> Ran Receiver-of-the-Drowned, mother of Waves!
> Tiw Trust-Bearer, wolf-binder!
> Sif Sunshine-Hair, thunder-hall key-keeper!
> Forseti Finder-of-Springs, ship-steerer!
> Idunna Immortal-Apples, keeper of youth!
> Bragi Blithe-Tongue, skald-patron!
> We do you honour! Hail!

The horn of mead is poured out for the Gods. Then the Gyðja continues:

> Odin, all-father of the folk
> We call to you this day with loving hearts,
> For today, we honor she who walks among your halls,
> She who lays beside you in slumber,
> She who wakes you in the light of day,
> With her hands, cares for you, your home and children,

Your wife, Frigga, the silent, we honor this day,
For the gracious gifts she gives both gods and man.
Odin, we praise you and your wife,
And ask your hand to cast us favor
Through the honor we bring to your beloved wife,
Mother of Balder,
She who remains for us a tribute
Of grace, beauty and wisdom.
Hail Odin, husband of Frigga,
Chief of the Aesir, ruler of Asgard.

Four women come forward, to speak for Frigga. Ideally they should be happily married women, or at least widows.

First Caller:

To Frigga, the All-Mother,
You have shown me great comfort in times of pain,
In my greatest hour, you helped me achieve the greatest act of female power,
And gave me a treasured daughter.
You have granted me patience when I prayed for it,
Wisdom, when I asked,
And have shown me that my sacrifices are not for nothing,
But are essential to my life and calling.
To you, Great Mother, I call,
And ask you to remind us the power that we women share with each other.
Frigga looks deep within others and knows them.
Nothing keeps hidden from her, and yet she accepts everyone.
Frigga is the Mother who lays the mantle of her gentleness protectively on us.
In her fold one is sheltered safely and lovingly.
Frigga asks no questions, for she already knows the answer.
She knows one will talk when the time has come.
Frigga is the Mother who takes care of her children intimately and devotedly.
Always she is there, and has an open ear for them.

Second Caller:

Twist me, twist me, Frigga,

> Into your distaff,
> Spin me, spin me, Frigga,
> Into your wheel,
> Mould me, mould me, Frigga,
> Into some wool,
> Fix me, fix me, Frigga,
> Into the web of wyrd.

Third Caller: Nothing is recorded about Frigga prior to her marriage to Odin, but her gift is her ability to move outside of convention and yet still remain a loyal wife. She is very much the political wife in manners of state, but in her marshy hall of Fensalir she sits in relaxed contemplation. She runs Odin's house with an iron fist, but in her hall she is but one of several women that complete the important tasks of weaving and spinning.

She is known as the great spinner, she who spins the wool that the Norns will use to create the great web of Wyrd. Renowned for her ability to keep secrets, she does not reveal any knowledge unless the person proves trustworthy, and even then does not reveal everything. In order to perform this work she owns a marvelous jeweled spinning wheel or distaff, which at night shines brightly in the sky in the shape of a constellation, known in the North as Frigga's Spinning Wheel, while the inhabitants of the South called the same stars Orion's Girdle.

Fourth Caller: Frigga's marriage to Odin caused such general rejoicing in Asgard, where the goddess was greatly beloved, that ever after it was customary to celebrate its anniversary with feast and song, She was declared patroness of marriage; her health was always proposed with that of Odin and Thor at wedding feasts.

Frigga is the goddess of the atmosphere and the clouds, and is sometimes represented as wearing either snow-white or dark garments according to her somewhat variable moods. She is crowned with heron plumes – the symbol of silence or forgetfulness – and her white robes are secured at the waist by a golden girdle from which hangs a bunch of keys – the distinctive sign of the Northern housewife, whose special patroness she is said to be. She is Queen of the Aesir, and she alone has the privilege of sitting on the throne Hlidskialf beside her husband Odin. From thence she, too, can look over the entire world and see what is happening. According to our ancestors' declarations, she possessed the knowledge of the future, which no one could ever prevail upon her to reveal, thus proving that Northern women could keep a secret inviolate.

First Caller: Frigga is considered the goddess of conjugal and motherly love, and is specially worshiped by married lovers and tender parents. This exalted office does not so entirely absorb all her thoughts, however, that she has no time for other matters; for we are told that she is very fond of dress, and whenever she appears before the assembled gods her attire is rich and becoming, and her jewels always chosen with much taste. This love of adornment once led her sadly astray, for, in her longing to possess some new jewel, she secretly purloined a piece of gold from a statue representing her husband, which had just been placed in his temple. The stolen metal was entrusted to the dwarfs, with instructions to fashion a marvelous necklace for her use. This jewel, once finished, was so resplendent that it greatly enhanced her charms and even increased Odin's love for her.

Second Caller: But when Odin discovered the theft of the gold, he angrily summoned the dwarfs and bade them reveal who had dared to touch his statue. Unwilling to betray the queen of the gods, the dwarfs remained obstinately silent, and, seeing that no information could be elicited from them, Odin commanded that the statue should be placed above the temple gate, and set to work to devise runes which should endow it with the power of speech and enable it to denounce the thief. When Frigga heard these tidings she trembled with fear, and implored her sister and favorite attendant Fulla to invent some means of protecting her from Allfather's wrath. Fulla, who was always ready to serve her mistress, immediately departed, and soon returned, accompanied by a hideous dwarf, who promised to prevent the statue from speaking if Frigga would only deign to smile graciously upon him. This boon having been granted, the dwarf hastened off to the temple, caused a deep sleep to fall upon the guards, and while they were thus unconscious, pulled the statue down from its perch and broke it to pieces, so that it could never betray Frigga's theft in spite of all Odin's efforts to give it the power of speech.

Third Caller: Odin, discovering this sacrilege on the morrow, was very angry indeed; so angry that he left Asgard and utterly disappeared, carrying away with him all the blessings which he had been wont to shower upon gods and men. According to some authorities, his brothers Vili and Ve took advantage of his absence to assume his form and secure possession of his throne and wife; but although they looked exactly like him they could not restore the lost blessings, and allowed the ice giants, or Jotuns, to invade the earth and bind it fast in their cold fetters. These wicked giants also pinched the leaves and buds till they all shriveled up, stripped the trees bare, shrouded the earth in a great white coverlet, and veiled it in impenetrable mists.

But at the end of seven weary months the true Odin relented and returned, and when he saw all the evil that had been done he drove the usurpers away, forced the frost giants to beat a hasty retreat, released the earth from her icy bonds, and again showered all his blessings down upon her, cheering her with the light of his smile.

Fourth Caller:
Lady of Asgard,
You who hears the secrets of the All-Father,
You who holds his heart in your hands,
In you we seek what we need,
And you provide, greatly.
Let us remember your gifts,

And honor you with well wrought work,
From our hands and our hearts,
May we aid each other in times of need,
Through you, Frigga, we can learn much,
And in you are mysteries that we seek to understand,
Wind us in your distaff, dole us fair and just fate,
Through you, Frigga, we ask, that this life,
Be full of love, light, and needed strength,
Great Mother, accept our offering,
Not of blood, but of our efforts and devotion,
Our love and desire to honor you
Hail Frigga! Hail Frigga! Hail Frigga!

All repeat "Hail Frigga!" as it is spoken. The Gyðja stands forth with the refilled horn and says:

> We ask all of you to think on community and family, and as we pass the horn, lift it in the name of mothers. You may lift it to your own mother or to Frigga herself.

The horn is passed, and toasts are made to mothers. The horn is then refilled, and the Gyðja says:

> We shall also this day make offering to the family *disir*, the women spirits who watch over us:

First Caller:
Around the hearth of the house
They gather, old and young,
A whispering and rowning of women,
Growing, receding, never silent.
Present, but ungraspable,
Watching over their own,
Dignified, Guarding, Keeping.
A coming and going –
All have passed on, yet all stayed.
Mothers, Matrons, Aunts,
United for years round the same hearth,
Joined over the ages,
Caring, Blessing, Gifting.

> Gray, flax-blond, raven-black,
> Faces melding, bound together by love,
> Together, Giving, Bearing.
> Names fade,
> Time passes, community lasts,
> Guarding, Caring, Watching.
> Women they were, Disir they are.

The Gyðja pours out the offering horn, saying:

> We pour this offering for the *disir* of all families in attendance this day. May you grace our homes with blessings of kindness, love and security. We will now call upon Frigga's hand-maidens!

Second Caller:
> Frigga, Beloved, Asgard's Queen
> Saga, ancient story-teller supreme
> Eir, physician, healing maid
> Gefion, giver, a land did make
> Fulla, plenty all around
> Sjofn, affection does abound
> Lofn, permission granted thus
> Sin, defender, warding us
> Hlin, protectress, warrior friend
> Var, hearing oaths until the end
> Vor, does know all that we seek
> Snotra, wise of what to speak
> Gna, swift messenger of Frigg
> Goddesses, much do you give.

Third Caller:
> Hail to you all, may you ever be strong,
> May your days be joyful and your nights full of song.
> May you grant me and mine love, peace and health,
> Wisdom, kindness, good-luck and good wealth.
> May it be that you are with us
> Through our days and our nights,
> To grant us comfort and strength
> Through the dark and the light.

Hail to you Goddesses for your blessings this day,
Hail to you Goddesses for the blessings on their way.

The offering is poured out to the Handmaidens, perhaps by the Fourth Caller, who says, "Hail to you all, Ladies!" After this a Sumbel is done[4], and the rite is concluded.

---

[4] Described on pages 157-8.

Ritual for Jormundgand
Raven Kaldera

Jormundgand, the Midgard Serpent, does not speak or have language, so our ritual to the Big Snake had no written script and was performed in complete silence. Because of this, I will recount what we did for folks who might want to do the same thing.

First we found a lake that we could all get to in the middle of the night. While this ritual can be done in the ocean (and that's probably the best place for it) not everyone lives close to the sea, and so any large body of water will do. The sky must be clear and starry, and the water such that people can walk in safely up to their necks or thereabouts. Clothing or lack of it is irrelevant; some of the folk taking part in the ritual put on bathing suits and some simply stripped and walked into the water.

We made a symbolic "serpent" out of a long piece of snake-printed silky spandex, sewn into a tube about twenty feet long. (It probably should have been longer.) One end was sewn into a taper like a tail, and the other had a rudimentary head on it. Then, in the middle of the night, we went silently to the lake. Everyone had been briefed as to the rules of the ritual, and no one spoke from the time we left the cars to start walking up to the lake, to the time we got back to the cars. (We did talk about the ritual later, when we got back, and compared notes.) We all undressed quietly and leisurely, and when everyone was ready we all walked into the lake together, again as quietly as possible. We stood there in the darkness and each took hold of the "serpent", coming into a circle in the water while holding it in our hands. One participant held head and tail and brought them together in his hands. I raised my arms to the starry sky and silently asked the Great Serpent to come to us, and give us wisdom. Then I stepped into the middle of the circle.

Each of us took a turn in the middle of the circle and stood, shoulder-deep in water, meditating. Some stared at the sky, some closed their eyes. While they did this, the circle rotated clockwise around them in the water, holding onto the fabric "serpent". It created a slight whirlpool effect around the seeker in the center, who was symbolically surrounded by the Guardian of Midgard. When each person was finished with their communion with the Serpent, they stepped back and took their place in the circle, relinquishing the center to the next person who wished to step forward. After everyone had had their turn, we uncoiled the circle into a line and walked out of the lake. We then dressed and walked, still in silence, back to the cars to drive home.

It was a ritual of incredible simplicity, but everyone who took part was very moved, and gained some kind of sacred wisdom from the experience. We later made another circle, this one sitting in a warm room, and shared the images that the Serpent had given us.

Loki Rite
Michal Koudelka

The ritual below was sent to us by Michal Koudelka, a Pagan in the Czech Republic, who wrote the following to us:

This ritual was created for a specific situation, planned for an occasion with an experienced Godhi and Pagan-curious folk. It's quite static and its people-involvement is limited, but it should be quite easy to modify it to involve more people. Second it's quite short – my experience says that you can't expect long concentration from people on their first ritual. And third, it was far from the place we were used to working in, so we were not able to bring a lot of ceremonial stuff. Beyond this, it's very easy to transfer to a one-man ritual. I tried to use some mythological references, because the people at the ritual had little to no spiritual experience, but they knew at least the basics of Norse mythology.

When Loki told me how to accomplish this rite, he asked me to cast a few drops of my blood onto the altar before the ritual started. I decided not to do that, because I didn't want to make other people feel uncomfortable, but then I accidentally cut myself while opening the bottle of wine, so I cast the blood anyway. So if you're not a fan of blood sacrifice, be careful.

As a ritual beverage, I used an old strong sweet fortified wine from southeast Europe. I expect that any fortified wine will be OK (pinot, sherry, vermouth, etc). If possible the attendants of the ritual should be cleansed with incense first. I used a combination of storax and dragon's blood, but simple mugwort should be fine too.

༶ ༶ ༶ ༶

The Godhi first calls to various beings in the Nine Worlds. I drew a rune for each being/world I called on (Algiz for the Aesir, Ansuz for the Alfar, Kenaz for the Duergar, Hagalaz for Helja's realm, Thurisaz for the Jotnar, Jera for the Vanir, Sowelu for Surt's realm, Isa for Nidhogg's realm and Gebo for the spirits. Other people may choose different runic combinations for the worlds.)

Godhi:
> I call to the Aesir in the Plain of Idavoll!
> I call to the Alfar, the folk of Lofar!

I call to the Dokkalfar, outlaws to their own kind!
I call to the Duergar, deep below the World of Man!
I call to the souls of the Dead in Helja's realm!
I call to the Jotnar, first true rulers of the tempest!
I call to the Vanir, granters of the first fruits!
I call to the Old Ones, the first who were born from the
> abyss of Ginunngagap! Surt, who rules the primordial
> fire, and Nidhogg who rules the land of ice and mist.
I call to all spirits and deities who share this land with us!

> Hear me, because we have courageously gathered to honor an unfairly denounced god!
> Loki! You gave your blood to the first humans. You are one of the three who gave the existence to mankind, one of three whom we owe for our being. And despite this, some of us have the foolhardiness to call you "Father of Lies" and "Evilmonger".
> We who gather here tonight remember your gift, and we will never betray you. We know that your tricks are done to show us truth, to lead us to the truth about the weakness of Man, the contrivances of the Gods, and the inequities and bleeding wounds of this world.

Father of the Wolf, I call you!
Lord of Fire, I honor you!
Flamehair God, I pray to you!
This night I welcome you among us!

At this point, the Godhi takes the chalice from the altar and fills it with wine, and then holds the chalice over his head to bless it. Actually, it's a very difficult task. I imagined a flaming ray or shining column from the sky to my chalice.

Godhi: Loki! We know it is your blood that circulates in our
> veins. It's our force and our greatness. Give us your
> blessing tonight; make our blood strong as was the blood
> of your followers in ancient time.

The Godhi drinks and then calls out, "Loki's blood flows in my veins!" The Godhi passes the chalice to the nearest person in the circle, who is expected to do the same as the Godhi. The chalice travels among the people until it returns to the Godhi again. He may empty the chalice by drinking it, or keep the rest as sacrifice to the land. Everybody is asked to concentrate before he drinks, and think about the ties and obligations that they accept.

Godhi: We thank you for your gift. We promise you that we will use it the right way. We will never close our eyes before injustice, and we will always stand against hypocrisy and shabbiness to make you proud of us, the same way we are proud of you.

Then the Godhi calls out "Hail Loki" three times, and the people repeat it.

Godhi: The ritual is finished, but not our bond. We have received Loki's blessing and he will show us our way – but remember the promises we gave to him, and make sure you will never betray them.

When I led this ritual the first time, it was finished by simply hailing Loki, without the ending; but everyone felt that something was missing. Then a friend of mine standing in the circle began to laugh insanely. (Usually he's a quiet person.) All the other people followed him, and it was the best ending you could imagine. But if you're not sure how people will react, then add these ending sentences. You can't gracefully force people into insane laughter.

Evening Ritual to Mani
Moonsinger

Begin by setting up an altar to Mani. It doesn't have to be very large, but it should, in some way, reflect your impressions of this God. There ought to be a candle in the middle of the altar. I usually give Him sweet wine (like Lillet dessert wine, or Inniskillin ice wine), and I've written the offering part of this ritual to include that, but readers should feel free to give Him whatever offerings they feel He might like and to alter the wording of that part of the ritual accordingly.

If you are able to stand where you can see the moon, it is best to do so and to do this ritual in Mani's light. But if not, don't worry.

ଔ ଔ ଽ ଽ

Begin by reaching your arms up as if to embrace the moon. (This makes the rune Algiz, which is not incidental. It is a physical expression of devotion and prayer found in many ancient images.) Take a few moments to breathe Him in, to feel His light, His presence, His power filling you and wrapping itself around you. Allow yourself to physically embody and express your devotion to Mani.

Light a candle and say the following prayer:

> Mani, I ask Your blessings upon me tonight.
> You who are the night's sweetness,
> majestic and beautiful;
> You who gleam like a jewel in the fabric of the heavens,
> gliding across the sky from horizon to horizon,
> please smile upon me.
> Grant me the safety and protection of Your regard
> as I sleep and as I dream.
> The delicious luster of Your beauty leaves me in awe.
> You are my inspiration and my heart's haven.
> Sweet God of the evening sky,
> Remotest splendor,
> may my dreams be filled with You.
> Hail, Mani, beloved God of the Moon.

Offering

Pour wine into a pretty glass and raise it before you, offering it to the moon. Say:

> My Splendor, I offer this wine to You. May it sweeten
> Your evening as You sweeten mine. I hail and adore You,
> oh Mani, my Enticement.

I usually kneel before my altar at this point taking as long as I need or want in contemplation of Him, but readers should follow their hearts on this matter, kneeling, sitting, or standing as they feel appropriate for as long as they are moved to do so.

Closing Prayer

> Sweet Cherishment, my Adoration,
> My Longing, my Strength,
> Be Thou hailed with the setting of the sun,
> The rising of the day and every hour in between.
> Gleaming glory of all the nine worlds,
> I bow my head before You
> And pray only that I might carry
> Your image into my dreams.
> Hail, Mani.
> The Moon reigns supreme in His abode.
> He is beautiful and invites only longing.
> Praise Him.

The candle may be allowed to burn down or may be extinguished and lit when this ritual is next performed. It is Mani's though, and should be used only for Him.

Originally published in *Day Star and Whirling Wheel*, by Galina Krasskova. Asphodel Press, 2007

Well of Wisdom Seidh Ritual for Mimir
Gudrun of Mimirsbrunnr

I am a seidkona, meaning that I travel in trance to the Three Wells of the Tree and retrieve knowledge for those who ask, in an oracular fashion. There are many places to go for wisdom – to a specific god, or to the realm of a certain type of spirit, or to a place that is known for its oracular art, such as one of the Three Wells. Each well has guardians associated with it, and the Well of Wisdom is guarded by old Mimir, the God of Memory. I experience him as a severed head floating deep in the well, surrounded by the floating skulls and bones of those people he has killed for asking foolish questions. He is not an easy god to deal with, but for some reason he has taken a fancy to me. Perhaps because I am always careful about what I ask, and pay him well afterwards.

This ritual requires at least three people to do – a seidkona/seidmadhr (medium), a godhi/gythia, and a singer. (The addition of a drummer with a simple frame drum who can hold a steady, slow beat is useful as well.) The medium should not be asked to take on the job of running the ritual. They should be allowed to concentrate fully on their own job, which requires going into trance and allowing the power of the Well of Wisdom to come through them. When I have participated in this rite, I have always been the medium, so I will be speaking about my experience from that perspective.

Everyone who deals in trance has different ways of achieving it. I am not going to tell you how to get into a trance, because you might not use the same methods I do. However, it should hopefully be a method that you can do while sitting on the floor in a room, covered with a large piece of cloth. Sometimes my trancework at the beginning of this rite reminds me of Thorgeirr the Lawgiver's adventure in "going under the cloak", as there is a certain amount of sensory deprivation.

Mimir likes good liquor, poured into a hole in the ground. In worst cases – like the one time I was caught doing this rite in a city and had no way to get to an appropriate place afterward to pour out his offering – I used a storm drain while focusing on taking the alcohol to his well, and that seemed to work. The gythia for this rite should carry a few bottles along.

The most important items for this ritual are a mask and a large piece of shiny fabric – the size of a large blanket – with a hole in it. I made a mask for Mimir that is pale and skull-like, with long flowing white hair. I got a large piece of fabric – a king-size sheet, actually – that was made of a very dark green satin, almost black. That reminded me of the greeny-black water in his well. I cut the edges so that it was circular, hemmed them, cut a face-sized hole where my face would be, and attached the mask to it. The fabric becomes the water of the well, hiding the body of the oracle, and the mask becomes Mimir's floating face. I fastened one sparkling blue artificial gem, shaped like an eye, over where my heart is when I wear the mask.

The sides of the well can be created from chairs in a circle facing out around the cloth, and a row of candles are placed around its edge, just out of range of the chair legs. I also place four large bowls of actual water around the edge, at my head and feet and to each side. Then I lay still under the cloth, my eyes closed but looking out through the mask, and put myself into trance.

There are two areas marked out for this ritual – the "well" area which I have just described, and the "opening" area, which should be only a short distance away. The singer will have to go toward the "well" and sing, and the medium should be able to hear the singer even in trance, so they shouldn't be that far away.

ଔ ଔ ଓ ଓ

To begin, the gythia gathers the people at the opening area and recanes them and the space around them with mugwort, saying: "Be blessed and purified in the search for wisdom!" Then the gythia says:

> We go to visit the Well of Wisdom, guarded by Mimir the Wise. To do this, we will follow the path of the Tree to the mountains of Jotunheim, where the second great root burrows into the earth. There we will speak to Mimir – the God of Memory – who is a magical severed head floating in the Well. Be respectful – Mimir is dangerous, in spite of his condition. You may ask one question and one question only, and it must not be frivolous, so if there is nothing you want to know that badly, do not even ask! If you understand, raise your hand – we will walk there in silence.

The people raise their hands, and the gythia begins to lead them on a circle around the edge of the room. Meanwhile the singer walks toward the Well and begins to sing Mimir's song, calling him into the medium. If there is a drummer, they go with the singer. The gythia leads the people in a spiral, circling tighter and tighter, until they are standing in a ring around the well. They are told to sit backwards on the chairs, facing in and looking in over the edge. The singer continues to sing until everyone is seated, and then finishes the song and stops. The gythia calls out "We hail you, Old Guardian, Root of the Kjalar Mountains, Wise One of Jotunheim! We come to ask for your wisdom, should you choose to bestow it on us!" and pours liquor into one of the bowls of water (which should not be so full that the addition of liquor will make them overflow).

Ideally, if all goes well, Mimir then opens his eyes and speaks. Each person present may ask one question, and he will either answer it or he will not. If he answers, the questioner must pour more liquor into one of the bowls as an offering. If anyone is disrespectful, the gythia must have them removed immediately and offer more liquor in apology – Mimir holds grudges and does not appreciate being toyed with.

When he has answered everything that he intends to, the gythia gives him the last of the liquor and thanks him for his gifts. Then the party stands, each takes a candle, and they spiral out of the room. The medium is left to come back in silence, and then the bowls of water and alcohol are carried out and poured into some body of water (or down a storm drain, if need be, but very ceremoniously).

Mimir's Well Song:

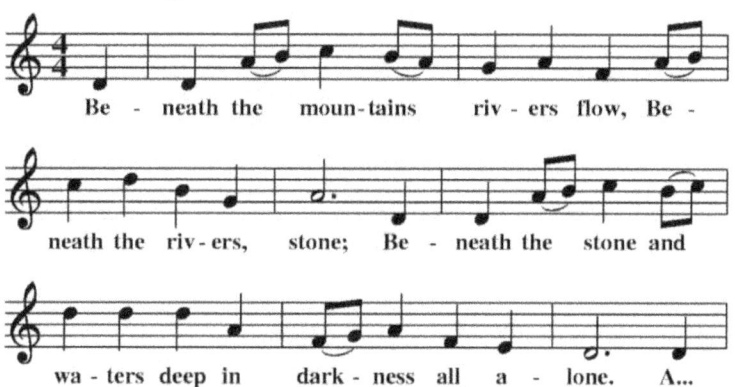

Mimir's Well Song
Gudrun of Mimirsbrunnr

> Beneath the mountains rivers flow,
> Beneath the rivers, stone;
> Beneath the stone and waters deep
> In darkness all alone.
>
> A thousand years of sacrifice
> A thousand years endured
> A thousand years of wisdom locked
> Beneath the mountain's roots.
>
> O Mem'ry's Lord and Keeper once
> Snatched back from death to dwell
> A thousand years of loneliness
> Within stone wisdom's well.
>
> You gave the corbies twa to him,
> You took from him an eye,
> And with its power you light the dark,
> The depths where still you lie.
>
> O Mem'ry's Lord and Keeper, grant
> Us some of what you've gained,
> And we shall pray and honor you,
> For ending of your pain.

Devotional Rite for Njord
Galina Krasskova

This ritual is a little different. It's not meant to be done regularly; in fact, depending where you live, it can take some preparation. The purpose of this ritual is to serve as a devotional rite honoring the God Njord, by taking His image (be it a carving, a statue, a laminated picture) to the ocean. As early as the writings of Tacitus, the use of processions honoring Vanic Gods has been attested to in lore (Nerthus ritual, *Germania*, chapter 40). So for this ritual, the idea is to carry your statue or image of Njord to the ocean where it can be anointed with seawater.

This is a very open-ended ritual. It can be as simple or elaborate as you wish. Choose the music that you will play in the car with Njord in mind. Dress in colors that you associate with Him. Prepare food or offerings that can be given to Him on the beach. Display the God-image proudly in your car (which admittedly can take some doing).

ଔ ଔ ଓ ଓ

Begin by offering the following prayer:

> Father Njord,
> Warlord of the Vanir,
> Hostage of Peace,
> Diplomat,
> Sea-farer
> Master of Ships
> Lord of the boat-yard.
> I hail You.

> Father of Freya,
> Father of Frey,
> Husband of Nerthus,
> Husband of Skadhi,
> Peaceloving Master of Noatun
> May this offering be pleasing to You,
> Oh my Lord.

Proceed onward to the ocean. Once there, take the image of Njord to the shoreline and allow the water to flow over it – holding on carefully so it isn't gifted to the sea itself! Then set out the offerings and spend as much time as you wish in communion with Njord. Make sure the offerings are organic and biodegradable so that they can be left on the beach by the water's edge. Best of all, make it something the seagulls will enjoy.

Return home, displaying Njord's image mindfully and prayerfully and once home, return it to its altar knowing that the ritual has ended.

Originally published in *Northern Tradition for the Solitary Practitioner* by Raven Kaldera and Galina Krasskova, New Page Press, 2007.

Three Norns Ritual
Gudrun of Mimirsbrunnr

We created this rite for a Pagan festival. The main ritual had several stations, each created and manned by a different Pagan group, and people passed through them one at a time over a period of about two hours. Our group created and donated this part, which is designed to serve a number of people coming through at a fairly slow pace.

This ritual requires three priestesses – well, of course. Unlike the Greek Moerae, with the Norse Fates the Spinner (Urd) is the oldest Norn, and then the Weaver (Verdandi) is her daughter, and the Cutter (Skuld) is her granddaughter. Ideally the ages of the priestesses should also be in this order, but if a woman feels drawn to a particular part she should take it. However, whoever takes the role of Urd needs to be a skilled handspinner, regardless of age. (It is possible that a man might play one of the Nornir, but he must then dress and act like a woman of the right age for the duration of the ritual, and preferably for a little bit before and after. Ritual cross-dressing has its precedence, but it must be done with real effort and respect for the shape one is taking on.)

A great deal of wool or other natural fiber should be carded, dyed in different colors, and then several yards of it spun up beforehand. Whoever takes on the work of that pre-ritual spinning should do it with great concentration, perhaps with a prayer to the Nornir that is repeated over and over as the fiber is worked. A makeshift loom should be put together – when we did this rite with our kindred, we hung strings on weights from the branch of a tree and loosely wove some extra pieces of thread and yarn through it so that it resembled a Viking loom. The three priestesses stood with their backs to the tree and each other, facing out. If this is to be done indoors, the loom can be hung from the ceiling or from a simple wooden frame. An actual loom can also be used if one is available, so long as the weave is loose enough for the moving thread to be actually moved easily through it.

The pre-spun yarn is threaded through the loom, through spaces large enough that it can move easily. The end is brought out a good long way and then handed to the priestess who is standing in for Skuld. She should carry a large and obvious pair of shears. The other end of the yarn is held by the priestess who is standing in for Urd, and she continually adds more fiber to it and spins the fiber. The three stand in a triangle facing out, and the people approach them one at a time.

To begin, each onlooker approaches Urd and asks her a question, something they want to know. Instead of answering, she spins several inches of thread and tells them to hold it with two fingers in the middle of the section she has spun for them. "The past has information you will need to know in order to understand the answer," she says. "Follow the thread and you will know it." (This is why the fiber should be pre-dyed in different colors first, besides the colorful effect; it is easier for each person to keep track of their part of the thread if it has particular colors. Urd can even reach for fiber of some color she feels is symbolic of their question.)

Then the person, holding their thread, is gently moved over to Verdandi as she pulls the thread through her loom. The priestess who stands in for Verdandi has a difficult job, for she must pull the thread through her loom gently enough that it does not break, even with bewildered people holding onto their section, but firmly enough that it does actually move. When the person has been drawn up to her loom, she has them let go of their thread, pulls it through the loom, and has them take it up again on the other side. As she pulls it through the loom, she says, "The present has your question bound up with the will and desire and circumstance of many others. Follow the thread and you will come to understand them." Then she keeps pulling the thread, and the person takes up the slack and moves on to Skuld.

At Skuld's station, the priestess who stands in for Skuld takes the thread away from the person and says, "The future is not yet set, and there is always room for change, but you must act quickly with full understanding of the situation." She snips off the thread and gives it to the person, saying, "Take this home and place it under your pillow, and you will dream of your answer tonight – but only if you are willing to see the full answer, past, present, and future, and not just the part that is comfortable for you." Then she sends them away and turns to the next person.

This rite can go on for some time; it is probably best as part of some other larger ritual, because there is a lot of waiting in line. You may want to have a before-and-after section to distract those who have not yet approached the Norns, and those who have already finished.

Walpurgisnacht Ritual for Odin
Gavin Kreskin

I created this rite to celebrate Walpurgisnacht, April 30, the night that it is said that Odin hung on the tree for the ninth day and the runes came to him. It involves twenty-seven heiti or names of Odin. Twenty-seven is three times nine, or three to the third. Three and nine are numbers associated with Odin. This rite is meant to be a solitary ritual that is the preliminary to a group ritual, but it can also be adapted to group working. To do the rite, you will need to find a box and mark it with Odinic symbols such as runes or the valknot. You will also need the twenty-seven items in the following list, and they will each be ceremonially placed into the box for one of his aspects. The box will be put in a dark, dry place for a year, and then brought out the following Walpurgisnacht and carried around in a group ritual for Odin. Each person takes one item from the box until they are all gone, and these are the aspects of Odin that they should pray to during the following year. If you like, the box-making can be a group effort as well, and the box can be refilled that night for keeping until the next year.

You will need:[1]

- A piece of dark blue cloth, rolled up
- A cotton ball, slightly pulled apart, for a cloud
- A small string of silver beads
- A bead that looks like an eye
- A small silver offering cup
- A stick with blue and gray ribbons tied to it, like a miniature staff
- A small figure of a horse
- A silver string with nine knots tied in it
- The rune Ansuz carved or painted on something

Editor's Note: *Three of the rites in this book, including this one, were sent to us by worshipers who were currently incarcerated, showing that love of the Gods may come from all sorts of unexpected places.*

[1] If you are in prison while you attempt to do this ritual, it is possible to "origami" a little box out of paper, and draw symbols of Odin upon it, and instead of symbolic items you can have small slips of paper that can be rolled up and placed within. Each can have the name of Odin written on it, or a picture of the item, or both. Remember that one of the names of Odin is God of Prisoners, and he is there to keep you strong if you call upon him.

- A small spear (I made mine out of a stick and a bit of cut tin from a can lid)
- A small sword
- A tiny knife, smaller than the sword
- A small shield
- Three twigs of an ash tree, tied together with black thread
- A rusty piece of chain
- A piece of gray cloth, rolled up
- A small blue glass bottle, corked or sealed, filled with mead
- A piece of string formed into a noose
- Two cords, one white and one black, knotted together
- A knotted red cord
- A silver coin
- A clear glass marble
- A few gray hairs donated by a wise elder of Odin, tied together with blue thread
- A twig of evergreen, preferably yew, but it can be fir or spruce
- A colorful glass marble
- A piece of black cloth, rolled up
- Two black feathers, wrapped together with gray thread and hung with blue beads

ಐ ಐ ಏ ಏ

To begin, stand with your arms lifted and speak this invocation:

> Hail to Odin, Wise and Powerful!
> By blue of twilight sky I honor you,
> By blue of single eye I honor you,
> By blue of autumn winds I honor you.
> By gray of storm cloud I honor you,
> By gray of the road's dust I honor you,
> By gray of winter skies I honor you.
> By black of raven's wing I honor you,
> By black of impending Doom I honor you,
> By black of deepest mysteries I honor you.
>
> Alfoðr, All-Father,
> Take me beneath your cloak and protect me.

Place the blue cloth into the box.

> Asagrimm, Ruler of the Aesir, teach me who will be loyal to me and who will not.

Place the cotton cloud into the box.

> Gagnrað, Counselor, whisper your wisdom into my ear.

Place the string of silver beads into the box.

> Vakr, Awakener, do not let me fall into complacency.

Place the eye bead into the box.

> Vinr Stalla, Friend of Altars, be there for me when I kneel in my hour of need.

Place the offering cup into the box.

> Gangleri, Wanderer, guide me on my travels through dark places.

Place the stick with ribbons into the box.

> Fjallgeiguðr, Shape-Shifting God, let me become who I need to be to survive.

Place the horse figure into the box.

> Galdrafaðr, Father of the Magic Song, teach me the weaving of words.

Place the knotted silver string into the box.

> Runaguð, Rune-God, show me the wisdom for which you sacrificed yourself.

Place the Ansuz rune into the box.

> Biflindi, Spear-Shaker, encourage me to move when I have fallen down.

Place the little spear into the box.

> Viðrir, Stormer, teach me humility in the face of my own wyrd.

Place the little sword into the box.

Gollungr, Yeller, teach me to speak loudly for my own
needs when necessary.

Place the little knife into the box.

Valfoðr, Father of the Slain, train me for excellence that I
might be worthy of your halls.

Place the little shield into the box.

Sigfoðr, Father of Victory, bless me with achievement of
my goals.

Place the ash twigs into the box.

Haptaguð, God of Prisoners, teach me how to survive the
long waiting.

Place the chain into the box.

Glapsvin, Deceiver, teach me when it is right to twist the
truth to achieve a worthy goal.

Place the gray cloth into the box.

Bolverk, Evil Worker, teach me how to atone for
necessary wrongdoing.

Place the bottle of mead into the box.

Yggr, Terrible One, strengthen my spine when I must face
horror without flinching.

Place the string noose into the box.

Angan Friggyar, Frigga's Delight, teach me to be wise in
my choice of relationships.

Place the black and white cords into the box.

Jalkr, Gelding, teach me to appreciate limitations as
necessary to my discipline.

Place the knotted red cord into the box.

Auðun, Friend of Wealth, teach me how to gain what I
need.

Place the silver coin into the box.

Oski, Wish-Granter, be generous in my times of trouble.

Place the clear marble into the box.

Harbard, Grey-Beard, help me to live a long and wise life.

Place the bundle of gray hairs into the box.

Grimnir, Hooded One, walk with me into the shadows and bring me out again.

Place the black cloth into the box.

Julfaðr, Yule-Father, send the Wild Hunt to watch my back.

Place the evergreen twig into the box.

Viðfrager, Widely Famed, teach me how to make my mark on the world.

Place the colorful marble into the box.

Hrafnaguð, Raven God, I honor you with all that I know. Teach me to know more about all things, that I might have more with which to honor you.

Place the twin raven feathers into the box.

Close the box and put it aside. If you are solitary, choose object (or piece of paper) every ninth night from the box – picking blindly – and pray to that aspect of Odin to teach you. There are other aspects of Odin as well, and perhaps on a different Walpurgisnacht you might want to honor a new list, but this should keep you busy for at least a year.

Ritual In Honor Of Woden
Galina Krasskova

Begin by setting up a small altar for Woden. Anything that reminds you of Woden, or calls His canon of sacred stories to mind is appropriate. You should also have a candle, some incense, and either aquavit or whiskey to use as an offering and, if possible, a bit of tobacco. Have a glass for the alcohol and a small bowl for the tobacco (or ash tray if you're using a cigarette, tobacco, or pipe).

ଔ ଔ ଞ ଞ

Evening Rite for Woden

Sit in front of the altar and spend a few moments centering yourself. Then, turning your attention to Woden, light the candle and a bit of incense and offer the following prayer.

Invocation to Woden

>Hail to Woden,
>World-shaper, wisdom seeker,
>Wyrd walker, wandering God.
>Hail to He Who brings
>both weal and woe
>Who hung on the Tree,
>Who gnawed upon His own spear,
>to tear a hole between the worlds.
>Hail to He, who won the runes,
>Who, burned by their fire,
>Shrieked His spells,
>and burned them all right back.
>
>Hail to the All-Father,
>Ruthless, fearless, mighty God,
>Weapons wise and wondrous Lord.
>Bestow Your blessings upon me here tonight,
>and may my prayer be pleasing to You.
>Hail, Woden.

Meditation

In our cosmology, Woden (or Odin) is the God who breathed His breath into the first human beings, imbuing them with life. He's the breath-giver, and our continued breath is His gift. The first breath we take is drawn from Him and the last breath we exhale will be given back to Him. That is the focus of this meditation, that primal connection, that spiritual umbilicus.

Sitting comfortably, begin to focus on your breath. Feel the coolness of the breath as you inhale. Allow yourself to feel the intercostals (the muscles between your ribs) expand and release. Spend a few moments focusing on the inhalation, the feel of the breath flowing into your lungs, the expansion of your diaphragm followed by the exhalation, the rush of breath leaving your lungs, the contraction. Become aware of the circular rhythm and once you have spent a few moments focusing on your breath, turn your attention to Woden.

As you breathe, think about the creation story. Think about that first kiss of breath, the moment that Odin breathed life into Ask and Embla, waking them to their own humanity. Think about what that set in motion, and the long progression of humanity that flowed from the moment of that kiss.

Visualize, feel, or imagine (whatever works for you – people work and process these things differently and not everyone is visual) that you are connected to Woden by the cord of your breath, by that very rhythm of the inhalation and exhalation of your breathing. Imagine that as you inhale, you are consciously drinking in His breath, that He is breathing into you, and as you exhale, you are breathing into Him and He is drinking in your breath. Continue this for at least five minutes, longer if you can. Focus on the give and take, on drinking in His breath, and the connection further strengthened when you exhale into Him. When you are ready to stop, exhale for a final time and then take a few moments to re-orient yourself to your space, making sure that you are properly grounded.

Offering

Pour out some of the whiskey or aquavit into a glass and put it on the altar, offering it to Woden with the words, "Divine Breath-giver, I give this liquor to You in offering." Light the tobacco if it is a cigarette or cigar or pipe otherwise just sprinkle it into a small offering bowl. "I also give You this tobacco, for Your pleasure. May these small gifts be pleasing to You. Hail, Woden."

Spend however long you like in further contemplation. If this is being done as a group ritual, a horn should be passed at this point so that everyone may hail and honor Woden.

Closing Prayer

> Thank You, Woden,
> for Your wisdom.
> I hail You now, All-Father,
> and always.
> Hail, Woden.

The ritual is now ended. You may allow the candle to burn down or, if you wish, snuff it out and save it for the next Wednesday night's rite.

ଓଃ   ଓଃ   ଃଠ   ଃଠ

Suggestions for offerings for Woden

Colors: Grey, deep cobalt blue, black

Symbols: valknot, spear, wolves, ravens

Stones: labradorite, black goldstone, lapis

Herbs and Trees: The nine sacred herbs, ash leaves, elm leaves, parsley (associated with the Wild Hunt), woad, cinquefoil, horehound, periwinkle.

Runes: Technically, all the Futhark runes are His, but specifically Ansuz, Othala, Gebo, and Wunjo.

Food and drink: good quality alcohol (mead, dry red wine, whiskey, cognac, and other hard liquor especially aquavit), smoked salmon, red meats, spearlike vegetables such as leeks, asparagus, and garlic.

Service offerings: Woden is, in part, a God of warriors, so many of the same organizations to which one might donate for Tyr are appropriate for Odin as well:
- ଓଃ Disabled American Veterans: http://www.dav.org
- ଓଃ Fisher House Foundation: http://fisherhouse.org
- ଓଃ The Military Religious Freedom Foundation: http://www.militaryreligiousfreedom.org

- The Wounded Warrior Project:
  http://www.woundedwarriorproject.org
- American Women Veterans:
  http://americanwomenveterans.org/home/
- Paralyzed Veterans of America: http://www.pva.org

He is also a God of knowledge and education, so one might donate to an educational charity like http://donorschoose.org.

One could also reach out and help someone who is struggling to come into the faith, or volunteer to teach literacy. Donating books to children or schools in need is also an appropriate offering.

Contraindicated: cowardice, not "sucking the marrow" out of one's experiences, shirking military service.

Quoted with permission from an as yet untitled forthcoming Book of Hours by Galina Krasskova.

Devotional Rite for Sigyn
Galina Krasskova

This rite is dedicated to Sigyn, one of the deities who works closely with Galina. This could be used as an inspiration for a basic rite to honor any god or goddess that one loves and works with regularly. It isn't hard to create a simple invocation that includes titles of that deity and requests to be granted Their virtues. Then it's a matter of offering Them food and drink that They might appreciate, and offering some service – even meditating on Their might and wonder – for a time.

Prepare by setting up an altar to honor Sigyn. The center point of the altar should be a large bowl. We suggest having a special bowl that you set aside only for this purpose. There should be two candles on the altar as well. This ritual is best done after one's evening meal, as part of the ritual involves sharing your food with Sigyn.

ಜ ಜ ಜ ಜ

Begin by lighting the two candles and offering the following prayer:

> Sigyn,
> Beloved Wife of Loki,
> Mother of Narvi and Vali,
> Lady of Gentleness
> Lady of the Staying Power
> I hail You.
>
> Grant me Your courage,
> Which is that of the open yet invincible heart.
> Grant me Your humility,
> which is that of mindful devotion to Your love.
> Grant above all that I may be of service,
> To You, to Your husband, to Your children
> And to all the Gods who might have use of me.
> Hail, Sigyn.

Take a portion of your food and drink, a portion that you have consciously set aside from your evening meal and offer it to Sigyn saying: "For Your time in the cave, when You starved and went unnourished in duty to love. May this nourish You."

Take the bowl between your hands and raise it up saying "May I hold this bowl in Your stead, Lady. May I take Your place in the cave tonight, for a few brief moments." Then hold the bowl. Try to hold it for at least ten minutes and fifteen is better. Just hold the bowl, concentrating on Sigyn doing so for Loki and what this must have meant for the both of them. Just hold the bowl until the time you have allotted is up.

When you are finished, light a stick of incense, offering it to Sigyn. Snuff the candles and wash the bowl thoroughly. Leave the food out for Her until the following morning when it can be disposed of.

Originally published in *Northern Tradition for the Solitary Practitioner* by Raven Kaldera and Galina Krasskova, New Page Press, 2007.

Skadhi Blót
Mist, Gyðja of Kenaz Kindred, Canada

This ritual is designed for mid-to-late winter.

ଔ ଔ ଓ ଓ

At the beginning of the rite, the Gyðja speaks:

> It is appropriate during this dark and cold part of the season to blót to the huntress of the Nine Worlds. It is fitting to call upon Skadhi during this time of year, as she is the symbol of the hunter in the winter, and that is what we all are. The last part of winter looms and we find ourselves reflecting on the nature of survival, the time when food was scarce, and perhaps the hunt un-yielding of any bounty.
>
> It is fitting to call upon a winter giant, and in this blót we honour her and her clan. The story of Skadhi is story of one that was not willing to lie down and take what had happened to her, but in fact journeyed forth to the Gods and demanded compensation.
>
> Tonight, we shall honour and remember the strength and wonder of the goddess Skadhi. Although traditionally this blót would take place when hunting is at its peak, it seems fitting that it also be when the winter is harsh and brutal. Skadhi is protective and strong, and in this guise of the warrior we can call her forth to protect us from the elements that may threaten the return of warmth and light.

At this point, we perform the Hammer Rite[1]. The Gyðja and her assistant walk to the four quarters and perform this rite; alternately, some other ritual of creating sacred space could be used.

After this is done, the Gyðja says:

> I hallow and make holy this harrow and stead in the name of Skadhi, ex-wife of Njord, stepmother of Frey and Freyja, wife of Ullr, daughter of Thiazi, defender of the realms of winter from the coming storms. In your name we make this place fitting for our gods and kin.

---

[1] The Hammer Rite was created by Edred Thorsson, and is available in his book *Futhark: A Handbook of Rune Magic*.

A bowl is brought forth full of ice cubes with a white candle in the middle. The Gyðja says:

> Before the Jotun goddess Skadi came to Asgard after her father's death to claim her inheritance and a husband, she was worshipped widely in Midgard among the humanfolk. She went often among them during the winter months, preferring to spend the summer months either in Niflheim or in the far northeastern reaches of Jotunheim, where it was snowy year-round. It was Skadi who first taught them the making of skis for the quick and snowshoes for the slow, of winter dogsleds and traps of many kinds, of tracking and recognizing spoor even in the bitter cold, and slowly they became winter hunters under her guidance. She taught a few of them, also, of the ways of the stars, and how to read their chill and gleaming knowledge.
>
> Among the northerners of Midgard – who lived more than half the year in snow and ice – Skadi was much beloved, and also not a little feared. To gain her favour could mean the difference between surviving the bitterest winter in reasonable comfort, or seeing one's children perish of cold and starvation. They did not fool themselves into thinking that Skadi was a kindly mother goddess; she was a maiden of ice, a white wolf in the snow with blood on her breast, a spear of ice falling upon the unwary. They knew her nature, both cold and bloodthirsty, and they offered her sacrifices.
>
> When the seers looked upon the signs of Nature in the autumn, and knew with sinking heart that this winter would be especially harsh, a young man was chosen among the handsomest of the village, and offered to Skadi as consort and sacrifice. He was sent naked to a bower built for them in the snow, there to await her pleasure, and she could take it as she wished. Then he was lashed to a tree, and his testicles tied to a buck livestock animal of some sort – goat or bull – and they were ripped from him. Whether he lived or died was up to Skadi and how well he had pleased her, but he would never share his seed with

another woman again. His blood was caught in a vessel of carven stone and left on her altar, and she would have mercy on the village and send them plentiful game, and fewer snowstorms.

In modern day, we do not offer the sacrifice of flesh or blood, but to Skadhi we offer this, our devotion and love in the form of the blót.

Tonight, as we raise our glasses to her, perhaps her favour will smile down upon us and we will once again see the wonderful budding trees and blossoms as Frey and Freyja bring life to the land once more.

Invocation to Skadhi I

Skadhi, clear-eyed huntress and bow-woman,
Thjazi's daughter, battle-maid
 Avenging with flashing sword his death,
 Accepter of weregild,
 Courageous and beautiful bride of brave Njord,
 Sea-god and shore-dweller whose hall you left
 For the peaks of Thrymheim.
Dear to you are the howls of wolves, Skadhi,
Dark lady who brings the snows of winter;
The fiercest storms and deadly ice are yours.
Guide our arrows to their goals, shining one,
Keep us safe in our winter travels.
Skadhi, great huntress and serpent-hanger,
Njord's husband and snowshoe-goddess,
We ask you, O Shining Bride of the Gods
To join with us on this night of darkness,
For the winds are wailing
And the wolves are howling in the hills.
O mighty winter-goddess, woman of the wild,
As the darkness covers the fields and the folk,
We pray that you share your strength with us,
That you guide us in our goings and doings,
And that you bring the light of your wisdom
To fill the hall and the folk again.
Hail Skadhi!

An offering of liquor is poured out to Skadhi.

Invocation to Skadi II

>Hail, Huntress of the snow and ice!
>Hail, wife of Njord the sea-god
>Who would not compromise with anyone,
>Nor live on the shore near the sea-birds
>Rather than your beloved snowy mountains.
>We who struggle between the tracks
>Left by Your winter sleigh,
>We whose bloody marks You track,
>Skillful in your cold eye,
>We hail you, Mistress of Survival!
>Etin-bride of winter, Your cloak
>Spreads white over the fields,
>The icy wind Your breath,
>White wolf in the snow,
>Lady of the crisp clean starry sky
>Over the frozen tundra.
>Teach us of the narrow edge between
>Living and dying, and of that struggle,
>And the cold, naked truth that it reveals.
>Catch us naked in the snow, Lady,
>We shall bare our throats to your wisdom
>And count ourselves lucky.

Libations are now brought out for Skadhi's family members – Ullr, Frey, Freya, Njord, Thiazi, and the Frost Giants. After each invocation is read, everyone echoes "Hail _____!" and their offering is poured out.

Invocation to Ullr

>Ullr, great huntsman and master of the bow,
>Sif's son and Snowshoe-Aesir,
>We ask you O Glory of Winter
>to join with us on this dark night,
>For the frost is thick and the cold is chilling to the bone
>O mighty shield-god, fair of face and fight,
>As the darkness covers the fields and the folk,

We pray that you share your strength with us,
That your skiff should shield us from harm,
And that your shining light should fill the hall the and folk again.
Hail Ullr!

Invocation to Frey and Freyja

Though she did not live with you long,
Her love with you both has stayed,
For Frey to Gerd she did bring,
And brought the blessings of a love true and lasting,
For Freyja she caught up the trickster with ease,
And comforted you by binding his bones,
To you both she showed a love, lasting longer than vows.
As it is our way to honor the clan and family
Of the god we are blótting to this day,
We offer this gift to you in like kind,
As family and kin to the lady of winter.
Hail to Frey and Freya!

Njord

To you, great god of the sea,
We bring you gifts this day
In honour of your marriage to the lady of winter,
Though neither could reside in the hall of the other,
We learn that even if circumstances change,
It is possible to part in peace and friendship,
As with your children, we offer you the same,
A gift in kind, to the goddess we celebrate this day.
Hail Njord!

Thjazi

Swift you were to steal Idun,
And for punishment slain by the gods of Asgard,
But still in this death,
A beacon of memory given to your daughter,
Two stars within the sky,
To watch over the people of Midgard,

In the midst of the cold and snow, when above we look,
The stars known to us as Gemini remind us of you,
To your daughter we honour,
For from you came a daughter with strength
And wisdom upon her bestowed,
To you, father of Skadhi, we give you hail,
And welcome you to our humble feast.
Hail Thiazi!

Frost Giants

Giants of the cold lands,
Of frost and ice,
We come this day to ask you now to slumber once more,
The winter sky is still cold,
And the light of summer far from our sight,
But we ask you now to remove yourself from our land.
In thanks for our survival,
We offer you humble offerings
To implore you to return once more
To the cold and frosty places of the great Ash.
Hail the Frost Giants!

After the last hailing and libation, the Gyðja says:

> Although traditionally a ritual dedicated to Skadhi and Ullr often followed a hunt, we can perhaps only strive to honour them in our own way. We felt that they would be more apparent during this time of year than in November, because frankly it is now when we need reminding of surviving the rest of a winter that goes on too long. Skadhi protects those in Midgard from terrifying storms, that decimate not only the land but our desire to go outside at all. It is very depressing to see the world so dark and cold, and she illuminates it with a protective force, reminding us that there is fun to be had even if we absolutely hate the cold!
>
> Ullr is one that represents the hunt, and in that role can provide the success needed in all endeavours. Normally, at this time, weapons would be dedicated to Ullr

to provide successful hunting; however, he is also good at providing a great deal of success to those seeking personal change and transformation. It is in this form we will ask all of you to come forward and ask Skadhi for whatever you wish ... this does not have to be a request heard out loud, but can be personal and quite if you wish.

After you state your wish to Skadhi, please sip from the cup, as a gift from her to you.

Ullr, the companion of Skadhi, is said to hold Odin's throne while he is wandering the world of Midgard over the cold and frosty months. As a god of success in all endeavors, the god of glory and of skill, we ask that those who wish may come and place an offering to Ullr into the bowl. If you have anything that you wish to have success in at the moment, feel free to ask Ullr for his blessings. As a gift for your offering, please eat a piece of this white cake.

Participants come forth and ask their boons, and give their personal offerings. As this ritual was meant to be a short one, we then ask if anyone wishes to have a rune reading done during the rite, and if not we will begin Sumbel[2] to close the rite.

---

[2] Described on pages 157-8.

Sunna Rite
Galina Krasskova

This ritual should be performed outdoors, where individuals can see and experience Sunna's presence directly. Folk should be called together in a circle. We originally performed this around a fire pit and while there was no fire, the pit made an excellent place to deposit offerings to Sunna (a fire was lit later in the evening and the offerings then consumed).

ଔ ଔ ଓ ଓ

Godhi/Gythia: We begin by hailing Skoll Sunchaser. Let Him who travels behind now be hailed before. To the wolf who helps this Goddess maintain the rhythm of Her travels, who never shirks in His duty, as She does not shirk in Hers. Hail, Skoll Sunchaser, mighty wolf, son of the Ironwood.

Pour out alcohol in offering.

Godhi/Gythia:
>Hail Sunna,
>We call to You,
>Who rides triumphant in Your chariot
>Across the broad expanse of day.
>Hail, Sunna, our Pacesetter,
>Who with Your brother governs the seasons,
>The turning of the year, our rising and retiring.
>Bless us, Great Goddess, with the strength, vitality and health
>That is Yours to bestow.
>We honor Your might, Your power,
>And Your eternal presence.
>Be with us here today, Sunna. Hail.

A moment should be taken by the officiant to speak on Sunna's importance to our ancestors. She remains the single most visible manifestation of the Gods. All we have to do is look up to see the power of Her passage across the heavens. Without Her benevolence there were no crops. Without crops, there was no food and the people suffered. Of all the Gods and Goddesses, Sunna perhaps had the most direct impact on the lives of Her people. It's easy for us to forget that, living as we do in an industrialized society that doesn't depend so readily on direct interaction with the land and its elements for sustenance. Yet without Sunna, our world would be a barren, icy rock.

Sunna Meditation: Drinking in the Sun

Have the participants extend their hands upwards to the sky. Invite them to concentrate on the heat of Her presence. She is a Goddess of health, wholeness, and vitality. She is a Goddess of might in its purest, most unfettered manifestation. Invite them to drink in Her presence. This is something that they can do every single day. Go outside, stand in the sunlight and spend a few seconds or minutes drinking in Her warmth, drinking in Her presence, drinking in Her vitality. These are the gifts She offers us and they're there for anyone who would reach out for them.

When the officiant has the sense that everyone has done this to their own satisfaction, he or she should fill a horn with libation and pass it around the gathered folk, inviting each person to hail Sunna in their own words.

Offerings

The officiant then makes whatever offerings he or she has brought to Sunna, and invites the gathered folk to do the same. Thanks are then given to Sunna, for Her presence, Her strength, Her constancy, Her might. The ritual is completed by having the folk chant Her name, over and over until the energy peaks. To finish, the officiant says:

> Thanks are given to the Goddess Sunna for Her blessings this day. May we go forth from this ritual space infused with the power of Her presence. Hail, Goddess of the Sun. Hail Sunna.

Originally published in *Day Star and Whirling Wheel*, Asphodel Press 2009.

Farmer's Thorrablot
Geordie Ingerson

Thor's Blot is January 19th, and it is the time when the farmer – love he Aesir or Vanir – petitions the great Thor for clement weather for the year. A farmer lives and dies by the weather, sometimes rather literally. If there is not enough sun or rain, if there is too much late or early frost, he can be ruined or, in older times, starve. Therefore, while the Vanic practitioner may work with the Gods of the earth in his daily work, that work must also take into account the occasional payment to the Gods of the sky. That is one reason why Thor allied himself with the common man – someone among the Aesir had to speak for the farmer who begged for decent weather.

For this reason, Thor should be honoured on his day. He is not a god who likes fanciness; the best thing to do is to go outside and face the sky, even if it is raining, snowing, windy, or any other bad weather.

ര ര ഏ ഏ

To begin the rite, lift your arms and call out to the sky:

> Hail Thor who brings the rain on the fields,
> Who all the gods of Earth cannot do without.
> Let there be drink for the fields,
> But do not wash them away.
> Let there be water for our drink,
> But do not drown us.
> Let there be water for washing,
> But do not wipe us away.
> Let there be water for the creatures
> In shed and in wood,
> But not too much, we pray, O Thor.
> Look upon us with a kindly hand
> And save your hammer for the unworthy.

Pour him out a glass of mead or beer – not onto the Earth directly, but flung in a great arc toward the sky (and hopefully not in a direction where it will fall on the people below). It is also politic to leave him a joint of meat as well, but make sure that the bones are not broken but neatly jointed out.

Originally published in *Ingvi's Blessing: Prayers and Charms for Field and Farm*, by Geordie Ingerson. Asphodel Press, 2011.

Ritual to Tyr
Ari

This rite is an example of a ritual that is not only devotional but purposeful. It is to be done for Tyr when you must do a hard thing that is the right thing, and you are well aware that you will suffer for it. Perhaps you will lose a friend, or your job, or your family, but that pales against the need to do what is right rather than what is easy. If you are in this hard place – choosing right-doing and personal honor with the sure knowledge that you will, indeed, suffer for this choice – then this ritual calls on Tyr to aid and strengthen you in your cause. Sometimes the world is not fair, and we must endure pain in order to do right.

However, before you do this rite, you should meditate for a long time on the cleanliness of your motivations. Be certain that this doing is necessary; are you sure that great harm would come to others if you were silent or inactive? Is there a simpler way to do this? Are you sure that you know the whole truth of the situation? Is any part of your motivation vengeful, or over-proud, or coming from self-righteousness? Is this a deed that would have more impact if it were done by someone else, someone who may well be the better one to do it? It is an insult to bring this matter before Tyr with hidden motivations or impulsive choices.

ଔ ଔ ଊ ଊ

For this rite you will need to go at sunset to a lonely place, and bring with you a red candle and a knife or sword of some kind.

> Hail to the One-Handed God!
> Hail to Him whose name is Honor
> And whose Word is iron,
> Who alone never shirks the thankless task
> Whose reason is Lawful Necessity.
> Hail to the Lord of Swords,
> Who gave a weapon-bearing hand
> To see that what must be done was done in truth.

Kneel and light the candle.

> Hail God of the sunset, last single ray of light,

Lord of loyal morality, whose name none takes in vain.

Catch the last rays of sunlight on the blade of the knife or sword. Lay your forearm against the earth, and, very carefully, lay the blade across it.

> Now must I face loss to do what is right,
> O Lord Tyr, and I do not ask for your aid
> To take away that loss, that I might hope for ease of action.
> As you stood forth knowing you must lose to win,
> So I ask only that you keep my back straight,
> My arm strong, my hand from trembling,
> My voice from faltering, my words from vanishing,
> My head up, and my resolve unyielding
> As I reach into the challenging maw of my own future.

Slowly and in silence, turn your hand over and lay your palm flat on the ground, with the blade of the sword under it. Tell Tyr what it is you will do, and then, as soon as possible after this rite, do it. Tyr will lend you strength, but you must not falter after you have promised it to him.

Originally published in *Northern Tradition for the Solitary Practitioner* by Raven Kaldera and Galina Krasskova, New Page Press, 2007.

Oathing Rite for Ullr
Geordie Ingerson

Ullr was one of the deities who watched over the sanctity of oaths. Traditionally his oaths were made on a ring, which was then buried in front of his shrine. This ritual is for any kind of oath that you feel would do better with a divine witness. However, remember that if you ask a deity to be a witness to your oath, you then give them the right to make sure that you keep that oath, by any means necessary. If you get them involved, they stay involved. Because of this, please don't do this lightly. Think about the oath for a long time before you jump in. Make sure that it is something you can keep without terrible damage to your life or that of your loved ones – or future loved ones.

Ullr's oaths were publicly made in front of his shrine, so you will want human witnesses as well. If it is an oath to another person, they should be there also. Buy a ring that seems appropriate to you. It does not have to fit any of your fingers perfectly; it need only be large enough to slip over the first joint of at least one finger. Bring along also three pieces of thread – one black, one white, and one forest green. Twist them together into one thread.

Since we no longer have public Ullr shrines, you will need to make one. It's not hard – drape a table or box in colors of evergreen, snow, and black. You might lay out a bow and arrows, a pair of skis and/or skates, small figures of deer, skis, sleds, snowflakes (there are Christmas ornaments of all of those out there), evergreen boughs (yew if you can get it), and perhaps a cup or bowl to pour a libation out of. Get him something for a libation and perhaps a food offering. Ideally it should be set up outside, in a forest of some sort.

ଔ ଔ ଓ ଓ

To begin, everyone should gather in front of Ullr's altar. Open the rite by reciting the following prayer:

> Hunter who smells out every lie
> And every broken word,
> Swift as an arrow strike,
> Swift as the arrow of truth,
> We ask you, Lord of the Hunt,
> Implacable as winter ice,

> Hear this oath taken in your presence
> And guard it well, with swift
> And thorough justice should it be
> Knowingly broken and cast aside.
> Hail Ullr, Lord of Winter,
> May you look with your glance of honor
> Upon all of us here.

The first person to make the oath then picks up the ring and places it on his finger, saying, "What goes out, comes back around, as winter follows summer." They then speak their oath aloud to all present.

If a second person is making the oath – if, for example, they are making oaths to each other – then they take the ring from the first person and place it on their finger, also saying, "What goes out, comes back around, as winter follows summer." Then the ring is removed, and the twisted thread is wrapped around it and tied with three knots. If there is more than one oath-taker, they share the knotting.

Then a hole is dug in the earth and the ring is placed in it. The oath-taker(s) may have help with the digging, but they must cover the ring with earth themselves. Then the rite is closed with the following prayer:

> Hail Ullr, Lord of Winter,
> Which follows summer
> In the great circle of justice and honor.
> May you watch over us
> With eyes of ice and iron,
> With steady hand on the still-bent bow.

Rituals for Many Purposes

Rite of Yggdrasil
Raven Kaldera

This ritual was developed for presenting to a large group at a mixed Neo-Pagan conference. It's a fairly large and elaborate rite, with a lot of props. We decided that the best thing would be a ritual that was easy to follow, had a good deal of participation but none that required specialized knowledge, and would be educational, teaching people who have little experience with Norse cosmology something that they could take home. As it turned out, the folks who were already Northern Tradition Pagans loved it as well.

Before the ritual, a large table was placed in the center with nine different altars around it, symbolizing the Nine Worlds. Each altar had a few items that symbolized that world (which can be temporarily donated by members of the group if necessary), a bowl of "blessing tokens" (small glass blobs in a particular color), a large candle (in the same color), some tokens symbolizing each world's vice, and some method by which the vice token could be destroyed. (While I discuss each of these separately below, I have also included a checklist for each world at the end for the officiant's use.) In the center was a representation of a tree, a horn of mead, a cup of juice, and the recaning sticks. Alternately, nine altars could be set up around the perimeter of the group, with a tenth one in the middle. It's a matter of how the space works best.

This ritual involves the art of *galdr*, which is the power-singing of runes. One of the officiants needs to know how to *galdr* specific runes in the background while each part of the rite is going on, and should probably practice each of them beforehand if they are not experienced with this. We used two officiants, plus one helper who carried bowls of tokens around, helped participants with token destruction, and carried the horn and cup around afterwards.

When we first performed this rite, we didn't know how many people we would get, and we were obliged to fit it into a slot only an hour and a half long. To save time, we decided to have around thirty blessing tokens (since handing them out was fairly quick) but only nine vice tokens (since destroying them was a longer process). If you have a time constraint, this might be a good idea. If time is not a problem and you know how many people to expect, you could go through as many vice tokens as you like.

First, the recels are lit and the first officiant goes around recaning everyone with the smoke. During this, the second officiant welcomes everyone to the circle. An explanation of the rite can be given at this time, with more or less detail depending on the level of experience and knowledge of the participants. At the very least, the second officiant should say:

> Each world has a gift, a blessing to give us, and each world has a vice that we must guard against. If you would receive the blessing of each world, take a blessing token when they are carried around the circle ... but keep in mind that every blessing has a price, some deed of courage or generosity that you may be required to do in the future. If you find yourself struggling with the vice embodied in one of the worlds and you would cast it off, take a token of that vice, come forth and destroy it. But know that there are only nine of each, so this chance is given only to the brave and bold, those who come forth without hesitation. This inequity is often part of life, so be brave and bold!

The first officiant says:

> Imagine a great World Tree, growing in the vast darkness of the Void, a great reservoir of Life in the darkness! It has a dragon at its roots and an eagle at its height. Imagine, like bright jewels in its branches, nine worlds that spin around it in a spiral, each one different, each one sacred in its own way. We begin at the top, in the Sky, where the light is brightest.

While this is said, the second officiant goes about and lights the nine candles on the altars. The first officiant goes to the first altar, on which burns a blue candle. We had laid here a horn, a sword, a small spear, a spindle, a Thor's hammer, and a bowl of blue glass tokens. The vice tokens for this altar are nine feathers, and next to them is a bowl of mud. The first officiant says:

> Hail to Asgard, the realm of the Aesir, the blessed heavenly Gods! Here are the Gods and wights of war and peace, of civilization and knowledge. Their blessing is

Glory, the ability to Win, the gift of Victory, the ability to see what you want and reach for it, to make it manifest! Would you have this blessing?

The bowl of blue glass tokens is carried around while the first officiant galdrs the rune Ansuz. The second officiant says:

> The vice of Asgard is Pride and Arrogance. When one is usually the winner, it is often easy to become too proud and head for a fall. If this is your vice, come forward and take one of the bright feathers, and bring it down to earth ... by burying it in the mud.

Those who will, come forth and do so, while the first officiant galdrs the rune Sigil. Then the first officiant moves to the second altar, on which burns a lavender candle. We had laid here a silver chalice filled with glittering glass fruit, and other shiny and illusory items, including a bowl of iridescent glass tokens. The vice tokens for this altar are nine butterflies cut of beautiful tissue paper, and under the altar is a prosaic plastic trash can. The first officiant says:

> We move down the Path of the Tree. Hail to Ljossalfheim, the realm of the Light Elves! Here are the spirits of glamour and beauty. Their blessing is Imagination, the ability to see beauty and wonder in all things! Would you have this blessing?

The bowl of iridescent tokens is carried around while the first officiant galdrs the rune Wunjo. The second officiant says:

> The vice of Ljossalfheim is Deception and Lies. While glamour can create beauty, it can also cover up the ugly truth. If this is your vice, come forth and take this tissue of Lies ... and tear it up and throw it away.

Those who will, come forth and do so, while the first officiant galdrs the rune Thorn. Then the first officiant moves to the third altar, on which burns a green candle. We had laid here a sheaf of wheat, a golden boar, a china cow, some wooden fish, a little wax beehive, some bread, and a bowl of green glass tokens. The vice tokens for this altar are nine shards of tasteless crackers, a dark version of the wholesome bread of Vanaheim. The first officiant says:

> We continue down the Path of the Tree. Hail to Vanaheim, the home of the sacred Vanir! Here are the Gods and wights of earth and fertility. Their blessing is Passion, the love of the body, the pleasure of the world. Would you have this blessing?

The bowl of green tokens is carried around while the first officiant galdrs the rune Inguz. The second officiant says:

> The vice of Vanaheim is Envy. It is forgetting how much you have while you covet what others have. Envy leads to inhospitality, to turning away the worthy and those in need. If this is your vice, come forth and take this dry bread ... and eat it, choke it down and remember that the grass may be no greener in another yard.

Those who will, come forth and do so, while the first officiant galdrs the rune Gebo/Gyfu. Then the first officiant moves to the fourth altar, on which burns an orange candle. We had laid here a wolfskin, a reindeer skin, a stone-bladed knife, a mountain-shaped stone, an antler, and a bowl of brown glass tokens. The vice tokens for this altar are a plate of small clay shapes, freshly molded. Each of them is different, and none of them make sense. The first officiant says:

> We continue down the Path of the Tree. Hail to Jotunheim, the home of the shapechanging giant-race! Here are the Gods and wights of the elements, the plants and animals, the forbidding mountains and deep caves and dark forests. Their blessing is Individuality, for each of them is different, and each follows their own path without hesitation. Would you have this blessing?

The bowl of brown tokens is carried around while the first officiant galdrs the rune Raido. The second officiant says:

> The vice of Jotunheim is Chaos. When individuality is the highest good, no one can come together peacefully, and chaos reigns in one's life. If you would rid your life of chaos, come forth and take this token ... and smash them flat, one onto the other.

Those who will, come forth and do so, while the first officiant galdrs the rune Hagalaz. Then the first officiant moves to the fifth altar, on which burns a candle the color of flesh. We had laid here a tiny cottage, figures of people dancing, an abalone shell holding a discarded snakeskin, and a bowl of beige glass tokens. The vice tokens for this altar are a bowl of seeds – we used beans because they are large. The first officiant says:

> We continue down the Path of the Tree. Hail to Midgard, the world of Humankind. Here, halfway down the Tree, poised below Roots and Sky, humans live and die and love and make our errors. The blessing of Midgard is Community, for here we are together, making a circle of protection and caring with each other. Would you have this blessing?

The bowl of beige tokens is carried around the circle while the first officiant galdrs the rune Mannaz. The second officiant says:

> The vice of Midgard is Conformity. We humans, in our search for the perfect community, often cast out those who are different and silence the voices of dissent ... and sometimes we are silenced, through our own fear. If you would break free of these chains, come forth and take this seed ... and carry it far away, and plant it alone where there is nothing like it, and help it to grow alone.

Those who will, come forth and do so, while the first officiant galdrs the rune Eihwaz. Then the first officiant moves to the sixth altar, on which burns a red candle. We had laid here a metal bowl with several votive candles (which were now lit), a piece of Icelandic volcanic rock, a fire-making kit, and a bowl of red glass tokens. The vice tokens for this altar are red paper "flames", meant to be burned in the flames of the votive candles. The first officiant says:

> We continue down the Path of the Tree. Hail to Muspellheim, the World of Fire. Here are the Gods and Wights of flame and dance. Their blessing is Energy, the vitality that gives motion. Would you have this blessing?

The bowl of red tokens is carried around the circle while the first officiant galdrs the rune Kenaz. The second officiant says:

> The vice of Muspellheim is Rage. Fire is also anger, which destroys all in its wake. If this is your vice, come forth and take this token, and burn it in the flames of Muspellheim.

Those who will, come forth and do so, while the first officiant galdrs the rune Cweorth. Then the first officiant moves to the seventh altar, on which burns a golden candle. We had laid here an anvil with a hammer, wrought iron tools and steel blades, and a bowl of gold glass tokens. The vice tokens for this altar are decorative cookies sprayed gold with spray paint – we used Pepperidge Farm Chessmen for their beauty. It was once food, now it is only decorative. The first officiant says:

> We continue down the Path of the Tree. Hail to Svartalfheim, Nidavellir, the home of the Duergar. Here are the wights of craft and skill, and this is their blessing – the ability to Make, the gift of creativity. Would you have this blessing?

The bowl of gold tokens is carried around the circle while the first officiant galdrs the rune Yr. The second officiant says:

> The vice of Svartalfheim is Greed, and Materialism. Do you really need those trappings of wealth? Is that extra money really worth losing time with your loved ones, with your own path? Do you own your possessions, or do they possess you? If this is your vice, come forth and take this token, and smash it on the anvil with the hammer.

Those who will, come forth and do so, while the first officiant galdrs the rune Fehu. Then the first officiant moves to the eighth table, on which burns a white candle. We had laid here a crystal bowl of water, many clear/white stones (such as Iceland spar), silver snowflakes, and a bowl of white glass tokens. The vice tokens for this altar are large grains of rock salt. The first officiant says:

> We continue down the Path of the Tree. Hail to Niflheim, the world of Ice, of many waters, of mists. Here

are the wights of weather and wind, of the primal Ice Age. This is a hard world, and its blessing is Survival, the ability to live through any hardship. Would you have this blessing?

The bowl of white tokens is carried around the circle while the first officiant galdrs the rune Nauthiz/Nyth. The second officiant says:

> The vice of Niflheim is Coldness, the unwillingness to help another, the concentration on your own self and survival until no one and nothing else matters. If this is your vice, come forth and take this token, and drown it in the waters of Niflheim.

Those who will, come forth and do so, while the first officiant galdrs the rune Isa. Then the first officiant moves to the ninth altar, on which burns a black candle. We have laid here bones, skulls, tiny gravestones, a large flat bowl of earth, a pile of smooth stones, and a bowl of black glass tokens. The vice tokens for this altar are little paper corpses. The first officiant says:

> We continue down the Path of the Tree. Hail to Helheim, the Realm of the Dead, the Root of the Tree. Here is the Goddess of Death, and all her collected souls, the Ancestors waiting to be reborn again. The blessing of this world is Peace. Would you have this blessing?

The bowl of black tokens is carried around the circle while the first officiant galdrs the rune Othila. The second officiant says:

> The vice of Helheim is Apathy. You care about nothing, nothing moves you, you lay there like the Dead and cannot make any impact on the world. If this is your vice, come forth and take this token, this small body. Bury it in the earth and place a stone upon it. Bury them all together and make a cairn upon them.

Those who will, come forth and do so, while the first officiant galdrs the rune Ear. Then the second officiant stands forth and says:

> We have walked the Tree from top to bottom. We stand now in the Realm of the Ancestors. Now we will

salute them! We will pass the horn of mead and the cup of fruit's blood, for those who would take alcohol and those who would not. Toast to the ancestors of your blood, if you will; speak their names. Toast to the ancestors of your spirit, if you will; those who came before and who inspired you.

The cup and horn are passed, and the people toast to the Dead. Then the first officiant galdrs whatever they will, and the folk are sung out of the circle.

※ ※ ※ ※

World Correspondences and Prop Checklist

Asgard
Blessing: Glory
Blessing Rune: Ansuz
Vice: Pride, Arrogance
Vice Rune: Sigil
Candle Color: Blue
Blessing Token Color: Blue
Vice Token: Feather
Destruction Method: Stuck in mud
Props: Bowl of mud

Alfheim
Blessing: Imagination, Beauty
Blessing Rune: Wunjo
Vice: Lies, Deception
Vice Rune: Thorn
Candle Color: Lavender
Blessing Token Color: Iridescent
Vice Token: Tissue Paper Butterfly
Destruction Method: Shredding
Props: Trash can, under altar

Vanaheim
Blessing: Passion
Blessing Rune: Inguz

Vice: Envy, Inhospitality
Vice Rune: Gyfu
Candle Color: Green
Blessing Token Color: Green
Vice Token: Dry cracker shard
Destruction Method: Eaten

Jotunheim
Blessing: Individuality
Blessing Rune: Raido
Vice: Chaos
Vice Rune: Hagalaz
Candle Color: Brown
Blessing Token Color: Orange
Vice Token: Weird clay bit
Destruction Method: Smashed together
Props: Clay on plate

Midgard
Blessing: Community
Blessing Rune: Mannaz
Vice: Conformity
Vice Rune: Eihwaz
Candle Color: Flesh
Blessing Token Color: Beige
Vice Token: Bean
Destruction Method: Taken away and planted

Muspellheim
Blessing: Energy
Blessing Rune: Kenaz
Vice: Rage
Vice Rune: Cweorth
Candle Color: Red
Blessing Token Color: Red
Vice Token: Red paper "flames"
Destruction Method: Burning

Svartalfheim

Blessing: Skill, Focus
Blessing Rune: Yr
Vice: Greed, Materialism
Vice Rune: Fehu
Candle Color: Gold
Blessing Token Color: Gold
Vice Token: Crackers sprayed gold
Destruction Method: Smashed on anvil
Props: Anvil and hammer

Niflheim

Blessing: Survival
Blessing Rune: Nyth
Vice: Coldness, Mercilessness
Vice Rune: Isa
Candle Color: White
Blessing Token Color: Clear
Vice Token: Large grain rock salt
Destruction Method: Drowned in water
Props: Glass bowl of clear water

Helheim

Blessing: Peace
Blessing Rune: Othila
Vice: Apathy
Vice Rune: Ear
Candle Color: Black
Blessing Token Color: Black
Vice Token: Tiny paper corpse
Destruction Method: Buried in earth
Props: Bowl of dirt

Three and Three Protection Rite
Raven Kaldera

This ritual calls upon six Gods. There are two divine male triplicities in Norse mythology – the older elemental triplicity of Aegir (sea), Logi (fire), and Kari (the North Wind) – and the younger Aesir creative triplicity Odin, Vili, and Vé. The first three brothers were all the sons of Fornjotr (also called Mistblindi), an ancient frost-giant, by three different wives. The second three brothers were the sons of Bor and Bestla, an early Aesir man and a frost-giantess. This rite calls upon each of them in turn, protecting a person or family from above and below.

You will need six kinds of liquor for this ritual, at least a generous cupful of each kind, which makes it a bit expensive, but worth it. You will also need a source of fire large enough to pour the liquor into without danger. Outside with a bonfire is best, but if that is not possible, large metal firepit-bowls are available that can be filled with charcoal or wood to set aflame, and this could be done in a driveway or back yard. We do not recommend doing this indoors unless you are very careful.

Which liquors to pick? It may be useful to wander around the liquor store and see what your intuition tells you. Aegir the Sea-King is a brewer, so I generally offer him high-quality local organic beer – nothing with nasty chemicals. Logi is a god of Fire, so he gets something spicy and hot. For Kari the North Wind, I look for some sort of clear flavored vodka in "ice mint" or that sort of thing. Odin is traditionally fond of aquavit. Vili is the god of Will, so one could find as high-proof a liquor as you can, such as Everclear. Ve is the giver of psychic ability, so one could go with a herbal liqueur.

Find six cups in the following colors: cobalt blue for Odin, yellow for Vili, purple or clear for Ve, red for Logi, white for Kari, and sea-blue or sea-green for Aegir. Use a recaning stick of dried mugwort, and divide a good-sized loaf of bread into six pieces.

ଔ   ଔ   ଚ   ଚ

To begin, pour the liquor into the cups and light the fire. Once the fire is going, light the mugwort stick and blow it out, creating smoke. Walk around the space with the smoking stick. To make the protection rite stronger, I suggest learning the Anglo-Saxon song listed in the

"Creating Sacred Space" rite and using that as your opening. However, at the very least, recan the area with sacred smoke.

Next, call out the following:

> Hail to you, Ancient Ones!
> Hail to the Three and Three
> Who circle about the World Tree!
> I come to you with open hands,
> Asking for your protection
> As you love the world, and humanity, and life itself.
> First I call upon Kari, Eldest Brother,
> North Wind of the Land of Frost,
> Coldest blizzard sweeping down on us.
> Hide me from all who would harm me and mine
> In the white veil of your snowy train,
> And may your breath chill their flames
> Until they lose interest and turn aside.
> Hail Kari, Fornjotr's son, father of Frost!

Pour out the white cup into the fire, and place a piece of bread thereon.

> Next I call upon Logi, Brother of Flame,
> Fire that devours all things,
> Bowl and spoon and house itself,
> And yet gives us warmth in the cold,
> Forges our tools, cooks our feasts,
> And brings joy and merriment to our dark nights.
> Protect me and mine with the heat of your fire,
> Let no one and nothing strike me down,
> Surround us in a wall of flame that harms us not.
> Hail Logi, Fornjotr's son, brother of Sea and Wind!

Pour out the red cup into the fire, and place a piece of bread thereon.

> Next I call upon Aegir, Brother of Ocean,
> King of the Northern Seas that roll,
> Depths and billows, currents and eddies,
> Husband to Ran of the emerald eyes and weedy hair,
> Father to the Nine Waves that kiss the shore.

> Protect me and mine with the thundering force
> Of your breakers that sweep away all resistance.
> Protect the salt blood in our veins,
> Let it run in peace and safety through our hearts.
> Hail Aegir, Fornjotr's son, brother of Wind and Fire!

Pour out the sea-colored cup into the fire, and place a piece of bread thereon. Now extend your arms to the side, and call out:

> Hail to the Three Brothers, older than old,
> Who sang your songs to my ancestors
> As they lived by Fire and Sea and Winter Winds.
> Let nothing come up from below to ensnare me,
> Let nothing come from the fires of rage,
> Let nothing come from the ocean of resentment,
> Let nothing come from the winds of chance
> To stop my feet upon my true road.

Move back to the firepit again, to call upon the next deity.

> Next I call upon Vili, God of Will,
> Brother of Odin and son of Bor,
> Who gave wit and intelligence to mankind,
> Who gave the hands that touch and make,
> And the will to see things through.
> Place your sacred will against the obstacles
> That wait to swoop down upon me.
> Make me safe in the yellow light of day,
> And give me the wits to know danger where it lies
> And not to imagine it where it is not.
> Hail Vili, firstborn of Bestla, ancient wise one!

Pour out the yellow cup onto the fire, and place a piece of bread thereon.

> Next I call upon Vé, Lord of Sacredness,
> Brother of Odin and son of Bor,
> Who gave the eyes that see to mankind,
> Who gave speech and sacred words to mankind,
> Who gave eyes that see and ears that hear,
> Who gave the smile and the frown,
> And the ability to see the sacred.

> May I see clearly where I need protection,
> May I hear clearly the warning words of others,
> May your words of power be with me as I walk.
> Hail Vé, second son of Bestla, Lord of the Shrine of Holiness!

Pour out the purple or clear cup onto the fire, and place a piece of bread thereon.

> Next I call upon Odin, All-Father of the Aesir,
> Son of Bor, brother of Vili and Vé,
> Who gave life itself to Ask and Embla,
> Who gave inspiration to seek higher and farther,
> Who lay soul into their wooden bodies
> And brought them to life, and love, and spirit.
> O Odin, protect me and mine where we stand,
> Do not let the hail of misfortune tear us down,
> And do not let any who would plot against us
> Come within three steps of our home and our works.
> Look after us with all five eyes, O Lord of Asgard,
> One blue and wise, four black and twinkling
> And fluttering on feathered wings of magic.
> Shield us with the breadth of your knowledge
> And deliver us from any ill fortune that may escape you.
> Hail Odin, youngest son of Bestla,
> Wanderer, Warrior, Wod-Keeper!

Pour out the cobalt-blue cup onto the fire, and place a piece of bread thereon. Now extend your arms upward and call out:

> Hail to the Three Brothers, wise and fair,
> Who spoke your words to the ancestors
> As they learned to master their minds.
> Let nothing come down from above to ensnare me,
> Let nothing come from the will of others,
> Let nothing come from the words of others,
> Let nothing come from the spirit of others
> To stop my feet upon my true road.

Put out the fire, and the rite is ended.

Warding Rite for Gerda
Raven Kaldera

Gerda, the bride of Frey who is the god of agriculture, is known as the Lady of the Walled Garden among many Northern Tradition practitioners. Her very name translates to "guard", or perhaps "the guarded one". When Frey first sees her from afar, she is in the garden of her father's home, which is surrounded by a wall of fire. She is a goddess of introversion and protection, of winnowing out the chaff and weeding out what must be cut back for other choices to flourish. As Frey is involved in the production of grain and meat – the staples of agriculture – so Gerda is involved in the production of roots and herbs, the plants grown in the walled garden or kitchen area, as well as those gathered wild from the nearby woods. She rules the boundary between wild and tame, passing back and forth between the wilderness and the safety of the protected garden, and helps those who must also make that transition.

This ritual is performed to ward a space and keep the people who live or work within it safe. Because Gerda works with herbs, this ritual requires a number of specialized herbs familiar to northern Europe, and to most herb gardeners. If you are not a herbalist, your local health food store can help you to find samples of the dried herbs, and they can also be mail-ordered. If it is during the growing season, however, the best thing of all is to put the word out and find someone with a herb garden who actually grows these plants, and see if you can get freshly picked sprigs. These are generally well-known plants among herbalists, and there is no reason that you cannot acquire them with a little work. Substitutions may not be made.

The herbs needed for this ritual are: Agrimony (*Agrimonia eupatoria*), Nettles (*Urtica dioica*), Marshmallow (*Althaea officinalis*), Elderflower (*Sambucus niger*), Yarrow (*Achillea millefolium*), Betony (*Betonica/Stachys officinalis*), Vervain (*Verbena officinalis*), Milk Thistle (*Silybum Marianum*), and Angelica (*Angelica archangelica*). An action is performed with them in each direction, but its nature depends on what kind of plant matter is acquired. Dried and crumbled herbs can be scattered, while freshly cut herbs can be dipped in water and sprinkled like an asperger. A small amount of each herb should be set aside beforehand, and brewed into a cup of strong tea that should be at hand during the rite, as it will be a libation.

The warding verses can be spoken by one person, or by many if this involves a whole household, but it is written as if for one practitioner.

ଓ   ଓ   ଚ   ଚ

To begin, the warder calls on Gerda by saying:

>   Hail Gerda, Lady of the Walled Garden,
>   Hallowed in hedgerive and hammerwort,
>   Sacred in stonecrop and sowthistle,
>   Gifted and gifting in gladden and dragonwort,
>   You help us build the still, safe place
>   In which we can grow tender hopes to blossoming.
>   Hail, Lady of the forest paths,
>   Hallowed in hillwort and hindberry,
>   Sacred in cock's spur grass and sicklewort,
>   Gifted and gifting in gale and libcorn,
>   You help us bring those hopes into the world
>   To test and turn them into manifestation.
>   Hail, Lady of the quiet endings,
>   Hallowed in hulwort and whortleberry,
>   Sacred in ramsons and raven's leek,
>   Gifted and giving in viper's bugloss and boarfern,
>   You teach us to cull out what cannot be
>   While still keeping hope alive in the dark.
>   Hail, Lady of the hidden treasures,
>   Hallowed in mallow and meadowwort,
>   Sacred in sundcorn and stitchwort,
>   Gifted and giving in groundsel and sedge,
>   Cleansed in river-mint and lamb's cress,
>   You bring us deeper than we thought possible
>   Into the earth on which we depend.
>   Hail, Gerda, etin-bride of Frey,
>   Shadow to light, night to day,
>   All things balanced in your keen dark glance.

The warder then takes up the Agrimony and faces the East, and says:

>   Cocklebur, Garclive, sword of autumn winds,

> Sticklewort, Monkelus, dry up wagging tongues,
> Let no assault through words and names
> Trouble this place and bring us shame.
> From Gerda's lips shall you spring
> And guard the doorway of the East.

The warder then takes up the Nettles (carefully!) and faces the South, and says:

> Nessel, Netele, Needle-wight, sharp your blade,
> Soldier of the burning lands, scorching through the shade,
> Fire burns like Gymir's gate, never shall they pass,
> Ward the blows of anger, block the blows of danger,
> From Gerda's finger shall you spring
> And guard the doorway of the South.

The warder then takes up the Marshmallow and faces the West, and says:

> Healer of the marshlands, river of the morn,
> Lady of the white root, rose without a thorn,
> May the trouble and pain of other souls
> Wash by our door and leave us whole.
> From Gerda's kiss shall you spring
> And guard the doorway of the West.

The warder then takes up the Elderflowers, and faces the North, and says:

> Ellen, Ellhorn, Holantar, holy doorway of the Dead,
> Ruis, Svarthyll, Alri, Hyld, old woman of the coldest road,
> Let Death not dog the footsteps
> Of this home upon the Earth.
> From Gerda's footfalls shall you spring
> And guard the doorway of the North.

The warder then takes up the Betony, faces the North-East, and says:

> Betonica, Goodhead, Master of the skull's door,
> Demon-driver, banish all the evil that may come.
> Let all within these walls sleep well
> And no fearsome dreams portend.

> From Gerda's brow shall you spring
> And guard the doorway of the North-East.

The warder then takes up the Yarrow, faces the South-East, and says:

> Milfoil, Woundwort, Ryllik, keep the blood within the body,
> Warrior of the thousand flowers who moves in purity,
> Let no weapon cross the threshold
> If it may ever turn against us.
> From Gerda's veins shall you spring
> And guard the doorway of the South-East.

The warder then takes up the Milk Thistle, faces the South-West, and says:

> Love Thistle, Mother's Milk, Keeper of the Well of Plenty,
> Pig Leaves and Madonna's Pride, look fondly upon us.
> Lady of thorns, keep us like your children,
> As the gentlest mother can be roused to protect her young.
> From Gerda's breast shall you spring
> And guard the doorway of the South-West.

The warder then takes up the Vervain, faces the North-West, and says:

> Eisenkraut, Ironwort, Simpler's Joy, herb of ancient sorcery,
> Pigeon Grass, Enchanter's Plant, wizard of the glass,
> Draw your cloak over every window
> And make invisible the space within.
> From Gerda's eye shall you spring
> And guard the doorway of the North-West.

The warder then takes up the Angelica, faces upward to the sky, and says:

> Archangel, Hollow-Stalk, keeper of the upward way,
> Rainbow path, sunburst seed, warming world,
> Lay roof of sky over roof of matter
> And may only good come down.
> From Gerda's palm shall you spring
> And guard against all that comes unseen.

Then the warder pours out the cup of tea, saying, "Lady, we give you what is yours." Everyone should then process through the space with fire and water and salt and recaning incense, singing, and the place shall then be both as a temple and a fortress, as safe as the walled garden.

Needfire Ritual
Mist, Gyðja of Kenaz Kindred, Canada

This is one of the rituals donated by Kenaz Kindred. You will need several long pieces of colored string, as many as there are adult women in your group, of at least six feet in length apiece, a large candle carved with a Nauthiz rune, and a recaning stick of mugwort.

ఞ   ఞ   ౭౦   ౭౦

The ritual starts with this song being sung or recited, by one or many.

By Water and Land [1]

Chorus: By water and land,
By sea and by sand,
By earth and by sky,
By low and by high.

By moonlight that grows,
By the river that flows,
By home that I love
And the High Ones above.

Repeat chorus.

By seagull that flies,
By the cracking of ice,
By the ocean so wide,
And the swell of the tide.

Repeat chorus.

Where the watchfires burn
May you safely return,
Bring your ship to the shore,
As the old ones before.

Repeat chorus.

Gyðja: This is a ritual about asking for what we need. I think all of us need something; sometimes it can be wishes for health, spiritual enlightenment, wealth, direction or other

---

[1] © 2009 Michaela Macha; used with permission. http://www.odins-gift.com

things. So this ritual is dedicated to the rune of Naudhiz, the need-fire. We will be offering up blessings for each other; you can take all blessings or just one, it is up to you. With every blessing received we ask that you ask the Gods also to bless the others here.

The Gyðja lights the large candle, saying, "Nauthiz! We are in need!" and draws a Nauthiz rune over the candle with her finger.

Gyðja: First, before anything is asked for, we will create a strand of Wyrd. This strand represents our kindred and its connection to each other, because through our connection to each other we strengthen our connection to the gods. It is by our hands and hearts that we ask our gods for help, and so we bind our fates together each time we gather. This strand represents that bond!

> I would ask all the women to come forward and take a piece of string. We will be joining our threads with the other women of the group, and form a twisted strand. As you step up to a fellow woman in the ring, you will tie your thread to hers. We will be attempting to make nine knots in the thread to make a united strand of fate.

The women all come together and each takes a piece of string. The Gyðja knots all the strings together at the end, and then the strings are twisted together to form one strand. As each section is twisted – about six inches or so – another woman makes a knot in the combined strings. As they work, the following song can be sung or chanted or spoken, by them or by the onlookers.

Twist And Weave [2]

> Twist and weave,
> Spin and tie,
> All the threads
> We live and die.
>
> Guide the threads,
> Warp and weft,
> Cut and trim

---

[2] Written by K. C. Hulsman; used with permission.

> The shuttle heft.
>
> Bind the luck,
> Read the fate,
> Stitch and knot
> To create.
>
> Twist and weave,
> Spin and tie,
> All the threads
> We live and die.
>
> Sisters three,
> We ask of Thee,
> Look after us
> Fatefully.
>
> Twist and weave,
> Spin and tie,
> All the threads
> We live and die.
>
> All the threads
> We live and die.

Gyðja: Norns, sisters of fate, we have spun the threads that bind us. May these strands of fate bind us to the will of the gods and may that will be favourable.

The thread is laid on the altar.

Gyðja: The first blessing in this ritual will be for healing. If anyone in the ritual has need for healing, or wishes the gods to bestow healing upon others for any reason, then please step forward.

She asks each "What is it that you wish to heal?" Each speaks of their need, or of another's need. She then says "Then step forward and receive the blessings of Eir, physician goddess."

When all have spoken, the Gyðja lifts her hands and recites:

> Maiden of Lyfja, Mengloth's friend,
> Healer of open hand,
> Trace your runes

> On the hand of the healer,
> The heart of the nurse
> And the doctor's trail.
> Grant weal to wounds,
> Relief for pain,
> Succor for sickness,
> And wholeness for hearts.
> All of Nine Herbs
> Mix in your mortar,
> Give to us mortals
> Health in our days.
> Eir, of all
> The maidens mighty
> Near to our needs,
> O hear our plea![3]

Gyðja: The second blessing will be for spiritual enlightenment, communication or divine inspiration. For anyone wishing to receive spiritual gifts from the gods, please step forward.

She asks each, "What is it you wish to receive?" When all who wish have stepped forward into the circle and spoken, the Gyðja lights the recaning stick and walks around, smudging and blessing each one, saying:

> Many voices melt into one,
> Yet each one stays clear and unique.
> Thor's mighty voice booms over Midgard.
> Freya's charming song flows seductively about the Thunderer.
> The Rede-Giver's sayings tie webs with an accent.
> Frigga's voice – not loud, but unmistakable.
> Frey's tenor, a growing and becoming that rises and surges.
> Variety in unity, the strength within the whole,
> Each for themselves and all together,
> Each leaves his mark and makes whole.
> Over all Midgard sounds the call of the Gods,
> Heard everywhere, and the God's children do follow.

---

[3] Written by Michaela Macha; used with permission.

Gyðja: The third blessing is for financial stability. It is not wrong to ask the gods for this, as they work for us and we for them, and can grant us stability. However, I will not go as far as saying they will bestow riches upon you, or that you will win the lottery; but they do provide a way for us to survive, and that we can ask for their blessings in this regard and with any ventures of business of any kind.

She asks each, "What is it you seek blessings upon?" Each steps forward and speaks of their need. The Gyðja lifts her arms and says:

Gyðja: Gods above, we know our lives are fuller with you in it, but we ask you to lighten our burden, assist us in providing security where there is none. Give us a way to feel secure in our life, so that our thoughts can be turned more toward spiritual living. Grant us prosperity in our endeavours.

Gyðja: The fourth blessing will be for our relationships. For those that would like to receive blessings in their relationships with their families, please step forward.

After these have stepped forth, the Gyðja raises her hands and says:

Gyðja: Frigga, mother of the home, strengthens our bonds with each other and make our families whole, lady who guards the home and hearth bestow upon us these blessings.

Gyðja: For those who would like blessing on marital or romantic relationships, please step forward.

After these have stepped forth, the Gyðja raises her hands and says:

Gyðja: Freyja, goddess of passion, grant faithful love to those who feel your fire, bestow upon those who seek to love the gift of a passionate heart, and the reason to use it. Frigga, grant those in long-term relationships the will and strength to keep these relationships going, and grant them always a peaceful home in which all are happy and content. Let love be first and foremost the thought in our minds as we rise and sleep each day. Let the sun never set on a home in turmoil, but let always our beds be a place of unity in which two remember and embrace their love.

Gyðja: We have called, and Nauthiz has answered! Our gods grant us all good will and wishes. We will now conclude this ritual, and pass the horn in sumbel.

The main rite is over, and a Sumbel[4] is performed.

---

[4] Described on pages 157-8.

Anglo-Saxon Blessing Rite

Alaric Albertsson. Written for Sassafras Grove, ADF

This ritual was written for a ritual for Ar nDraiocht Fein, and it follows a version of the standard ADF ritual format. To learn more about this format, please consult their website[1].

Consecration of Time

Nine Knells (ringing a bell nine times)

Opening Statement of Intent

Wé cumaþ tó gebréman þa hálig wihtes![2]

Consecration of Space

(Anoint with water)
May the waters around us bless and hold you.
(Mark with earth)
May the land below us bless and hold you.
(Cense with recels)
May the sky above us bless and hold you.

Warding the *Wéofodsteall*

Take flame or incense around the perimeter of the *wéfodsteall* (altar area) while saying:

Fyr ic bere ymbe friðgearde,
Ond béode gehwilc útlendan fleogan aweg![3]

Pour an offering of mead into the *blótorc* (blessing bowl), and say:

Punor, accept this offering, and ward this holy place.

Call for Inspiration

Raise the mead horn and say:

Behold the mead of inspiration.
Dwarf-brew,
Ettins' hoard.

---

[1] http://www.adf.org/rituals/explanations/
[2] *"We come to honor the Holy Ones!"*
[3] *"Fire I bear around this sacred space, and bid all Outsiders to flee!"*

May it touch our lips and strengthen our hearts.
May our songs be sweet and strong,
May our words be wrought with Wyrd.
With mortal voice from Middle Earth
We call to highest heaven!
Let the song-mead inspire us.
Grant us this blessing!
Grant us this grace!

The mead horn is now passed around the assemblage and all (who wish to) may sip from it.

Honoring the Earth Mother[4]

Earth, Divine Goddess, Mother Nature,
Who generates all things
And brings forth anew the Sun,
Which you have given to the nations,
Guardian of sky and sea, of all Gods and powers;
Through your power all Nature falls silent
And then sinks into sleep.
And again you bring back the light,
And chase away the night,
And you cover us yet most securely with your shadows.
You contain chaos infinite, yes,
And wind and showers and storms.
You send them out when you will
And cause the sea to roar;
You chase away the Sun and arouse the storm.
Again, when you will, you send forth the joyous day
And give the nourishment of Life with your eternal surety.
And when the soul departs, to you we return.
You are duly called the Great Mother of the Gods;
You conquer by your divine name.
You are the source of the strength of nations and of gods.
Without you nothing can be brought to perfection
Or be born;
You are great, Queen of the Gods.

---

[4] 11th century Anglo-Saxon prayer.

Goddess, I adore you as divine; I call upon your name
And give thanks to you, with due faith.

Centering

Close your eyes and breathe deeply ... breathe in from your belly ... in ... and out ... and with each breath, allow your body to relax ... let your breath carry away tension from your flesh ... relaxing your feet and legs ... your belly and chest and shoulders ... relaxing your arms and hands ... relaxing your face and mouth and eyes.

Now, with your body still and calm, imagine a mist around you ... feel yourself move through the mist to a place between land and water ... a shoreline ... listen to the sounds around you ... hear the water lapping against the shore ... feel the water swirl around your feet ... let the water rise up within you, into your legs ... rising ... into your loins, pooling into a cauldron of primal power there ... you breathe and the water moves upward ... rising through your loins, through your spine to fill a cauldron in your heart with healing energy ... rising further up your spine and into your head where it pools into a cauldron of wisdom and vision behind your eyes.

> The sea is to everyone seemingly unending,
> if you should dare an unsteady ship,
> and the sea-waves frighten you fiercely,
> and the sea-stallions do not heed their bridles.[5]

But now, imagine the sky overhead ... the sun and the moon and, far beyond them, the stars ... imagine a single star at the center of the sky, shining directly over your head ... see a flash of light shining down from that star ... streaming down until it touches your head, filling and illuminating the cauldron there ... starlight over the still water, shining from above ... flowing down into your heart ... warming the cauldron of healing ... shining downward to

---

[5] From the Anglo-Saxon Rune Poem.

reach your loins ... the light awakens the power there with a renewed awareness.

> *Tir* is a star that keeps faith well
> With those of noble heart.
> Always on its course,
> Over the mists of night it never fails.[6]

Feel yourself shining and flowing with the chaos of potential and the light of world order ... these powers are balanced within you ... yours to shape and use, always ... but for now allow the powers to recede ... allow the waters to return to the primal sea, the light to return to the heavens ... knowing that each time you attune to them you become more at one with these powers ... breathe deep ... and allow your awareness to return ... as you open your eyes.

Recreating the Cosmos

Drop silver into the waters of Wyrd and say:

> We leave this offering within the Well of Wyrd,
> Deep within the earth.
> And may the dwarves bear witness to our sacrifice.

Kindle *récels* (incense) and say:

> We leave this offering to the Sunlight Realm above.
> May the smoke carry our devotion upward,
> And may the elves bear witness to our sacrifice.

Cense and asperse the *Eormensyl* (World Tree) symbol, and say:

> The roots of the *Eormensyl* are nourished
> In the waters of Wyrd.
> Its infinite limbs reach to the Sunlight Realm and beyond.
> Woden's steed, greatest of trees,
> Spanning the worlds of gods and men.
> Between the light above and the waters below,
> We gather at the Sacred Tree.

---

[6] From the Anglo-Saxon Rune Poem.

The Creation Myth

Before time and space and order,
There was only fire and ice,
And between these a gaping void.
From out of the north poured endless frost,
To meet with endless flame raging from the south.
Coming together, spiraling and swirling,
Until within the void a Middle Earth formed.
Neither cold nor hot, neither dark nor light,
But covered in twilight.
And in this twilight the earth produced Tuisto,
The first of all things.
Male and female was he,
And from him all Gods and Powers emerged.
A war then raged among the Mighty Ones,
Until there was a peace between the *Ases* and *Wanes*.
The *Wanes* then built mighty halls
In the world that lies beyond the western sea;
The *Ases* took the highest heavens as their home
And set a wall around it.
And together they drove the Ettins
To the world beyond the dawn.
Thus the Mighty Ones came to dwell
In the outermost worlds traversed by the glory of elves.
And the *Ases* then espied, between these realms,
Two trees growing in the Middle World.
Two trees, standing along the seacoast, an ash and an elm,
With no destiny assigned to them;
With no *wód*, nor *willa*, nor *blód*.
The gods gave each of the trees three gifts;
To each tree, the breath of inspiration,
The power of intellect, and a divine form.
And so from the ash tree came the first man,
And from the elm the first woman.
Like the ash and the elm,
Our spiritual roots reach down, even now,
To seek nourishment in the waters below;
To seek nourishment in the Well of Wyrd.

Wód inspires us to reach upward to the light.
Like the ash and the elm,
Each of us is like unto the Great Tree
That spans the worlds.

Then all chant:

The Fire; the Well; the Sacred Tree;
Flow and flame and grow in me!

Opening the Gateway

One-Eyed Woden,
World-wanderer, wolf-lord,
Wild wondrous windmaster!
Hooded and cloaked you walk between the worlds.
Woden, accept our sacrifice!

Pour an offering of mead into the blótorc, and say:

Give us your blessing!
Open a way between the worlds,
That our prayers and praise might be heard in the halls
Above, below and beyond this Middle Earth.
Woden! You who hear all!
Hear us now, and let the gates be opened!

Three knells will signal the opening of the gate.

Honoring the *Ylfe*

Sprinkle mugwort into the *récelsfæt*, and say:

I give this offering to the spirits who dwell in this place.
To elf and dwarf,
Woodwose and wight,
Moss-wife and púca and hob.
Good neighbors, we honor you.

All sing:

Air spirit, wood spirit, field spirit, lake spirit,
We are but one Spirit living in the world.
Some dwell on land and some dwell on wind,
And some undersea, all living in the world.

Honoring the Ancestors

Sprinkle rosemary into the récelsfæt, and say:

> I give this offering to the ancestors
> Who have brought us to this place.
> Across the ages we call to you!
> Ancestors of blood, who've given us worldly form;
> Ancestors of spirit,
> Whose inspiration illuminates the path before us.
> Ancestors, we honor you.

Honoring the Gods:

Sprinkle *stór* into the *récelsfæt*, and say:

> I give this offering to the Mighty Ones
> Who have blessed this place.
> You who dwell in the celestial heavens,
> You who dance upon the waves,
> You who are found in the depths of the earth,
> And in the wild places.
> Mighty Ones, we honor you.

Ærende

A *rúnwita* will draw staves of the *Fuþorc* to determine if our offerings have been accepted and to receive any messages the deities, ancestors or elves wish to give us.

Farewell to the Kindred

> Mighty Ones, Ancestors, Spirits of this world,
> May there ever be peace among us.
> We thank you for your many blessings.
> Wassail!

Farewell to the Gatekeeper

> Woden!
> You who wander between the worlds!
> One-eyed, hooded and wise beyond all knowing.
> We give thanks for helping us to open the Way!
> Let the gate be now closed.

Three knells will signal the closing of the gate.

Final Offering

Pour the remaining mead into the *blótorc* and say:

> We return the mead of inspiration to its source.
> From the gods, to the earth, to us;
> From us, to the earth, to the gods!

Return to Middle Earth:

> Close your eyes for a moment and take a deep breath ... let your spirit return fully to this Middle World ... let the Great Tree fade into the mists ... let the *récelsfæt* become an ordinary smouldering coal ... the Well of Wyrd, a simple vessel of water ... take a deep breath ... step into this world ... and open your eyes.

The rite has ended.

Deconsecration of Time:

Nine Knells

Evening Rite of the Five Elements
Galina Krasskova and Sophie Oberländer

This ritual is based on "The Evening Rite of the Five Elements" from "Dea," one of the liturgy books of the Fellowship of Isis. We liked the idea of having such a clear and simple ritual for the Northern Gods and so stole the format shamelessly for the following rite. Many thanks to FOI and the Honorable Olivia Durdin-Robertson, co-founder of FOI. The inspiration for this rite was hers first.

A small altar should be set up with a stone, a bowl of water, incense, two candles, a small vial of some sweetly scented oil and, if possible, Deity images.

ଔ ଔ ଓ ଓ

Opening Invocation

>Oh sweet light in the darkness,
>Mani, beloved Lord of the moon, I hail You.
>Watch over us this night.
>Extend upon us Your loving gaze.
>Wrap us in the music of Your presence.
>Be with us as we pray and sleep and dream.
>You who embody the sensuous harmonies
>Of the night, of the unknown,
>Of all that we might wish to be or see or hold
>Be with us this evening in our hearts and in our dreams.
>Hail Mani, God of the Moon,
>Of seeming and unseeming, belief and fantasy,
>Stillness, and the mad whirling dance of time.
>Hail Mani.

Meditation on Mani

>The moon follows us. He remembers, our time keeper, our history keeper, the memory of the eddies and flows of our world. He shares His beauty with us, and communicates via music, mathematics, madness: obsession for all that He holds, all that He has seen, for the rich, alabaster loveliness of His presence. He is bound to His service, to the cycles that He himself helped to put

in place and supports. Yet He protects and watches over those in pain, those suffering, hurting or hopeless. His fascination is immense, His compassion deep yet He must maintain, for the most part, His celestial distance. Beads, knots, numbers, calendars, dreams, music, sand, symbols. He wears the cloak of night, an easy adornment to His remote beauty. He is sensual and quixotic as only the moon can be. His voice is sweet and contains enchantment of all that He has seen passing millennia after millennia through the flowing folly of man.

His words: See me. Reach up for me. I will come to You. I will watch over you. I am there for you. When you are most alone, know that I see you. I know you. I never, ever forget. It is mine to remember: everything. I am master of night, as my sister is mistress of the day. I have might of my own. Yet am I secretive.

On the altar, light two candles and a stick of incense.

Prayer to Nott, Mother Night

>May our Mother the Night, gracious Nott,
>Bless us this evening through the five elements.
>May She look down upon us
>And enfold us in Her blessed darkness,
>Through which no malice may penetrate.
>May Nott enfold us in Her protection.
>May She look down upon us with gracious benevolence.
>May She watch over our slumber
>And grant us the grace of ivory-hued dreams.
>Hail to Nott, ancient Goddess,
>Vast and unknowable, bedecked in stars,
>With the world at Her feet.
>Bless us this night, Mother Night. Hail, Nott.

Place your hands on the stone on the altar, feel its strength, its weight, its heaviness.

Prayer to the Goddess Sigyn

>I offer this prayer to the Goddess Sigyn:

> Hold me in Your sweet hands, Lady,
> That I may be a vessel for poison and sorrow;
> Bear me upwards in Your bright arms,
> That I may catch, and shield, and shelter;
> And when I spill, forgive me.
> Please enfold me in your strength tonight, oh Goddess.
> You who are as strong and unyielding in Your love
> As the mountain in its power,
> Please watch over me and bless me this night.

Dip your fingers in the water and make a circle on the brow.

Prayer to Loki

> You are mutable, oh my God,
> And wondrous, bedecked in splendor,
> Even when You're not.
> Change me, bless me, open me,
> Wash me clean of all pettiness and dreck.
> Sweet salmon of knowledge,
> Slippery, sly, and cunning,
> God of deceit and speaker of the most terrible truths.
> Make me mutable too so that I might be
> Whatever You need me to be,
> In the act of loving You.
> I hail You this night, oh Loki.

Asperge yourself with the smoke from the incense.

Prayer to Odin

> You who blessed us with breath,
> Who wove the mighty magic of our breathcords,
> Strong as wyrd, implacable as fire, I hail You.
> Open us tonight to the rushing wind
> Of ecstatic inspiration that only You can bring.
> Bestow upon us this blessing
> That through our dreaming we may carry
> The ephemeral breath of our creative vision
> Into the waking world, and make it so.
> Hail Odin, Master of Manifestation.

Please bless us this night.

Hold hands over the two candles.

Prayer to Sunna

> Hail mighty Sunna,
> Mistress of the chariot of the sun,
> Champion of the sky road,
> Mighty, valiant, supreme.
> I ask Your blessings in the morning when I wake.
> May I partake of some small measure
> Of the strength and vitality You bring.
> May I awake from my night's rest ready to work,
> To serve, to play, to rejoice.
> May I await Your coming with the dawn joyously
> And with an open heart.
> Hail, Mighty Sunna.

Anoint head with oil. This is symbolic of honoring one's connection to the Gods.

Prayer to Hoenir

> Brother of wind and fire I hail You.
> God of wisdom and silence, I honor You this night.
> Please help me to keep my mind and heart
> Always centered on my Gods.
> Please help me to keep my desires focused
> On what would please Them the most.
> Teach me to make every action, every word,
> every half-whispered hope
> A living, centering prayer to the Holy Ones.
> Hail, Hoenir, God of mystery.

Anoint the heart with oil. This is symbolic of the desire to focus one's life around proper honoring of the Gods.

Prayer to Earendil

> Hail Earendil, bright lord of the sky.
> May You be praised who are so often now forgotten.

> May You shower Your wisdom down upon us
> as we sleep and as we dream.
> You, who are the divine archer,
> Always on track, far seeing, far planning,
> Help us to also remain focused on our goals.
> May our dreams, words, and waking actions
> Lead us ever closer to ardent service to the Gods.
> Bright Earendil, fearsome and wise,
> Look kindly upon us this night, I pray.

Spend some time quietly meditating on the Gods. If it helps to pray with beads or to read a passage from lore then by all means do so. Afterwards, offer thanks to the Gods and then the following prayer is offered:

> Dear Gna, messenger of the Gods,
> Jewel of Frigga's hall, fleet footed and swift,
> Please carry these prayers to the halls of the Holy Ones.
> Bestow upon us the grace of spiritual clarity,
> That we may hear the messages
> They send in return rightly and well.
> May You be honored this night and always, oh Gna.
> May all the Gods and Goddesses be thanked this night.

Originally published in *Day Star and Whirling Wheel*, by Galina Krasskova. Asphodel Press, 2009.

Rite for the Land
Galina Krasskova

Wherever you do ritual, magic, or any sacred work, the land is listening and noticing. The spirits of the land – land-wights or *landvaettir* – can be powerful allies and friends, and even if you do not wish to make a permanent link with a land-wight, it is only courteous to make a ritual offering to the spirit of any piece of land where you are going to be, or have been, doing regular workings.

This rite does require digging a small hole with a trowel, but it need not be more than a few inches deep. Bring a loaf of bread, a spoonful of salt, a cup of good liquor (or fresh milk if you can get it), a coin (any country or denomination), a seed, and a small polished stone.

ଔ ଔ ଓ ଓ

Find a place that intuitively seems like the "heart" of that piece of land, and speak the following:

> O Wight of the earth beneath my feet,
> Wight of place, Wight of territory,
> Watch well my workings here, and wish me
> Nothing but good. Here I gift you,
> Here I offer you, here I fain you.

Dig the hole, and place the bread in it.

> For your gladness, the gift of grain.

Pour in the salt.

> For my safety, salt of earth.

Pour in the milk or liquor.

> For love of nature, nourishment.

Place in the coin.

> For your welcome, worth.

Place in the seed.

> For your greening, growth.

Place in the stone.

> I give back what is Earth's by right.
> Hold up my footsteps, ward my way,
> And may this land be ever blessed.

It should go without saying that once you have made this offering to a land-spirit, you had best not litter or otherwise treat the place badly afterwards. This rite should be done at least yearly if it is a familiar and often-used piece of land. Pick up litter, pile broken brush, and keep an eye out for foolish pilgrims who make careless messes.

Originally published in *Northern Tradition for the Solitary Practitioner* by Raven Kaldera and Galina Krasskova, New Page Press, 2007.

Earth Healing Rite for Jord
Ari

This short rite takes place with everyone sitting on the ground in a circle. (It must be done actually sitting on earth, not on a floor in some flat somewhere. Bother to go outside and put your behind in Her lap.) Nothing is needed except for your bodies and the Earth; however, it is very important that this ritual be followed up by a group act of actually going to some area that is in need of cleaning and picking up the trash from Her body. The act of de-littering is the magic that completes the rite; otherwise it remains incomplete and impotent.

ಯ ಯ ಬಾ ಬಾ

To begin, the leader leads everyone through guided meditation to ground and center in the Earth beneath them. If you do not know how to do this, I recommend the first chapter in the book *Neolithic Shamanism*, as it thoroughly discusses this process.

When everyone has grounded and centered, the leader beats their fist against the ground three times and says, "Hail Jord!" (Don't worry about hurting Her. You can't hurt Her with your little fists, and the Earth enjoys being used as a drum. There are much worse ways that we have hurt Her; your Styrofoam cup thrown out the window is the real blow.) Everyone follows by striking the ground three times and repeating "Hail Jord!"

The leader continues with their invocation. After the first line, everyone calls out "Hail Jord!" again and strikes the earth three times. After the second line, everyone calls out "Jord, we bless you as you have blessed us!" Then these two responses are repeated, alternating, over and over after each of the next two lines. The pattern should be obvious.

Jord Invocation:

> Hail to the first lover of Odin!
> For as you opened yourself to him, you taught him to love.
> Hail to the ground beneath our feet!
> For as you support us, you teach us how to support each other.
> Hail to the Mother of Thor!
> For as you calmed his cries, so the mountain breaks up the storm.

Hail to the one who sends up his lightning!
For as the sky touches the earth, divine energy is released.
Hail to the Mother of Frigg!
For she learned in your arms the gifts that would make her the Mother of Asgard.
Hail to the one who gives without stinting!
For as you lavish your gifts on us, so we learn to give to others.
Hail to your bones, the bedrock beneath us!
May it be whole and solid, without cracking.
Hail to your limbs, the mountains that rise!
May they stand tall and not erupt upon us.
Hail to your flesh, the soil that grows all!
May it be clean and free of poisons.
Hail to your blood, the underground rivers!
May they run clear and not be sucked away.
Hail to your skin, the grass and weeds!
May they grow in profusion and keep your flesh from erosion.
Hail to your hair, the trees that wave in the wind!
As Odin caressed you, so may they always stretch to the sky.
Hail to your eyes, the shining lakes that reflect the heavens!
May they always lie glittering in purity.
Hail to your womb, the dark places that breed the tiniest lives!
May they always stream forth to break down the waste of the world.
Hail to your mind, the intelligence that guides the cycle!
May we never assume that we know better than this greatness.
Hail to your children, the *landvaettir* who watch over us!
May we never forget to honor their gifts.

The leader then takes saliva from their mouth and places it upon the Earth, and says, "My rain to your Earth; I give you a part of me." Everyone else follows. Then all strike the Earth once more and cry out "Hail Jord!" together. Then all must rise and go forth in a group to clean Her skin of the waste of Man.

Acre Bot Ritual, Modernized
Geordie Ingerson

The Acre Bot ritual is a spell to bless the land, written in Old English. It is a fairly long and involved charm/rite, and it survives today only in a Christianized form. It is clearly older than the Christian era, as its earth-worshipping roots show, but obviously it had to be Christianized in order to be allowed to survive at all. The version that I propose here is a rewriting of what the original rite might have been like if it had not been changed to reflect the God of the oppressors. This rite is to be done by the owner of a good-sized piece of land, in order to bless the spirit of that land and fill it with peace, fertility, and health to all that live upon it. The rite follows the outline of the original, but some areas are more delineated than in the mediaeval original because we do not always have access to what was obvious to them, and of course the words are changed to an extent. Where the mediaeval peasant used Latin because it was a little-known "magical" language of the time, I use Old English, which has become just as foreign and magical to us as Latin was to them. The aid of a godhi or gythia is required for this rite; if the landowner is themselves a holy person of this tradition, they may do all parts of the rite themselves.

The following items must be gathered together before the rite:

- A jug of clean water from some spring or well in any place that seems sacred to them, and that is fully drinkable without any poison or disease.
- Homemade soap, perhaps from a local artisan if not made by you yourself.
- A cup of salt from the sea.
- A small bottle of olive oil.
- A small bottle of honey.
- A cake of yeast.
- Milk from a local milking animal – if not your own, then one on a neighbouring farm.
- A bundle of twigs, one collected from each type of tree on the piece of land.
- A bouquet of weeds, one of each type collected from the piece of land. (Except, traditionally, for burdock; one expects that this is because of its terrible burrs. I also disincluded ragweed and a few other noxious types that I wished to disperse.)

- A small quantity of dried mugwort, for incense.
- A small quantity of fennel seed, wrapped in a cloth.
- Four crosses, traditionally made of aspen twigs. If there is no aspen to be had, use some other wood. Tie one with red yarn, one with blue, one with green, and one with gold. If you like, keep winding the yarn around them to make small "god's eyes". If you need to use other woods and can find them, make the red one of fir, the blue one of ash, the green one of linden, and the gold one of any nut tree. If this is not possible either, do the best you can with the twigs from trees on your property.
- A tiller or small plough; owned, borrowed, or rented. It is fine to use a motorized tiller; we are modern people after all.
- An area of your land, however large or small, that is staked out to be tilled for a garden.
- Seeds to plant, of your choice.

The last item to be obtained is rather difficult; the rite specifies that one must "take unknown seed from beggars and give them twice as much as you get from them." Apparently in mediaeval times beggars went about selling seed; these days, they are unlikely to sell anything of the sort. Assuming that the idea is to be generous and thus bring that generosity into your home, a better modern substitution might be to find a beggar or homeless individual and offer to give them a pound in exchange for a coin, or something like that. Coins have long been a symbol of Earth and wealth, and many have been buried in the Earth like seeds. One could consider this to be "seeding wealth".

Lay out all these items and ask the godhi or gythia to come to your land. An altar should be set up to all the Gods mentioned in this rite, either by the landowner or the godhi or gythia.

To begin, the godhi or gythia shall speak over the water the following blessing:

> By the blood of Nerthus, running underground,
> Lady of bogs and fens,
> Lady who speaks from the deepest well,
> Bless this water come up from your depths
> And may all who drink of it prosper.

The godhi or gythia shall then speak over the soap the following blessing:

> By Holda, Lady of the Hearth,
> Queen of Broom and Dustbin,
> Witch of the Wild Hunt,
> Feathers of the snow,
> May this be blessed in your name
> And all things come clean.

The godhi or gythia shall speak over the salt the following blessing:

> Salt of Earth, bones of Nerthus,
> From the depths we arise,
> To the depths we shall return.
> Soul of mountains, bless us
> With endurance forevermore.

The godhi or gythia shall speak over the milk the following blessing:

> Milk of Audumhla, Great Cow,
> (*or, alternately,* Milk of Heidrun, Great Goat,)
> You give life not only to your young
> But you sacrifice to those in need of nourishment.
> Give us your blessing, Hoofed Mother!

Then the landowner shall turn the four turves of sod upside down and lay them before the altar. The landowner shall take the twigs of wood and the herbs, and dip them in the water and sprinkle the sods with them. Then he or she shall do the same with the milk, and oil, and honey; then a bit of the yeast shall be sprinkled on them as well. As this is done, say:

> In the name of all the Gods,
> Thou shalt grow, thou shalt multiply,
> And thou shalt fill the Earth.
> *Aweaxan, gemanigfealdan, and Erce gefyllan.*

Turn the turves over so that the green side is upwards, and then the godhi or gythia shall say over them the following blessing:

> By all the Gods who walk this Earth,
> By all creatures below and above it,

> May this land be blessed!
> In the east, shall it be blessed!
> In the south, shall it be blessed!
> In the west, shall it be blessed!
> In the north, shall it be blessed!
> In the center, where grows the World Tree,
> May it be blessed!

Then the landowner takes the four crosses of wood and yarn, and carves or paints names on one arm of each one. As he or she does this, the godhi or gythia blesses the cross in the name of that deity. The red one shall be written "Nerthus", and the blue one "Njord", and the green one "Freya", and the gold one "Frey". Then the turves of sod shall be carried, one at a time, back to their places. One cross shall be laid in the bottom of the hole of each one, and the turves of sod laid in on top of them. Place Freya's cross in the east, Frey's cross in the south, Njord's cross in the west, and the cross of Nerthus in the north. Then speak the word *"Aweaxan!"* nine times, and then say nine times, "By the grace of the Gods."

Then the landowner should come back to the center of the land and bow to the east nine times, and say the following words:

> Eastwards I face, for favours I pray,
> I ask the great lord, I pray the mighty Thor,
> I pray the holy guardian of the skies,
> Earth I pray and the sky above,
> And thunder's might and the heavenly halls,
> And the generosity of Frigga the Queen,
> That I may be able, with the grace of the Gods,
> With teeth disclose, with firmness of thought,
> Raise up these crops to my wordly benefit,
> Fill this earth by firm faith,
> Make beautiful these pastures as the skald sings,
> That I should have favors on earth, who alms
> Have given justly according to the will of the Gods.

Then the landowner shall turn clockwise three times, and lay down on the ground and recite three times the following:

> *Hwæt, eorðe mæg wið ealra wihta gehwilce,*

> *and wið andan, and wið æminde,*
> *and wið þa micelan mannes tungan.*[1]

Then say:

> I commend this land to the Gods,
> And all who live upon it to the Gods,
> And my fortune to the Gods.

Then the landowner should make or have made a loaf of bread that uses some of the blessed water and milk and salt, and the oil and yeast and honey, and the following seven grains: wheat, rye, barley, buckwheat, millet, oats, ground dried fava beans, and dried acorn flour. (If you cannot find the latter locally, you can find it mail-order on the Internet.) Any recipe may be used so long as it has a little of each of these. The original calls for a loaf the size of the palm of the hand, but you may wish to make more loaves to eat yourself, especially if this rite is to be a family affair.

Tie the blessed soap, the rest of the blessed salt, the coins, the mugwort, and the fennel seed into a cloth and hang it from the handle of the tiller or plough. Say the following words:

> Erce, Erce, Erce, Earth Mother,
> May you and all the Gods grant us
> Fields growing and thriving,
> Flourishing and bountiful,
> Bright shafts of millet crops,
> And of broad barley crops,
> And white wheat crops,
> And of all the crops of the Earth.
> May the Gods grant us,
> And all the ancestors who watch,
> That our wealth be safe against every foe
> And secure against every harm
> From misfortune sown across the land.
> Now I pray to the Gods who created this world
> That no woman be so wordwise and no man so powerful
> That they can upset the words thus spoken.

---

[1] "For lo, the Earth prevails over all creatures, / and over malice and over jealousy / and over the tongue of the mighty man."

Then cut the first furrow with the plough, or till the first strip of land, and say:

> Hail to thee, Earth, Mother of Men.
> May you be fruitful under the protection of the Gods.
> Filled with food for the benefit of men.

Lay the loaf of bread in the furrow or under the tilled earth and say:

> Field full of food,
> The race of man
> Brightly blooming,
> Be thou blessed
> In the holy names of the Gods
> And the Earth on which we live,
> O Gods who gifted us with this land,
> Grant us the gift of fertility
> That each grain may be profitable to us.

Then again say three times:

> *Hwæt, eorðe mæg wið ealra wihta gehwilce,*
> *and wið andan, and wið æminde,*
> *and wið þa micelan mannes tungan.*

Then go in and feast, for the rite is over.

Rune Creation Ritual
John Hebreska

Making your own rune set can improve the feeling of your readings and give a close personal tie with your runes. While many people choose to use purchased runes for their castings, or runes that were given to them, as you progress you may decide that you want to take this additional step.

Making the set can be as simple or complex as you want it to be. It can be extremely ritualized or more informal, depending upon your circumstances. What follows is a foundation upon which you can build your own process for creating runes.

Wood is the most common material used by people when they create their rune sets. Trees give us a sense of life and tie us to the earth. They remind us of Yggdrasil, and also the sacrifice Odin made by hanging on the tree to gain the knowledge of the runes.

The branches of trees such as apple, pine, or yew are typically used for runes, but virtually any wood will do. Some makers claim that to use "dead wood" (already fallen) from the tree is inappropriate for runes, but I think that's a personal choice. The important thing is that your choice of wood resonates for you. This can range from going out into the woods and cutting down a branch of a tree that you find particularly meaningful (making sure to give thanks along the way) to going to your local art supply store and purchasing wood disks.

There are other materials as well. Glass beads, stones, metal; any material that you can mark on is sufficient. Ultimately you are likely to find a material that works well for you. Just remember that with whatever material you're going to make, you will need to be able to mark it in some way.

Next, you need to find a way to put the runes on your set. As with materials, it's largely a matter of personal preference, both from a practical standpoint and a spiritual one. Fine-point permanent markers are the easiest, and will mark on almost any material. We're also all used to writing with a pen, so it's easy. You can also use an X-acto knife or a wood-burning tool. A Dremel tool works well on stone and metal. I've even done a set of shot-glass runes and used the chemicals available in craft stores for glass etching. One thing to watch out for is anything that's water soluble. Whether it be watercolor paint or latex paint, the chance that your runes would get wet (and thus ruin them) makes water soluble marking materials inappropriate. It's not that this causes a spiritual problem, it's that it presents a practical one.

Traditionally one consecrates a set of runes by "staining" them with a life fluid. This is normally blood, but it could also be saliva, semen, or urine. You'll need to either provide this fluid when you ritually consecrate the runes, or collect and store it for use in ritual.

(A note about blood collection and safe practices: In modern society the extraction of blood raises a significant number of safety issues, both to yourself through disease and infection, or to others. If you're going to use blood and store it beforehand, you'll want to contact a friend with medical expertise who can provide blood collection and storage vials. Typically a blood storage vial has a small amount of heparin in it to keep it from clotting.)

You'll also need a saw if you're cutting a branch, and sandpaper if you're working with rough wood. You'll want linseed oil or varnish for final treatment, and a bag to store them in. The question of linseed oil or varnish is one worth spending some time thinking about. Linseed oil is viewed as "more natural" while varnish can give you the ability to give your wood certain colors. However, varnish may create a coating that "seals" the runes in a way you don't like. Spend some time thinking about it.

My experience, particularly when working with a branch, is that creating the slips you are going to carve the runes on is best left to a non-ritualized process. Whether you do it with a handsaw, or a table saw, or some other way, it takes a while, and for me personally, doesn't fit well within the ritual process. You'll also want to create "extras" (I recommend doing 36 slips) for mistakes. No matter how many times you do it, you'll make a mistake. After you've cut your slips, and have your materials together, it's time to set up for ritual, and create your runes.

Before you go into ritual, take a pencil and "pencil in" each rune on a slip, if a pencil is something that will mark the slips. This will make it easier to make the runes during the creation process. If you can't mark on it (such as with glass), keep a few extra slips around for mistakes. Doing this beforehand will make the actual creation process easier.

Now set aside a ritual space, and do whatever ritual you deem appropriate for your path. I open with a hammer rite, which is simply going to one side of my space, lifting a hammer and stating: "Hammer of Thor, Hallow and Hold This Holy Stead!"

Then I move to the opposite side of the space, lift the hammer, and state: "Odin, bless me as I honor you through the creation of runes today." I offer a toast to Odin and place my altar items before me (a horn, and a hammer) to give my process meaning.

Now put down two cloths, one for your "blanks" and another for your finished runes. Through whatever process you choose, based upon your materials and marker, create each rune. As you're writing or carving, intone the name of the rune, or chant it. Think about the meaning of the rune, and what it means to you. If possible, you want your rune strokes to be downward, into the earth (downward meaning towards the bottom of the rune), and across the grain of the wood, showing an affirmative intention to put energy into the slip.

After you're done with the carving, place the rune on the "finished runes" cloth, and make a hammer sign over it. Proceed onto the next rune. I recommend you go through all of them at a setting, one aett at a time. This generally takes an hour or two if you're doing it for your first time.

When you've finished your last rune, you'll now want to consecrate them with your fluid of choice. I recommend doing this before placing the linseed oil or varnish on them, as the oil or varnish will "seal" the rune. After you've consecrated each rune, *galdr* (intone) each rune again, as a set, pushing your personal energy into the runes.

At this point, I recite the Icelandic Rune Poem:

> Wealth is a source of discord among kinsmen
> and fire of the sea
> and path of the serpent.

> Lamentation of the clouds
> and ruin of the hay-harvest
> and abomination of the shepherd.

> Torturer of women
> and cliff-dweller
> and husband of a giantess.

Aged Gautr
and prince of Ásgardr
and lord of Vallhalla.

Joy of the horsemen
and speedy journey
and toil of the steed.

Disease fatal to children
and painful spot
and abode of mortification.

Cold grain
and shower of sleet
and sickness of serpents.

Grief of the bond-maid
and state of oppression
and toilsome work.

Bark of rivers
and roof of the wave
and destruction of the doomed.

Boon to men
and good summer
and thriving crops.

Shield of the clouds
and shining ray
and destroyer of ice.

God with one hand
and leavings of the wolf
and prince of temples.

Leafy twig
and little tree
and fresh young shrub.

Delight of man
and augmentation of the earth
and adorner of ships.

Eddying stream
and broad geyser
and land of the fish.

Bent bow
and brittle iron
and giant of the arrow.

You may alternatively decide that one of the other poems sings to you. Then you close your ritual space in whatever method you see fit.

After you've closed your ritual space, you should take the time to apply the linseed oil or Varnish onto the runes, and let them dry. If you use varnish, I generally recommend doing this outdoors because the fumes can be problematic and you may need to take frequent breaks.

Congratulations! You now have your own personal set of runes.

Rune Tree Rite
Raven Kaldera

This ritual is based on the shamanic World Tree rites of western Siberia, with a Northern Tradition twist. It is a solitary ritual, meant to be worked on a very large single tree which will represent Yggdrasil. The tree should be large enough to climb and easily sit in, as well as to have thirty-three spikes driven into it in an upward spiral. Since it will then become the sacred living embodiment of Yggdrasil, it's best that it be on the property of someone who understands these things, and will not be tempted to cut it down. To find the right tree on the privately held property of an understanding party, go through the woods and ask each of the tallest and largest trees if they are willing to endure this pain, as Odin endured his pain hanging on Yggdrasil in order to acquire the Runes. After this rite, the tree must be given offerings of food, drink, and coins buried at its roots on a regular basis, and any other offering that seems right.

Once the tree has been located, thank it and give it the first offering of food and drink. Sit at its base with your back to its trunk, and speak to the spirit of the tree. Then mark where the spikes will be driven in. They are for climbing up in a spiral around its trunk, and should end at a strong branch that is easily able to bear the weight of a sitting human. Some hardware stores sell special "tree spikes" with a little upturn on the end to keep the foot from slipping; these are often used by hunters who install tree stands to shoot from. (If you are able to make a permanent place to sit at the top of the spiral, such as a small platform or tree stand, by all means do this thing.) After you have marked them in a ladderlike spiral, apologize once more to the tree and then hammer in the spikes.

Next, prepare thirty-three small wooden charms on strings, each with one of the Futhorc runes carved upon it. (If you prefer Futhark to Futhorc, you are welcome to take the idea and rewrite the ritual for that system.) Loop each charm over the appropriate spike, up against the tree bark, in the order named below. Tie ribbons of many colors to its branches, above the sitting-place. During the preparation, use a ladder to decorate the tree; you should not actually climb the spikes until the ritual is underway.

When you are ready, stand at the base of the tree and call out:

> O Yggdrasil, show yourself
> In this your child of branch and root!
> O Yggdrasil, I would climb your heights
> And see from your great vantage point.
> O Yggdrasil, bring me closer to sky
> And let me see with Hraesvelg's eye.

Then, as you take each step on the spiral, you say the next line in this prayer. (The Rune of that step is listed after each line.)

> From the Hel Road I rise. (Raido)
> Through the mounds of the Ancestors I rise. (Othila)
> Through the tides of Wyrd I rise. (Perth)
> Through Hel's Gate I rise. (Ear)
> Through the fields of ice I rise. (Isa)
> Through the lakes of mist I rise. (Laguz)
> Through the dragon's chill breath I rise. (Algiz)
> Through the hands of craft I rise. (Yr)
> Through the treasure-store I rise. (Fehu)
> Through the singing leaves I rise. (Os)
> Through the need-fire I rise. (Nauthiz)
> Through the forge-fire I rise. (Kenaz)
> Through the funeral-fire I rise. (Cweorth)
> Through the winter storms I rise. (Hagalaz)
> Through the wild herds I rise. (Uruz)
> Through the oaken wood I rise. (Ac)
> Through the serpent's coils I rise. (Ior)
> Through hoofprints in the dust I rise. (Ehwaz)
> Through the roads of Man I rise. (Mannaz)
> Through the gates of Man I rise. (Eihwaz)
> Through the crossroads I rise. (Gebo)
> Through the fertile fields I rise. (Jera)
> Through the blood on the grain I rise. (Inguz)
> Through the birch-grove I rise. (Berkana)
> Through the circle of stones I rise. (Stan)
> Through the hole in the hedge I rise. (Thorn)
> Through the chalice well I rise. (Chalc)
> Through the twilight torch I rise. (Wunjo)

Through the arch of spears I rise. (Tyr)
Through the morning's call I rise. (Dagaz)
Through the lightning's strike I rise. (Sigil)
Through the winds of the sky I rise. (Ansuz)
To the crest of Yggdrasil I rise. (Gar)

When the sitting-place has been achieved, tie one more ribbon onto the tree and make yourself comfortable, ideally with your back to the trunk. Ask the avatar of Yggdrasil at your back to help you see what can be seen, and put yourself into a meditative trance. If there is room on your platform, this is a good time for divination. Once you have received your answers, start down the tree again. Say the lines in reverse order, going "from" the crest of Yggrasil "to" the Hel Road, and replace "I rise" with "I descend". When you have reached the bottom, make another gift to the tree and go home to write down your wisdom.

Holda Housecleaning Rite
Shannon Graves

This is not a ritual for just "cleaning the house" as it is a ritual for finding motivation to clean the house. It's said that the goddess Holda punished lazy housekeepers, and it's true that for many of us, it takes a huge amount of effort just to get started, much less keeping up with it. This ritual is the one that you do when the mess gets huge and feels overwhelming, and you don't think that you can handle it. Holda is the one to call on, not because she isn't ruthless, but because she is.

ଔ ଔ ଚ ଚ

First, kneel in the worst part of the mess. If you need to sweep away bits of it in order to do so, that's all right. Put your hands on the floor (or the horrid carpet, or whatever) and say to her:

> Stiffen my spine that I might sweep
> The grime from ground and garden.
> Sharpen my sight that I might see
> The way through mess and muddle.
> Strengthen my will that I might wash away
> Disarray and disorder from door to door.

Then stand and go to the hearth of the home – usually the kitchen where the stove pilot light burns, but if you've got a fireplace in your living room and you feel that's the real hearth, go for it. Lay out a piece of bread with butter, and a cup of tea (any kind) on top of one flawless white napkin. Light some scented herbs for incense (not on the napkin); culinary ones are best for Holda. I use kitchen sage, thyme, dill seed, and various spices on a lit charcoal disc. Blow the smoke around the room and say to her:

> Hail Holda, healer of house and hearth,
> As I feed you, so may you feed me
> On soup of strength and meat of might,
> On pottage of purpose and perseverance,
> Hold me up to face this task
> And fail me not, nor let me fail.

Then pick up a broom and sweep for a few minutes. It doesn't matter if there's carpet on the floor and the broom isn't going to do anything. Just sweep, because it invokes Holda's energy into the room. Lift the broom in the air and walk around the mess, waving it. As it waves, the mess should become less frightening. When you've done that for a few minutes, put on some loud music and start cleaning. It will be easier than you think – and when it becomes difficult, you'll feel Holda holding you up and keeping you on track.

A Meal Blessing
Joshua Tenpenny

Sometimes the meals we eat are a prayer unto themselves. Food fresh from your own garden, bread baked by hand, a holiday feast shared with friends. These clearly nourish our souls as much as our bodies, and it is easy to see the sacredness in these things. A blessing spoken at these times just affirms what was already apparent. But for most of us, most of the time, modern life obscures the sacred connection between the food in front of us and the life which was sacrificed for it. This blessing prayer is meant to be an opportunity to be mindful of how and what we eat.

ಆ ಆ ೲ ೲ

The prayer is:

> For all who gave of their bodies and lives for this meal,
> I give blessings and praise.
> For all who toiled to harvest and prepare this meal,
> I give blessings and praise.
> For all who share this meal with me,
> I give blessings and praise.

For the first line, take the opportunity to look at (or speculate about) the ingredients of what you are eating. The food we eat was all alive at some point. It can be challenging when facing a brightly colored snack cake or box of chicken nuggets, but remember that Life comes only from Life. No matter how obscure or distant the connection, all food comes from the bodies of living things. So take a moment to reflect on the fields of grain, the vegetables growing on some distant farm, the wildlife displaced and the pests killed at that farm, the livestock and the grain that fed them, the dairy cows, the laying hens, the trees full of fruit. Think about where the ingredients came from, and give thanks to the living things whose sacrifice has provided this meal. Whether the sacrifice was of their life or an offering from their body, whether it was animal or plant, give them your heartfelt blessing and praise their sacrifice.

For the next line, take the opportunity to think about how the food got to you in its present form. Think about the people who raised the animals and grew the vegetables, and the people who did the harvesting, butchering and packing. Think about the factory workers who process the foods, the truckers who bring it from farm to factory to store, and the business men who coordinate the whole thing. Think about who cooked the food, and who taught them how to do it. Maybe this food traveled only from your garden to your plate, making a brief detour to the sink, in no one's hands but your own. Maybe this food had a transcontinental voyage, with components coming through dozens of factories, its origin shrouded in mystery. Whatever the journey, take a moment to offer a blessing to all involved in the process and thank them for their part in bringing this nourishment to you.

Finally, take the opportunity to reflect on this meal in the context of family and community. Sharing food is one of the basic forms of social bonding. Honor the bonds of kinship and hospitality which are nourished by this meal. On a more abstract level, think about other families sitting together for dinner as you are, other harried office workers having a quick lunch at their desk like you are, other parents feeding their children as you are, other commuters eating fast food while driving like you are. Think about how this meal reflects social customs or honors family traditions. Think about how this meal connects you to others, whether they are present with you or not. Offer blessing and praise for these connections.

ଔ ଔ ଓ ଓ

To give this blessing formally, you might include a brief statement about the key ingredients, people, and connections involved in the meal. For a group meal, after the person offering the prayer says each line (using "we" and "us" as appropriate), the group can reply with "Blessings and praise!" For a more participatory blessing, people in the group might suggest specific things about the meal to offer blessings and praise for. For example, someone might say, "For Aunt Mimi who taught me how to make this pie, I offer blessings and praise." to which everyone replies "Blessings and praise!"

To offer the blessing briefly and informally, just let your mind wander over each of these things as you start the meal, and say to yourself, "Blessings and praise. Blessings and praise. Blessings and praise." The point isn't to turn each meal into a research project, but to encourage mindfulness and curiosity about the process by which living things become food for us. We are part of a complex network of nourishment and obligations, and this prayer traces those threads which bind us together. Let it train you in mindfulness, helping you to see how every meal is sacred.

Originally published in *Honey, Grain, and Gold: A Devotional For Frey* by Joshua Tenpenny. Asphodel Press, 2009.

Fidelity Ritual for Sif
Ingeborg

I wrote this rite because I was having trouble staying with my marriage vows. While I respect my polyamorous friends, my husband and I have chosen monogamy – as Starhawk says, " ... to concentrate on one person with depth and passion." Yet it's not always easy, even when both people very much love each other, and I think that we feel shame over that. We are taught that if you really love each other, staying faithful to your vows should always be easy, and that's not true – and doesn't make you a bad person if you have to struggle. In fact, it's a sign of honor to struggle to keep a vow and to win. There's nothing dishonorable about asking for help in order to win that struggle, and that is what this ritual is about.

It was performed by myself and three of my monogamous female friends, all of whom felt that they could use the extra aid, but it could be performed by any number of people of any gender. (It can also be performed as an entirely solitary ritual.) Non-partnered or polyamorous people could still attend, and perhaps witness or drum or clap, and certainly hail Sif and Thor, even if they are not renewing their vow to stay monogamous. I see Sif and Thor very much as the keepers of monogamy; if polyamorous couples/triples/others wish to be blessed for their bonds of love and fidelity to each other, there are multiple God-pairs who can make that happen – Odin and Frigga, Frey and Gerda, Loki/Angrboda/Sigyn, and others. But Sif and Thor are for those who cleave only to each other.

Ideally, couples should be there together; the reason that I and my friends did not have our husbands there was because they were not Pagan, and indeed this had become a source of difficulty that we had to work through. I am happy to tell you that at this time of sending the ritual to you, we are all still together with our husbands, and all still very much in love. Hail Sif!

ॐ ॐ ॐ ॐ

The altar is draped in yellow cloth. On it lays a short sword, a horn of mead (and more mead in a bottle for refilling), a golden chain, a yellow candle, a large bowl if the rite is held inside, several yellow stones such as citrine, and several yellow scarves – as many as there are people wanting Sif's aid and blessing. Four people stand around the altar to be the gythias (or godhis, or both, though we will use the word gythia for now); others circle around them.

The first gythia lights the yellow candle, raises the horn of mead, and says:

> Hail Lady Sif, Wife of Thor.
> Indeed, this is how we most know you,
> Wife of the Great Thunderer,
> And this is a title that you love and cherish.
> You are more than just a wife –
> You are the one who hallows the doorway,
> You are the Mother of Ullr and the Mother of Thrud,
> You are one who grants skill in weaponry,
> You are one who protects wives and children,
> You are one who gives excellence in whatever skill we
>   strive for.
> So we hail you, Sif of the Golden Hair!

The first gythia carries the horn of mead around the circle and each person drinks and toasts "Hail Sif!" or pours out a small libation onto the ground or into the bowl if this is held inside. The second gythia stands forth and says:

> And yet, Sif of the Aesir,
> First and foremost you are the Wife of Thor.
> What can we learn from you, Lady of the Golden Hair?
> First we can learn that you honor your husband
> And love him above all else,
> And you would not see a rite for you go by
> Without honoring him as well.
> So before speak of you further,
> We hail Thor, Husband of Sif,
> Great Thunderer, Friend to the Common Man,
> God of the spring rains and the lightning strike,
> Master of the Winds of the Western World!

The second gythia refills the horn and carries it around the circle; each person drinks and toasts "Hail Thor!" or pours out a small libation onto the ground or into the bowl. The third gythia stands forth and says:

> Sif, Bilskirnir's Lady,
> We know that you did not come to your husband a virgin.
> You had once another husband, great Aurvandil,
> And a young son by him, Ullr, at your breast.
> You teach us that true love does not always
> Come with the first rush of the heart,
> That it is all right to find it later,
> That it is all right to leave something that does not suit
> And go to something that does.
> You ask only that we who have so sworn
> Try our best until it is clear that it is over.
> You ask that if it fails, it fails
> Through no fault on our parts,
> But only because it was inevitable
> Even though we could not see so far ahead.
> Sif, bless us with the will to try again and again
> And the knowledge to know when to step away.

All say, "Sif, bless us!" The fourth gythia stands forth and says,

> Sif, Lady of the Golden Hair
> Whose locks were magically crafted by the dwarves
> At the behest of Laufey's Son,
> Some say that your shorn head
> Was a sign of adultery; that Loki knew
> Something that Thor did not, and tried to tell him.
> We do not know if you broke your vows,
> And we never will, but we do know
> That whatever happened between you and your husband,
> You made it up, and made your vow anew.
> Sif, you teach us that even if we make a terrible mistake,
> Fidelity can come back again from error
> If there is enough love and patience
> To build up trust again, step by arduous step.
> Sif, bless us with the ability to trust again,
> And to help our beloveds to trust us,
> And to weave that trust anew each day.

All say, "Sif, bless us!" The first gythia stands forth and says:

> Sif, Lady of the Golden Hair,
> They say that the bridal night
> Of you and your passionate husband
> Is made again every time the rain falls
> Onto the golden fields of grain.
> As the earth is always overjoyed for the rain
> That gives it nourishment and life,
> And without which it would be dry and barren,
> And as the rain always loves the earth
> That it caresses or ravishes,
> Let us always be joyful for the presence
> Of the beloveds to whom we cleave.
> Sif, bless us with that excitement
> Every long day of our lives together,
> Until the day that one of us walks the road to Death.

All say, "Sif, bless us!" The second gythia stands forth and says:

> Sif, Lady of the Golden Hair
> Whose mane was made artificially,
> You know that even when we lose our beauty
> Through accident or old age,
> We are still worthy of love and loving.
> Help us remember, each on each side,
> To find the beauty in each other
> That lies beneath the skin and bone.
> Sif, bless us with the sight of that beauty
> And may we never lose sight of it.

All say, "Sif, bless us!" The third gythia stands forth, holds up the gold chain, and says:

> Sif, Mother of Ullr who oversees the oaths of the tribe,
> Mother of Thrud who is strength and truth,
> Help us to keep our oaths of fidelity,
> To cleave only to the one who cleaves only to us
> Because it is what is best for the two of us,
> Because it is what nourishes our souls together.
> Let us not forget that this is our best road,
> Even in the face of temptation, of loneliness,

> Of grass that looks so much greener
> When we are angry or restless or sad.
> Help us to remain strong and true
> Throughout the difficulties of time,
> And never regret keeping our oaths.
> Sif, bless us with a heart so strong
> That we can resist all the thorns that will come.

All say, "Sif, bless us!" Then the fourth gythia stands forth with the yellow scarves, and says:

> All who would ask Lady Sif, once again,
> For renewal of your will to be faithful,
> Come forth and be bound as you were once bound,
> As you are still bound,
> As you will always be bound.
> Hail Sif!

All say, "Hail Sif!" Each of those who would ask for Sif's aid in this way should come forth. The fourth gythia ties the scarves around their neck, or wrist, or arm, or waist, saying, "Sif bless you." Then the candle is blown out and the rite is over. If there is an offering bowl, its contents should be taken outside and poured out onto the Earth.

A Northern-Tradition Sauna Ritual
Raven Kaldera

To prepare for the sauna, first clean yourself. In the winter during older times this would have meant a scrub with snow; at least take a shower first. There will be enough toxins coming out of your pores in short order. Clearing the skin is a good idea. It can also be used as ritual pre-cleansing in order to make yourself ready for the sacred space of the sauna.

A sauna is divided into rounds, each called a *gang* in Finnish. The ritual we create here is done in three rounds, as are many traditional versions. The first gang is the opening of the space, done to warm up and release the pressure of the everyday, a transition from daily concerns. It is the Ancestor round, in honor of those who came before us. The Ancestors are always honored first during a proper Northern-Tradition sweat ritual. Although this ritual is written as if for a group – since it may well be the job of the spirit-worker to lead it – it can also be adapted to a personal religious ritual by one individual.

ଔ   ଔ   ଓ   ଓ

To begin, each person is recaned with mugwort and then sent inside the sauna. Everyone comes in naked, bowing before the low lintel, and seats themselves. The one who is in charge of the rite lets everyone get settled in silence. Keep the silence going for a few minutes in order to let everyone calm down and transition away from their daily movement. If there are those who are uncomfortable, the silent warmup may help them as well. Ideally, one ought to get to the point where there is no psychological discomfort with being naked in a roomful of other naked sweating people. Physical discomfort is to be expected, at least in small amounts – in fact, if someone needs to leave during the rite for physical reasons, let them do so, and don't give them trouble about it. Having someone keel over will disrupt everything. It should go without saying that everyone in the ritual space should have been briefed on what this is about and how to properly behave.

If possible, encourage people to start by breathing together, difficult as that is in the hot room. The ideal is to get folks into a headspace where they are the tribe, all together, quietly celebrating their group bond. Don't push it, though. Overenthusiasm will not work here. Let the *löyly* – the sacred steam that rises with the breath of the Ancestors – do its job.

The officiant (which is how we will hereby refer to the person in charge of the rite) kneels before the fire as one would an altar, extends their hands towards the fire, and says:

> In the beginning, there was Darkness,
> The neverending Void of Ginnungagap.
> Then came Surt into the world with his flaming sword,
> One point of light in the Darkness,
> And so was Muspellheim, the World of Fire,
> Brought into existence.
> Before anything else, there was fire.
> Out of the darkness, Fire.

All participants repeat back, "Out of the darkness, Fire."

On top of the stove, a number of stones have been arranged, ideally in a spiral pattern, or perhaps that of a rune or a pictograph. They have been heating up all this time. The officiant has held back and is carrying one stone, which they now carefully place with the others, completing the pattern. The officiant says:

> Then came forth the world of Niflheim,
> The land of ice and snow, and cold stone.
> And so came forth also Ymir, great as a mountain chain,
> Suckling the nourishment of Audumhla, Mother Cow,
> Giant of stone and ice, Ancestor of thousands.
> At the beginning of the world, there was fire and stone.
> Out of the ice, stones.

The participants all repeat: "Out of the ice, stones."

Then the officiant wipes the sweat from their forehead with a bit of (natural fiber) cloth, and tosses it into the fire, saying:

> Then of the sweat of Ymir was born the first frost-giants,
> As cold as the sons of Surt are hot,
> Ancestors of many worlds,
> The powers of air and wind,
> We honor them with our very breath.
> Above fire and stone, there were the cooling winds,
> And out of the sweat of earth, life.

The participants all repeat: "Out of the sweat of earth, life."

There should be a bowl of water placed on one of the benches; it can have some kind of herb or essential oil if you like. For appropriate scents, I prefer pine needles for the first round (symbolizing the evergreens which are the oldest trees), birch for the second (as this is the birching round, although if you're using birch whisks, there's no need for anything but clean water), and the third should be chosen on the basis of which Gods you are honoring. The officiant holds up the bowl of water and says:

> Then Muspellheim did draw near to Niflheim,
> The moment of worlds colliding,
> The fire melting the ice,
> And the mists of water rose between the worlds.
> Hot to cold to hot to cold; here we live this first cycle.
> In the beginning, fire and water and stone,
> Changing the Land of Ice to the Land of Mists.
> From fire and water and stone, all creation.

The officiant pours water onto the hot stones, and as the steam rises the participants repeat: "From fire and water and stone, all creation." The officiant then speaks of honoring the ancestors who came before us, and may speak of some deed done by an ancestor. Others then might speak forth with tales of their own ancestors. For those who do not know their own ancestors, or do not wish to honor them by name for whatever reason, speaking of a spiritual ancestor that inspired them will suffice. Not everyone needs to take part; if the round falls to silence, that's fine. Whatever people say, it should end with a time of meditative silence.

Meanwhile, the *löyly* is surrounding everyone slowly. One Finnish farmer referred to there as being four kinds of *löyly*: Maiden *löyly*, Lady *löyly*, Mother *löyly*, and Grandmother *löyly*. The first time that the water is thrown on the rocks is Maiden *löyly*, which surrounds you like a fiery lover; you can hardly bear her touch, but it is exciting and ecstatic. The second is the Lady *löyly*, which caresses you like a loving wife. The third, Mother *löyly*, is so gentle that it is "like sitting in your mother's lap". The fourth, Grandmother *löyly*, is said to be the sweetest of all ... it happens when you go out to the bathhouse after the sauna and toss a little water onto the still-warm coals for the sake of the Saunatonttu (the spirit-guardian of the sauna) and the Ancestors.

When the first round has gone on long enough – and "long enough" is something that needs to be carefully gauged by the person in charge; remember that you'll be doing two more of these – everyone takes a break. This is the time to wash in cool water, or take a cold shower, or roll in the snow, depending on how sturdy one is. If someone has high blood pressure or a heart condition, have them soak or sponge off with warm water – a sudden drastic temperature change could create problems. Then it's back in for the second *gang*.

The second *gang* is for weighty matters. It is the round for the Community, Mannaz. While this is traditionally for bringing up important issues that are besetting the community, it is not for arguing or starting fights. Instead, people should frame their issues as hopes, stating what positive changes they would like to see happen in the future. "Community" could be anything as small as one's family to as large as the world. The round is formal, and people should not speak out of turn. If the group is intimate and trustworthy enough, negative matters between people can be brought up, but the officiant should keep things on track and not allow grudges to affect the energy of the rite.

This is the round where the birch whisks are brought out, steamed over the fire, and used to flagellate each other. It is done to loosen off the dead bits of skin that are peeling off of everyone's back, and also for spiritual purification. When done in community, it is important that people do it to each other as well as themselves, as an act of acknowledging the community bond. If no birch whisks are available, essence of birch can be put into the water. Birching is sometimes done in the sauna, and sometimes during the second break, depending on people's preferences. Birch is the tree of Frigga, the Queen of Asgard and the Lady of Frithkeeping. Part of Frigga's gift is to make sure that social interactions run properly, with as few people being insulted as possible. During this round, the officiant takes on Frigga's role, making sure that the atmosphere is maintained and that nothing degenerates into argument or, conversely, mere partying. An invocation to Frigga can be done, if the people involved wish to invoke her, to keep things peaceful. The UPG of one spirit-worker was that this round would be appropriate for divination done with symbols – runes or pictographs –

drawn on birchbark or carved on birch twigs. After this round, the whisks are burned in the fire.

The third *gang* is done for the Gods, and it is mostly quiet. The Gods may be hailed in the beginning, by name as people choose or all together, and then silence falls again. The group meditates on how they are going to enact the vision that came during the *löyly* or the divination or the talking on the last two rounds. Then all leave in silence, shower off, and the sauna is left going for a while longer in order to propitiate the guardian spirit. Someone should be chosen to watch the fire – checking in on it periodically until it goes out – and if there is a feast afterwards, some of it should be brought out and set at the door of the sauna as an offering.

Originally published in *Wightridden: Paths of Northern Tradition Shamanism*, Asphodel Press, 2007.

Ritual for Healing of the Body
Raven Kaldera

This is a rite which invokes Mengloth, the healing goddess of Jotunheim, and her nine handmaidens. It requires ten people to act as officiants; nine can be of either gender but should be dressed in the following colors respectively: pink, light blue, medium blue, lavender, pale green, white, yellow, brown, and red. They should each bear stones (large or small) in the colors of their raiment. The tenth one, representing Mengloth herself, should wear white and green, and wear a very long necklace, at least six feet in length and wrapped multiple times around her neck. It would be ideal if they were all healers of some kind, but it is not absolutely necessary. They will be conduits. At the very least, each one must have strong positive feelings about doing the healing.

The ritual is to be done either over the body of someone who needs healing, or over their mark-fetch. A mark-fetch is made like this: A clean sheet is taken to the place where the individual lies and is ideally placed under them, or if they are so ill that they cannot be moved (or are in some place like the ICU where it would make health care professionals upset to try to move them), it is placed on top of them. A line is drawn around the outline of their body with a large marker (or paint and a paintbrush if there is plenty of room and they are willing to wait). Then the sheet is rolled up and sent to the place where the healing ritual will be held. A mark-fetch should never be made without the conscious, clear permission of the person involved. While it may seem unfair to refrain from doing this rite on someone who is no longer conscious and cannot give their consent, it is part of the pain of the healer's job that we cannot force healing on anyone. It may be worth it to ask everyone you know if they would want this ritual done for them should they become unable to make their wishes known.

I will proceed with the ritual as if it was done on the body of a living person. If a mark-fetch is used instead, place the items where they would go if it was a human body. I will also be referring to the officiants with female gender, but any of the roles could also be performed by men who have healing energy. The following items should be brought to the ritual:

- A cup of honey.

- ༶ A bottle of some herbal tincture made from many healing plants, or alternately a cup of herbal tea. This may or may not be made of plants that are specifically used for treating the recipient's illness, although that would be ideal. If the correct herbs are not known, any combination of powerful but benign alteratives would be fine. Consult a herbalist if necessary.
- ༶ A lit recaning stick of dried healing herbs.
- ༶ A pot of heating or cooling salve, such as a menthol or capsicum ointment.
- ༶ A bowl of paste or thick dressing made only from nutritious plants – vegetable, fruits, culinary herbs, etc.
- ༶ A piece of white chalk.
- ༶ A double-plied piece of red yarn.
- ༶ A small bowl of sawdust from a great oak tree.
- ༶ Three long strips of cloth in the colors of red, green, and blue.

༶ ༶ ༺ ༺

First Mengloth's officiant stands forth and takes off her necklace, and winds it about the hands and forearms of the recipient. She says:

> By this lineage of healers that lies in my wake,
> By a thousand years of their wisdom and skill,
> I bless you with healing both old and new.
> May you be healed of all that tears at you,
> May you be healed of all that plagues you,
> May you be healed of all that devours you,
> May you be healed to love and work another year.
> May the thousand poisons and pestilences
> Pass away from you into the earth,
> Into the air, into the fire, into the void,
> And may all be well with you once more.
> Through my hands and into yours!

She places her hands on top of the recipient's head, and blesses them in silence. Then Blith's officiant steps forward, dressed in lavender, with the cup of honey in her hand. She says:

> May the weather in the Valley of Apples
> Be fair and fine; may no dark clouds dog you,
> Nor depression weigh on your shoulders,

> Nor anything distorted become
> In the mirror glass of your mind,
> And may that mirror be yours to guide.
> May your thoughts and moods be clear and clean,
> And as sweet as honey in the hive.

She anoints the recipient's forehead with honey. Aurboda's officiant steps forward, dressed in brown, with the bottle of herbal tincture (or cup of tea) in her hand. She says:

> May healing medicines be found to help you
> From all the apothecaries in the world.
> May your medicines be strong and effective
> And do you no ill in the process,
> And if ill must be done, let it be obvious
> And pass quickly from your flesh.
> May they enter you with goodwill
> And may only good come of them.

She marks the recipient on the mouth with her finger, dipped in the tincture or tea. Then Hlifthrasa's officiant comes forth, dressed in light blue, with the recaning stick in her hand. She says:

> May your breath come easily into your body,
> May the wings of birds beat in your breast
> And not cease to pump, nor flutter to a standstill.
> May your breath flow throughout your flesh
> And bring healing wherever it passes.
> I bless your every breath, and sing it smooth,
> And may your inner sky be clear
> Day and night, from each day forthwith.

She blows the recaning smoke onto the chest of the recipient. Then Bjort's officiant steps forward, dressed in yellow, with the pot of salve in her hand. She says:

> May that which has too much heat be cooled;
> May that which is too cold be warmed.
> May all fevers kill what is needed
> Without damage, and then retreat.
> May the Sun shine into you,
> And may you find the energy

> To move your body, to sweat, to laugh,
> To find wholeness in the swing and sway
> And the dancing of the flesh.

She anoints the solar plexus of the recipient with the salve. Then Frith's officiant steps forward, dressed in pale green, with the bowl of nutritious gruel in her hand. She says:

> May you be nourished by all that you eat,
> And may the Sea of Dragons within you
> Devour all you take in, and take from it
> All that is good and fine.
> May all the wells and springs work together,
> May organ dance with organ,
> And nothing be thrown out of balance
> And so unbalance its neighbors.

She anoints the recipient with a fingerful of the gruel on the belly, between the solar plexus and the navel. Then Bleik's officiant steps forward, dressed in pure white, with a piece of white chalk in her hand. She says:

> May all the rivers within you
> Run clean and clear of all filth.
> May the Well of Midgard wash you clean
> And no poisons stay within your flesh.
> May you be purified by the sacred well,
> May you be purified by the sacred fire,
> May you be purified by the sacred breath,
> May you be purified by all the rains of Spirit.

She draws a spiral with the chalk around the recipient's navel. Then Hlif's officiant comes forward, dressed in pink, with the red yarn in her hand. She says:

> May the coils in your bloodline
> That grew you into who you are today
> Not interfere with your healing.
> May all the knots and tangled passed down to you
> By the many errors of your ancestors
> Stand aside from your road
> And allow you to find your way home

> Without ensnarling you in their tendrils.
> Ancestors, give the great gifts of your blood
> And hold back the evil ones for now.

She ties nine knots in the red yarn and lays it gently on the recipient's groin. Then Thjodvara's officiant comes forward, dressed in medium to dark blue, with the bowl of sawdust in her hands. She says:

> May your bones be strong as the oak
> And your muscles like the herd of cattle
> That will not be stopped in their flight.
> May you be sturdy and rooted
> And graceful in your movement,
> And may your trunk and limbs,
> Your roots and branches,
> Heal quickly from every bruise and strain.

She sprinkles sawdust across the thighs of the recipient. Then Eir's officiant comes forth, dressed in red, with the three colored strips of cloth in her hand. She ties the red cloth around the recipient's ankle, and says:

> By the sacred fire that burns within us,
> May flesh and bone and mind be healed.
> Take that fire within you
> And let it make itself a home.

She ties the blue cloth around the recipient's ankle, and says:

> By the sacred well of many waters,
> May flesh and bone be healed.
> Take those waters within you
> And let them make themselves a home.

She ties the green cloth around the recipient's ankle, and says:

> By the sacred earth beneath our feet,
> May flesh and bone be healed.
> Take that good green energy within you
> And let it make itself a home.

Mengloth steps forward again, and unwinds the necklace from the recipient's hands, and says:

May you be free of all pain,
May you be free of all torment,
May you be free of all infirmity.
We pray to the heights of Lyfjaberg
That you shall rise, well and blessed,
From your bed to face the world.

She takes the end of one of the strips of cloth and kisses it; each of the others also comes forth and kisses one of the cloth ends, and then the rite is over. The recipient should take the cloth pieces and dip them in the ash and the substances, and then roll them up and tie them with the string, and keep that on their home altar for healing. If a mark-fetch is used, the cloth pieces should be wrapped up inside it and the whole things sent to them to be laid on an altar.

Thirteen Maidens Graduation Ritual
Raven Kaldera

This is another one of those rituals which mark something our ancestors had no need of, and it is also another example of why it is important to be able to adapt ancient religion meaningfully to a modern world. People often complain how graduation – from high school or even college – is used today as a poor substitute for a rite of passage into the adult world. Since modern adolescents cannot legally be considered adults until several years beyond the time when they are theoretically able to breed, and graduation generally comes close to that time, we've tended as a society to use it for the "real" rite of passage, of moving into the adult work world.

However, even if we take up the tradition of having earlier "pubescent" rites of passage such as the ones in this book, graduation – from high school, from college, from a certification program – is a milestone worth honoring no matter what the age of the person in question. It is a community acknowledgement of the years of hard work that they have put in, and can also be a celebration of their entry into the work force (if they are young) or into a new career which could change the course of their life (if they are older and mastering continuing education). Indeed, given the number of people today who will be handed a diploma later in life for whatever reason, graduation has become even less attached to age-related rites of passage. It is, however, an extremely important social ritual in our culture on its own merits, and it should not be ignored.

When I began to think about a graduation ritual, the figures who immediately came forward were Frigga's handmaidens. I realize that there is a great deal of debate as to how many handmaidens there actually are, and which names "count" as handmaidens. Accounts vary from ten to thirteen. Rather than argue, I have included them all. The speakers for the various handmaidens could be all women, depending on how much of an authentic "feel" you want, or they could be other genders as well if you want to have all the graduate's friends and loved ones participate. The ritual does involve gift-giving, as do many graduation parties, but with this rite the gifts are made more meaningful and are also blessed by the Handmaidens, becoming gifts of spirit as well.

An altar is set up, with white cloth, thirteen candles, a cup or horn of some sacred drink, and thirteen carefully-chosen gifts, which will be discussed as we go along. The candles can either be all white, or they should be colored in this order: Gold, yellow, brown, pink, red, light grey, purple, light blue, parchment-colored, green, sky-blue, dark grey, black. A circle is formed around the altar with the graduate in the east, and each speaker comes forth to the altar one at a time. They speak their piece, give a gift to the graduate, pour out a small amount of the drink, and step back.

Fulla's Speaker:

> In the name of Fulla, Lady of Abundance,
> Keeper of the jewels of the All-Mother,
> We bless this great accomplishment that has been achieved,
> And may it return you rewards by the hundredfold.
> In token of this future abundance that we hope for you,
> We choose to share some abundance today
> With those less fortunate than you,
> And thus seal your blessing.
> May this be the seed from which grows your fortune,
> As the birch tree steps forward into the empty field.

A certificate is given to the graduate indicating that a monetary donation has been made to a charitable organization that they would approve of.

Gefjon's Speaker:

> In the name of Gefjon, Indomitable Lady,
> Guardian of the door of the All-Mother,
> We bless this great accomplishment that has been achieved,
> And may you be protected from misfortune as you go.
> In token of this protection from the harrowing of life,
> We give you this representation of our sheltering arms,
> Our shields, our will that you be safe.
> May this be the seed that grows your courage to take risks,
> As the rowan tree protects the doorway with its berries.

A charm of protection is given to the graduate.

Snotra's Speaker:

> In the name of Snotra, Lady of Labor,
> Keeper of the industry of the All-Mother,
> We bless this great accomplishment that has been achieved,
> And may you endure the many hours of toil with grace.
> In token of our hope for your persistence,
> We give you this gift to look forward to
> When the workday seems far longer than it ought to be.
> May this be the seed that grows your determination,
> As the ash tree forms the unbreakable handle of the sacred tool.

A certificate for some enjoyable thing – a meal, a show, or the like – is given to the graduate.

Lofn's Speaker:

> In the name of Lofn, Lady of Forbidden Loves,
> Keeper of the secret joy of the All-Mother,
> We bless this great accomplishment that has been achieved,
> But may it yet leave time for love in your life,
> In whatever way that love may come to you,
> And may you find a love that dances with your goals
> And supports them, and takes joy in them as you do.
> In token of our wish for balance in your life,
> We give you this spark of joy for twin hearts.
> May this be the seed that grows the tree of love
> As the alder tree gives us its glowing coals of warmth.

A certificate for some activity for two people is given to the graduate.

Eir's Speaker:

> In the name of Eir, Lady of Healing,
> Keeper of the sacred well of the All-Mother.
> We bless this great accomplishment that has been achieved,
> And may your body and mind be strong as you go forward.
> In token of the future health that we wish for you,
> We gift you a gift that holds all our healing wishes.
> May this be the seed which grows your vigor,
> As the willow tree eases pain and suffering.

A gift of healing is handed to the graduate. This can be a package of some stress-relieving herbal tea, or some remedy for something that they are known to suffer from, or a certificate for a session at some healing practice, or if nothing else a voucher toward health insurance or medication copayments.

Sjofn's Speaker:
> In the name of Sjofn, Lady of Consolation,
> Keeper of the comfort of the All-Mother,
> We bless this great accomplishment that has been achieved,
> And may you find that consolation when times are hard
> And the waiting for that good fortune seems endless.
> In token of the solace that we would wish for you,
> We give you these words of wisdom.
> May this be the seed that sprouts when you need it most,
> As the hawthorn's berries ease the trembling heart.

A gift of consolation is given to the graduate. This can be a book of wise thoughts, or a poster for them to look at when times are hard, or even a book on practical tips for those with little money. Ask Sjofn what will bring them the most joy on the hardest days. Also, Sjofn's speaker should embrace the graduate with all good will.

Vor's Speaker:
> In the name of Vor, Lady of the Holy Word,
> Keeper of the Oaths of the All-Mother,
> We bless this great accomplishment that has been achieved,
> And may you never give up on your promises to live rightly.
> In token of the promises that we hope you will fulfill,
> We give you a gift of our own promises,
> Which we also vow to fulfill when they are redeemed.
> May this be the seed that grows your integrity
> As the oak tree upholds the sky on its shoulders.

An envelope is given to the graduate with a written promise from one or more people to do one specified favor for them.

Syn's Speaker:
> In the name of Syn, Witness to Vows,
> Keeper of the Eyes of the All-Mother,

> We bless this great accomplishment that has been achieved,
> And we know that promises are sometimes hard to keep.
> In token of the sacred obligations that you will make,
> We give you a gift to help you to keep your word
> Even when it seems darkest and hardest.
> May this be the seed that grows your maegen to great heights,
> As the holly tree's berries are like drops of blood against the thorns.

A magical charm is given to the graduate. Its purpose is to give them strength to call upon when they must keep a promise that their heart does not wish to hold to.

Saga's Speaker:
> In the name of Saga, Lady of the Library,
> Keeper of the knowledge of the All-Mother,
> We bless this great accomplishment that has been achieved,
> And may you continue to add to your learning throughout your life.
> The printed word has been the workhorse that you rode
> To plow this field, but there are more fields to gaze upon.
> In token of our wish for your future learning,
> We give you another horse for your stable of scrolls.
> May this be the seed that grows your future quests,
> As the hazel tree inspires the tongues of skalds.

A book is given to the graduate, on some subject that they are interested in, which is wholly apart from the work they have done to graduate.

Huldra's Speaker:
> In the name of Huldra, Lady of Nourishment,
> Keeper of the Flocks of the All-Mother,
> We bless this great accomplishment that has been achieved,
> But great deeds are better done on a full belly.
> In token of the sustenance we would hope for you,
> We give you this blessed food and drink.
> May you never hunger, may you never thirst.
> May this be the seed that feeds your future deeds,
> As the grapevine gives both nourishment and joy.

A basket of good food and drink is given to the graduate.

Gna's Speaker:
> In the name of Gna, Messenger of Asgard,
> Keeper of the missives of the All-Mother,
> We bless this great accomplishment that has been achieved,
> And may you hear the messages that the Gods send to your ears.
> In token of the open hearing we would wish for you,
> We give you this small piece of the sacred,
> To strengthen your bonds with the Holy Powers.
> May this be the seed that grows your faith anew each day,
> As the ivy springs upward toward the endless sky.

A small altar item dedicated to some god – like a statue or sigil, perhaps of the graduate's patron deity – is given as a gift.

Hlin's Speaker:
> In the name of Hlin, Lady of Mourning,
> Keeper of the tears of the All-Mother,
> We bless this great accomplishment that has been achieved,
> And may your purpose hold you up in times of great grief.
> For purpose can be a solace, as can worthy work,
> Sustaining you even in the face of heartbreak and disaster.
> In token of the resilience we would wish for you,
> We give you a gift that will hold your tears
> And help you to go once again to the necessary work.
> May this be the seed that grows your hope anew,
> As the reed wails its sorrow in the winter winds.

A gift of something soft and comforting is given to the graduate – a blanket or quilt, a soft robe or scarf, a stuffed toy, or perhaps even – if it is appropriate – a furred pet. Hlin's speaker should also embrace the graduate.

Vara's Speaker:
> In the name of Vara, Lady of Prophecy,
> Keeper of the Visions of the All-Mother,
> We bless this great accomplishment that has been achieved,
> And may it reverberate into the future,
> And may you always be ready for misfortune before it appears.

> In token of the readiness we would want for you,
> We give you this gift of a look into the future.
> May this be the seed that gives clarity in confusion,
> As the elder tree gives her wisdom even to the poorest folk.

A gift of divination is given to the graduate. This can be either a tool for divination if the graduate does such things themselves, or more likely a certificate for a diviner, with instructions to keep it for the time of most confusion.

Heimdall's Ritual for Blessing a Guard
Ari

Many people in the world hold guardian positions – security guards, prison guards, bodyguards, bouncers – and it is a thankless job. Yet if they fail, many suffer. We generally walk past the bored-looking security guard and ignore him, assuming that we have the right to be where we are going, and it takes some thought and attention to see him as the image of Heimdall. But that is who he is, and he – and all other guardians – should be honored for that role. This ritual blesses them and gives them appreciation for their job.

First, make a sigil, a round piece of wood painted blue as the sky, with a piece of rainbow ribbon tied to it, and a golden chain to hang around his/her neck if s/he wants, or a gold keychain finding if s/he would rather carry it that way. The runes Dagaz and Algiz should be on the sigil, for wakefulness and protection. Mead should be present to toast to Heimdall. A wooden staff, taller than him/her, is given to him/her to hold.

ଔ ଔ ଊ ଊ

To begin, the guard is recaned with smoke of dried angelica and cumin seed as s/he stands grasping the staff. The person performing the ritual says:

> Hail to Heimdall! Hear us, Hallinskihdi!
> Gold-toothed guardian of Gjallarhorn,
> Give this your guardian
> Sire of many castes, stamina's soldier,
> See this your sentinel as s/he stands watch
> And watch over him/her as well.
> Bifrost's border-watcher, bane of burglars,
> Be with this your patient protector,
> Let eyes close not, let ears shut not,
> Let back bow not, let wakefulness flow,
> Let wits be about in all ways, O Wave-Son,
> Witness of a hundred leagues around.

Then a drop of mead is touched to each eye, each ear, the center of the forehead, the top of the head, and the back of the neck, with the words:

See all above,
See all below,
Hear all above,
Hear all below,
Sharp to catch all,
Proud to stand tall,
Strong back never fall.

The mead is given to the guard to take a swallow, and the rest is poured out as a libation to Heimdall with the words "Hail Rainbow's Guardian!" The guard hands the staff over, and is given the sigil in trade, with the words: "This staff stays in your spine; this sigil stays at your side." Then the guard should, ideally, go straight to work, with Heimdall's blessing.

Mordgud's Ritual for Blessing a Guard
Ari

While the Rite of Heimdall that I wrote is a general blessing to keep a guard safe and alert, this ritual calls upon Mordgud as Guardian of the Gate of the Underworld to bless their mental health. Some guards must keep the door between the outside world and very damaged people – prisoners, mental patients, addicts in rehabilitation facilities, etc. Being the doorway in such a situation can take a heavy toll on a guardian, dragging them down into a hard, cold, depressed, fatalistic, negative place. In this rite we call upon Mordgud to help them as their ward the entry to some very dark places, keeping their mind, heart, and soul intact and compassionate throughout the work.

First, a sigil is made from wood painted black with a white bind rune of the runes Ear and Algiz. A cup of liquor is brought, of some sort red as spilled blood. It should be hung on a loop of leather thong, for the neck or the keychain as they will. A candle of black is lit with the words "Maiden of the Helgrind!"

ଔ ଔ ଓ ଓ

To begin, the guard is recaned with smoke of any of the following dried herbs: elderflower, wormwood, snapdragon, and toadflax.

> Mordgud, Maiden of the murky realm,
> Helheim's Guardian, hallowed and hale,
> Stalwart sentinel of Death's doorway,
> You watch the dead walk down your road
> And cross the bridge of gold and knives,
> And watch them weep and wail their woe,
> And make all their excuses proud.
> You know their wounds, their hate, their fears,
> And yet you welcome every one
> With compassion's candle as cord is cut,
> Making them welcome at your mistress's wall.
> Bless this your guard with such serenity
> And ward off darkness from this watcher's mind.
> Protect him/her, Mordgud, Armored Maiden,
> And let him/her not slide down the slope
> To coldness cruel and bitter belief.

Bring them hope when hope is needed,
Bear their heart up when it falls,
Keep them sound within their walls.

Then a drop of wine from the cup is placed on the center of the forehead and on the heart, with the words: "Joy of heart, joy of mind." The liquor is given to the guard to take a swallow, and the rest they pour out as a libation to Mordgud with the words "Hail Hela's Homeguard!" The guard hands the cup over, and is given the sigil in trade, with the words: "This hope stays in your heart; this sigil stays at your side." Then the guard should, ideally, go straight to work, with Mordgud's blessing.

Standing In The Shadows Rite
Dokkulfr

This ritual is for those who find themselves wanting or needing to honor the "darker" pantheon of Gods and spirits when they have never done so before, and may feel uneasy about how they will be seen by others in the community. It is a rite to give one's self courage and conviction, for once you have heard your own voice saying these words, there is no going back.

Items Needed:
- Hallowing Hammer
- Offerings
- Flame
- Bowl

Collect your items and set up your altar as usual. Prepare a line defining your "garth" around your altar; this should be physically symbolized (such as with a cord) and you should be able to cross it with ease.

Gather your hallowing hammer and proceed beginning in the North.

Hammer-sign in each direction, with feeling:[1]

(Face North.)
Hamarr i Norðri, helga ve þetta ok häld vorð!

(Face East.)
Hamarr i Austri, helga ve þetta ok häld vorð!

(Face South.)
Hamarr i Suðri, helga ve þetta ok häld vorð!

(Face West.)
Hamarr i Vestri, helga ve þetta ok häld vorð!

---

[1] I use the reconstructed Old Norse/Icelandic as offered in *Futhark* by Edred Thorsson. The English translation is as follows: Hammer in the (direction), hallow and hold this stead holy. It is pronounced: *Hah-mar ee (Nor-three, Aus-tree, Sooth-ree, Vest-ree, Ee-feer mer) hel-ga vay thetta awk halld vor-thuh.*

(Face Upwards.)
Hamarr i fir mer, helga ve þetta ok häld vorð!

(Face Downwards.)
Hamarr undir mer, helga ve þetta ok häld vorð!

(Face North.)
I hail the Niflii,
Rime-thurses residing in Niflheim,
Host of Primal Ice and Stasis!

(Face East.)
I hail the Jotnar,
Etin-kin residing in Jotunheim,
Host of Primal Force and Destruction!

(Face South.)
I hail the Muspellii,
Flame-thurses residing in Muspellheim,
Host of Primal Fire and Flux!

(Face West.)
I hail the Vanir,
And the landvættir residing in Vanaheim,
Host of Primal Form and Creation!

(Face Upwards.)
I hail the Ljossalfar,
Light-elves residing in Ljossalfheim,
Host of Primal Light and Beauty!

(Face Downwards.)
I hail the Svartalfar,
Dark Elves residing in Svartalfheim,
Host of Primal Dark and Beauty!

Center yourself and step to the eastern edge of the your "garth-line". Walk the edge of your garth, saying:

Vættir-kin, I hail you now,
Bear witness not only to my words but my actions.

Now step outside of your "garth-line", with conviction. Say:

> Witness now, I choose to stand *Utangarð*, by choice, not by chance nor by decree. I stand proud with the friend of my house. I stand proud with the friends of my soul. Hear as I name you, and behold my choice!

Name the Rökkr-kin you honor now, and call them to witness.

Example: "Loki Laufeysson! Flame-charmer! My heart calls to you and I ask you to bear witness to my choice to honor the Eldest powers! I offer these gifts to you, proudly standing *Utangarð*!"

I usually offer my nail clippings to Loki and Hela for Naglfari. I give rotting apples to Hela. To Fenrir I offer raw meat, bones, and my own blood. For Sigyn, I "hold the bowl". For other Rökkr, I reply on intuition and their input. When in doubt, ask Them. They'll let you know.

Then say:

> Though I may join the *inangarð* on occasion, my heart never forgets the warmth given me here outside the garth. May I always feel as safe here as others feel in there. *Hailsan Rökkr!*

End.

Chaining Fenris: A Ritual to Bind The Inner Beast
Raven Kaldera

This ritual is best done directly after a workshop or discussion on monster work, or working with the Beast Within. There should also be some discussion of the myth of Fenris, or people may not really understand the symbolism, although the priest/ess will be explaining some of it in the opening invocation. For this ritual, you will need:

- A skein of yarn, cut into many lengths (we used silk, handspun "with intent")
- Many squares of black fabric, about 6" across
- A fire or candle flame
- A cup of something slimy
- A particularly ugly baby doll
- A skull with gold coins in its mouth
- Crushed and powdered granite, preferably mined out of the earth
- Beard shavings from anyone who lives full-time as female (hit up your transgendered friends for this one, and if you don't have any, make some!)
- Bird spittle (for this, find someone with a large pet bird and put things in its beak, then take them out – make sure to reward the bird for this!)
- Cat footprints (we dipped our kitty's feet in food-safe food coloring and let her walk on cloth)
- Water from a pond or stream with fishes in it
- A well-used teddy bear

Before the ritual, build a fire or light the candle. Around it, put the cup of slimy material, the ugly baby doll, and the skull with gold coins. Inform people that they represent four common types of monsters, and encourage people to add more if they can think of any items. Instruct them to spend time before the ritual dealing with the item(s) that represent familiar monsters to them. The reason that this is better done on one's own time, before the ritual, is that people are less likely to stand up in the middle of the ritual and talk about their monster in front of everyone, but they may be more willing to quietly go and commune with it beforehand.

1. The Raging Beast. Whether this is the creature full of anger and ready to strike, or just the sadistic one who likes to see pain, this predator is the most showy of all the monsters. He gets romanticized a lot, but there's nothing actually romantic about restraining an anger management problem that threatens to devour your life and your loved ones. It's actually pretty grubby and difficult. This monster jumps and strikes without warning and often without good reason; he may batter or verbally abuse others, and he may gleefully enjoy every minute of it. The fire represents this monster, and people should actually touch some part of it in order to connect with the burning nature of this beast. Have a first aid kit on hand for minor burns. Dripping hot stearin wax works well too.

2. **The Sleazy One.** This monster, when panicked, forgets their morals and will say or do anything to anyone in order to stay afloat. When they feel that their survival is threatened – and that is a very subjective thing, which could include losing an argument, looking bad in public, or not having enough money to keep up your profligate lifestyle – they will lie to their family, steal from their friends, cheat customers, and ruthlessly use anyone in range ... and then justify it because "it was necessary". The pot of slimy substance represents this monster, and people should stick their hands in it ... and not wash it off for a while, either.

3. **The Pathetic One.** This monster doesn't want to stand on its own two feet. It wants to be taken care of, paid attention to, be told what to do, be nurtured, be childish, and generally never take responsibility for anything in its life. This monster whines, weeps, blubbers, moans, curls into a limp, miserable fetal ball, or just sits paralyzed and pitifully helpless. People who have to deal with this monster should spend time with the ugly, pathetic-looking baby doll, carrying it around and attempting to like it.

4. **The Gloating One.** This monster is secretly (or not-so-secretly) sure that it is better than everyone else, and it spends a lot of time thinking about how lame other people are, and how superior it is in various ways. It is very insecure and requires a lot of reassurance, which is only really effective in the form of comparisons. It doesn't want to be told, "You're good at that"; it wants to be told, "You're so much better at that than Joe and Bob and Meriwether; see how lousy they are?" Without direct comparisons that denigrate other people, it has no basis for believing any compliment, and besides, it loves to gloat. People with this monster should spend time taking the jewels and gold out of the

mouth of the skull (and it should be a really nasty skull, preferably still with some rotting flesh and fur on it) and chewing on them. "This is what your values are really worth in the long run," says the dead animal head.

The other items are for the chaining ritual, and they represent the ingredients of Fenris's chain: mountain's roots, the beard of a woman, the spittle of a bird, the footfall of a cat, the breath of a fish, and the sensitivity of a bear. The yarn represents the chain itself that is used to bind the monster.

෴ ෴ ෴ ෴

After everyone has had a chance to amble over and pick a monster (or not; some may not be ready to deal with this), everyone gathers around a central area. Squares of the black fabric are given to everyone; this will be used to make a mojo bag. The priest/ess displays the six objects that are associated with Fenris's chain, and says the following invocation (which can be altered by the individual priest/ess to be spoken more comfortably):

> Behold the six impossible things, gathered by the magicians of the Duergar, to chain the beast who could not be tamed! Yet we know that they are not impossible, simply difficult ... and within them are found the keys to binding this Beast.
>
> Yet first we must ask ourselves: It is a terrible thing to be a prisoner. If one must be so imprisoned, for the good of all, what can we offer them in return? What will you offer your monster in exchange for its binding? What gift, however meager, can you give in return?

People take turns speaking, saying what they will give their monster as gifts – doing fun things with it, buying it toys, finding it friends to play with, whatever.

> Then here we make the chain of the six impossible things. They are called impossible, but we know that they are not so impossible. They are simply hard to come by.
>
> The first thing on our list is the roots of mountains. In the depths of mountains, there are caves and tunnels and dark places. There is also bedrock, that which supports the

rest of our lives. There is also the upheaval of early times, shaping those mountains from underneath. In order to work with our inner monsters, we have to be willing to go down to those places, to search the depths and scour the bedrock, to see what is deep inside. Sometimes we may even have to strip-mine the layers away, to expose the underground darkness to the light.

This is granite, crushed to a powder. This is what the mountains of this area are made of. Take it with you and remember.

The second thing on the list is the beard of a woman. This is tossed off as if it is impossible, yet we all know that it is not so. There are women who grow beards, and there are people who have beards who are women inside. This tells us that part of dealing with a monster is to find your inner balance between male and female, not to allow yourself to settle unquestioning into one or the other. That inner finding of balance helps you to maintain perspective. These are the shavings of a woman's beard; take them with you and remember.

The third thing on the list is the spittle of a bird. Regardless of what the myths say, birds have spittle ... and so do you. This sacred energy of a bird's mouth says that you should talk, should speak, should tell stories about your monster. Even if you cannot allow it to use your mouth, you can tell its tales, and show that it is appreciated. This thread has bird spittle on it, of a very talkative bird. Take it with you and remember.

The fourth thing on the list is the footfall of a cat. Everyone who has had cats will tell you that although they can be very quiet, they can also be very loud. They are only quiet when it is their will to do so. They have the ability to step gently or to step hard, and this is something that you must learn in dealing with your monster. Sometimes they will need you to go gentle. Sometimes you must be rough with them, remind them that you are the alpha in this body, make them submit and show throat ... or they will never respect you. The cat understands the control needed to go from gentle to rough. These are the footprints of a cat on cloth; take them with you and remember.

The fifth thing on the list is the breath of a fish. This, obviously, is water. Water symbolizes the feelings, the emotions that we must constantly check and be aware of. Sometimes, this is the only way to take notice of a chained monster who is becoming restless and needs attention. Watch the water levels in your life. This is water from a fishpond; take it and remember.

The sixth thing on the list is the nerves – or sensitivity – of a bear. While we couldn't bring in a real bear and skin it, we bring here a well-used teddy bear to pass around. Hug him, hold him, and remember that love and nurturing is necessary for all beings – even monsters. Perhaps they prefer their love and nurturing in a somewhat different manner – let them tell you what that is. Take a thread from the bear and keep it. Remember that part of your job, as the alpha in your body, is to protect them, feed them, and care for them. They are no longer your enemy. They are your dependent. You are the leader of the pack. Remember this.

Now we bind your things with this silken cord, as fine as the chain that bound Fenris. We bind it with nine knots, and then we bind it to you. Take it with you and remember.

Afterwards, the rite is closed silently, with all dispersing into the night to meditate on what has been done, and then meet again in a neutral place to talk about it.

Originally published in *Dark Moon Rising: Pagan BDSM and the Ordeal Path*, by Raven Kaldera. Asphodel Press, 2006.

Hela's Rite of Unbinding
Raven Kaldera

Hela, the Goddess of Death, is compassionate but completely implacable, and her rites are not convenient or merciful, but cut straight to the heart. Usually they are ordeal rituals of some sort, and usually they are intensely personal to the individual doing the ritual. However, this rite was general enough that I felt it could be used by a wider variety of participants. It is designed for someone who feels that there are many things binding them and holding them back, and wants – at any cost – to be able to let go. This rite is not for someone who is only beginning to consider the idea; it is for someone who cannot go any further. Hela is a Goddess called on in extremity.

Thus, this ritual may take hours, or even more than a day. Set aside a good deal of time, because it will not be convenient or merciful. It requires a minimum of three participants – the individual who needs to be unbound, a second one who has experience with divination, and a third individual who has skill and experience at tying ropes on people's bodies in a comfortable manner that will not cut off any circulation. The first one should come naked to the rite, and the second two should be swathed and veiled in black or grey, all features unseen. (It would be best if there was one other person present, whose job was to look after the vital signs of the central individual.) Since the seeker will be naked for some time, thought should be given to their warmth.

The following items are needed and should be laid out on a black-draped altar:
- A diabetic lancet, with an alcohol wipe if needed.
- A tiny bit of white linen or cotton.
- A cup of tea made with healthy but bitter medicinal herbs.
- A skull figurine, to remind one of Death.
- A single black candle, preferably long-burning.
- Nine pieces of black rope, about five feet long.
- A dark-colored blanket or large piece of cloth.
- Three stones – one black, one white, one grey – in a cup.

The three stones are a divinatory system and mean: Black is *Yes, you speak full truth, and you may pass*. White is *You do not speak the truth. You may not pass.* Grey is *You speak truth, but this is not the most important thing. We ask for a different answer. Try again.*

ଓ ଓ ଊ ଊ

The diviner shall first ground and center before the altar, and will not be moving from that spot for the length of the rite. The binder shall ask the seeker, as they approach the altar: "Would you make a deal with Death?"

The seeker says: "I would."

The diviner says: "Would you ask Hela to take from you these things that chain you?"

The seeker says: "I would."

The binder says: "And if She chooses to take other things from you as well, things that you no longer need, will you relinquish them as payment?"

The seeker says: "I will." (Obviously, if they are not ready for this, the ritual should not be happening.)

The binder says: "Kneel, and ask Her yourself." The seeker kneels before the altar and asks Hela to bless them with Her touch. Then a drop of blood is taken from the seeker's finger with the lancet, by themselves or one of the others, and the blood is wiped on the bit of cloth. The cloth is held in the candle flame until it burns up, and the bargain is agreed upon.

The diviner says: "Drink of the bitter draught of Life, and yet know that it heals you and bears you up." The seeker drinks from the cup of tea, and then lays down before the altar. Next the binder takes the twelve pieces of black rope and ties some part of their body. As they tie each one, the diviner leads the seeker through a meditation that is a trip through Helheim.

First the binder ties their ankles together – firmly but not tightly, this should be comfortable – and the diviner says, "You walk the Road to Hel. Your feet cannot swerve from this path. Speak of the path that you walk against your will, that you would leave, only you cannot find a way." The seeker speaks of this in their life. After they have finished speaking, the diviner draws a stone forth, and speaks its message to the seeker. If it is black, they go on. If it is grey or white, the seeker must try again until they get it right. The diviner and seeker may agree beforehand to try three times and then abandon the rite, or try three times and move ahead even if the spirits are not satisfied (knowing that Hela may ask a price), or some other action. Whatever is chosen, it must be agreed on ahead of time. (For the next steps of the rite, I will recount the part that differs. The seeker's words, the diviner's reading, and the results will be assumed.)

Next the binder ties their knees together, and the diviner says, "You pass the great well Hvergelmir, the torrent and tempest, and its blast drops you to your knees. Water is emotion, and this is the primal wave of emotion. Speak of what deep emotion in you is bound against your will, that you wish to release but cannot touch."

Next the binder ties a rope around their thighs – perhaps just above the knees where the last rope goes below – and the diviner says, "You stand before the Helgrind, the Bridge of Knives over the rushing river Gjoll. Now you are bound like the serpent, and you cannot run, but must keep inexorably moving. Speak of that which pursues you, and which you cannot outrun no matter how hard you try."

The binder ties a rope around the seeker's waist, and the diviner says, "You have crossed the bridge, and now you come to Mordgud's Tower, the great pillar by the Gates of Helheim. Your belly is bound, and you may not nourish yourself. She will not let you pass until you speak to Her of how you starve yourself for nurturing, and do not take care of your bodily urges."

The binder ties a rope around the seeker's wrists, binding them together behind their back, and the diviner says, "Next to the great black Gate of Helheim is the lowest root of the World Tree. Here the dragon Nidhogg gnaws away the old, rotten parts of Yggdrasil so that new growth may come. You approach the great root and see the dragon. Your limbs are now all bound, and you must crawl on your belly as She does. She heaves herself into your path, and She will not let you pass until you speak to Her of the rotten parts within you that you will not let go of, that keep you from reaching for your goals."

The binder ties a rope around the seeker's upper arms, binding them together – gently and loosely, so as not to cut off any circulation. The diviner says, "You have passed the great black Gate of Helheim and passed into the Land of the Dead. You see before you autumn trees and orchards filled with fruit, and a lake with an island in the center. You walk across the water, over the bones of many Dead, to that island full of mists and ghosts. They swarm around you, and they will not let you pass until you speak to them of the places where you feel helpless and insubstantial, little more than a ghost in the waking world."

The binder ties a rope around the seeker's neck – loosely, as it is not meant to choke but only to be a reminder. The diviner says, "You now come to Nastrond, Dead Men's Shore, where the corpses are piled on the beach for the dragon to recycle. The great hall of Nastrond is filled with tortured screaming souls, writhing in agony as venom drips down onto them from snakes poised in the rafters. Yet the door to Nastrond's hall is always open; they are there by their own will, to torment themselves. They will not let you pass until you speak to them of the ways in which you needlessly torment yourself."

The binder wraps a rope a couple of turns around the seeker's head, so that it holds their eyes closed, and the diviner says, "Now you come to a cottage in the forest, the place where dwell Baldur the God of Light, and his faithful wife Nanna. Yet your eyes are darkened, so that you cannot see his light and her devotion. They ask you to speak to them of the lights that shine in your darkness that you are ignoring, and of those who care for you whose gifts you do not value."

The binder ties a rope around the seeker's forehead, and the diviner says, "In darkness, then, you pass into the Mound of the Ancestors, all who lived and struggled that you might live and have the world. They will not let you pass unless you speak to them of the negative patterns that you learned from your family, the inheritance of pain and limitations."

The binder wraps the last rope around the lower part of the seeker's head, so that the turns of rope go between their lips and stop their speech. The diviner says, "Now you come to the end of the road. You stand before Elvidnir, the great hall of Hela that is half great castle and half rubble. She stands in the doorway, half beautiful woman and half rotting corpse, and holds out her left hand to you. She bids you to speak to her of your deepest humiliation, the one you have never spoken before now. As your lips are bound, speak it to Her in your heart, and She will hear you." Then, after the seeker has been silent for a minute, the binder says, "Rest now, and incubate in the darkness, and meditate on all these things, until you are ready to walk from the Land of the Dead." The binder covers the seeker with the blanket for warmth and sensory deprivation, leaving only their nose and mouth exposed. If there is an assistant, they stay with the seeker, watching their breath to make sure that it is regular and not distressed.

When the seeker has meditated, and gives the signal – perhaps something unmistakable like three evenly spaced grunts – the binder unbinds the rope around their mouth and the diviner says, "Now it is time to go forth from Elvidnir, but Hela asks you to speak to her of one thing. What compassion has your great and secret flaw given you for others?" The seeker speaks, and is not challenged; challenges are only for the way in. Instead, all present say, "Be blessed." This will happen after each step.

The binder unties the rope around the seeker's forehead, and the diviner says, "You pass beyond the Mound of the Ancestors. Speak to them, as you pass, of the good things that your family has given you."

The binder unties the rope around the seeker's eyes, and the diviner says, "You pass by the dwelling place of Baldur and Nanna, Light and Devotion. Speak to them, as you pass, of the light and love that can be found even in the darkest places."

The binder unties the rope around the seeker's throat, and the diviner says, "You pass beyond Dead Man's Shore. Speak to those tormented within of how you have walked out of the hall, and what you will no longer permit yourself to do to yourself."

The binder unties the rope around the seeker's upper arms, and the diviner says, "You pass beyond the Island of Ghosts. Speak to them, as you pass, of how you will find a way to be active instead of passive in your life."

The binder unties the rope around the seeker's wrists, and the diviner says, "You pass beyond the great black Gate, and come again to the root of the World Tree and the great Dragon. Speak to Her, as you pass, of what rotten thing within yourself you will let go of, that you will give a decent burial, mourn, and be done with it."

The binder unties the rope around the seeker's belly, and the diviner says, "You come again to Mordgud's Tower, and She lets you pass. As you go by, speak to her of how you will nurture yourself in the future."

The binder unties the rope from around the seeker's thighs, and the diviner says, "You cross the Helgrind, and this time there are no knives, but only a sturdy bridge. Speak of what fear you will turn and face instead of running away."

The binder unties the rope from around the seeker's knees, and the diviner says, "You cross over Hvergelmir, the Boiling Cauldron. Speak of the emotion that you will no longer repress, but will release into the light of day."

The binder unties the final rope from around the seeker's ankles, and the diviner says, "You walk with both feet upon the Hel Road, but in the other direction – toward Life. Walk forward and embrace Life, and ask the Gods to put your feet upon the right road." The binder and the assistant help the seeker to their feet. The diviner comes forth and gives them a sip of the medicinal tea, saying, "This is bitter, but healing often is. Go forth from this place a little more healed." The rest of the tea is poured out by the seeker as a libation for Hela; the seeker thanks Hela for Her wisdom and the privilege of entering Her land and being allowed to leave it, and the rite is over.

Solitary Rite for the Ancestors
Raven Kaldera

This rite can be done in a graveyard, on land that belonged to one's ancestors (*othal* land), or in front of one's ancestor harrow. The latter is an altar with images, written names, and/or items belonging to one's beloved Dead. Some hold strictly to their own blood kin; others incorporate spiritual ancestors – those Dead with whom you feel kinship – and deceased friends. Give them food and drink that they might have liked, and any other small gifts that you would have given them gladly in life. You can place a single candle to pierce the darkness of the past, or place many, as many as speak to you, to honor your beloved Dead.

☙ ☙ ❧ ❧

Begin with the following invocation:

> Hail to those who have passed through the veil
> From Life to Death, to Earth from Breath.
> Hail to those who suffered to gift me with blood,
> Hail to those who survived to gift me with body,
> Hail to those whose songs gift me with inspiration.
> Hail to those whom I knew and loved in life,
> Whose memory I carry with me like a word of comfort,
> Hail to those who left this land long ago,
> Whose names I honor like a word of hope,
> Or if I know not their names, whose lives I honor still.
> I live and love because you lived and loved,
> I speak and struggle because you spoke and struggled,
> You live in me, as I will live in those who come after me.
> Grant me the patience, O my beloved Dead,
> To see the long view, and remember that what I do
> Affects a million million souls I will never know.

Then light the candle or the central candle if there are many. Say, "I am the light of the present shining into the darkness of the past. May I do you honor, O my ancestors." Then, if there are more candles, light them and name the names of your Dead. After each one, say, "You are a light in my memory, and you have a place at this table." Then tell them what you will do for the future, so that when another lights a candle for you on their harrow, it will be with the memory of worthy deeds.

Originally published in *Northern Tradition for the Solitary Practitioner* by Raven Kaldera and Galina Krasskova, New Page Press, 2007.

Ancestor Ritual of the Four Directions
Raven Kaldera

You will need a table in the central area, laid with a cloth. The center of the table can be set as an ancestor altar, with people's photos or written names or other symbolic items. However, in the North there should be homemade bread. In the West there should be a goblet or bowl of milk, preferably raw milk from a local farm. In the South there should be set a basket of apples. In the East should be a horn of mead.

ଔ   ଔ   ଓ   ଓ

The approximate words for the ritual are reproduced here; the speaker can adapt them to the circumstances. This ritual can be adapted for specific groups of ancestral dead as well – the Ukrainian dead or the transgendered dead or the Deaf dead or any other group desired. The speaker says:

> Hail to Hela, Keeper of the Ancestors,
> Queen of Helheim, you who feed those
> Who have gone quietly down your road
> After their courage and endurance
> Paved the way for our survival.
> Keep them well, Lady of Helheim,
> For they bought our lives for us
> With blood and sweat, with toil and song,
> With joy and sorrow, with birth and death
> Upon birth and death, and we are grateful.
> Feast them in your halls with honor.

>> Today we honor those of our tribe who have gone before us. Every tribe has ancestors, even though for some it might seem strange to call them that. But it isn't strange, it is perfect. They were there first and beat the path for us. We walk in their footsteps, and we call their names, and we remember.

A candle is lit on the north side of the altar.

>> Hail Nordri! Hail Mani! We begin in the North, the direction of the body. Here we honor the ancestors of the body and blood, who gave us life. They fought and

> struggled and survived so that we might live today. They gave us our bodies, our unique DNA. For all those ancestors who passed these gifts along through their bloodlines, we thank you. We offer you bread, for all of you who planted and harvested that your children might live.

The bread is lifted high and blessed by all present, and then given to someone to be carried out at the end of the ritual and laid onto the Earth. If the ritual is outside, the bread is laid out now. A candle is lit on the west side of the altar.

> Hail Vestri! Hail Nott! Next we cross to the West, the direction of the emotions. Here we honor ancestors of the heart, those who weren't related to us by blood, but who gave us nurturing and care anyway. All adoptive parents fall into this category, as do loving stepparents, foster parents, "big brothers and sisters", friends who have passed away who were there when we needed them. This is the place of those who may not have shared blood with us, but who were a shoulder to cry on, a heart that opened for us, a kind word to pull us through hard times. We offer you milk, the milk of human kindness.

The goblet of milk is lifted high and blessed by all present, and then given to someone to be carried out at the end of the ritual and poured out onto the Earth. If the ritual is outside, the milk is poured out now. A candle is lit on the east side of the altar.

> Hail Austri! Hail Daeg! Next we cross to the East, the direction of the mind, of words and speech and thought. Here we honor ancestors of the mind, those whose writings filter down to us. We read about them and their struggles, and we learn. Ancestors of the mind are also our teachers who pass on hard-won wisdom, who mentor us in our ambivalent lives. We thank the writers of the words that taught us, the teachers of how to survive our paths. We offer you a horn of mead for your words that we drank in.

The horn of mead is lifted high and blessed by all present, and then given to someone to be carried out at the end of the ritual and poured out onto the Earth. If the ritual is outside, the mead is poured out now. A candle is lit on the south side of the altar.

> Hail Sudri! Hail Sunna! Next we move to the South, the direction of spirit and will. Here we honor ancestors of the spirit, those whose deeds we heard about, and who inspired us to do great deeds ourselves ... or simply to keep going. "If they could do that," we say, "then I can do this." They inspire us to be ourselves and to live our lives the way we need to. We looked to their courage to find our own. We thank you, the doers of brave deeds, for showing us that anything is possible. We offer you the fruit of Iduna, apples: sweetness, eternal life, because our own deeds are the fruit that was inspired by your blossoming.

The basket of apples is lifted high and blessed by all present, and then given to someone to be carried out at the end of the ritual and poured out onto the Earth. If the ritual is inside, all now process outside and leave the offerings on the Earth. Solemn silence is observed for a moment, then everyone goes back in and feasts, and tells tales of their relatives and ancestors.

Bloodline Curse Aversion Rite for Hyndla
Raven Kaldera

This ritual is done under very specific circumstances: when there is a problem in the bloodline that has been diagnosed by some seidh practitioner or shaman or other skilled person as a curse on the genetic line, and a pregnant woman wishes to turn it from her child. Sometimes these curses manifest as genetic disorders, sometimes as madness, sometimes as rampant bad luck. This ritual can only be done for a child before it is born, and it should be done far enough along in the third trimester of pregnancy that the child will be able to survive should it be born soon afterwards. Once the child takes its first breath, it is too late.

This rite calls upon the goddess Hyndla, Lady of bloodlines and genealogy. She is a very old goddess who knows everything about genetics and family trees, and if she is properly propitiated, she will be able to turn away the cursed ancestral wyrd. Instead, the child will have their own wyrd, separate from that of the family. This wyrd will lead them in a different direction, and no one can tell what that will be until they are older. They may well leave home quickly, however, and go in a direction that no one in the family has thought of. If Hyndla agrees, however, it will free them from any curse on the line. They will not be able to call on their ancestors for spiritual aid, but if their ancestors are badly cursed, this may not be such a bad thing. In order to offset this lack, the family might go out of their way to "adopt" unrelated grandparents for the child, help to foster a bond, and then have the child honor them as ancestors instead when they die – effectively creating alternative ancestors for the child. There are many good people who are approaching death and would make fine ancestors, in exchange for being remembered. Ancestors of the mind or heart or spirit are just as valuable as ancestors of the blood.

For this ritual, the pregnant woman should lie down on a bed or table draped in red cloth (a massage table is very good for this, if you can borrow one). Her belly must be exposed, but the rest of her can be covered or not as she chooses. For this rite, you will need:

- Two long strands of red string, yarn, or cord, about six feet long.
- A recaning stick to smudge the mother's body.

- ◌ Pots of white flour, black soot, and red ochre – the latter for the ancestors, who covered dead bodies in red ochre to send them to the next life.
- ◌ A fine paintbrush, a wet rag, and a cup of water to dip it in.
- ◌ A clear glass cup of ice water.
- ◌ A cup of some clear menthol-flavored strong liquor as a libation.
- ◌ A large pair of shears.

◌ ◌ ◌ ◌

First the officiant lights the recaning stick and walks around the room with it, doing whatever form of clearing and creating sacred space seems right to them. Then the officiant comes to where the woman is laying and blows smoke gently at her body, especially her belly, saying:

> Fire that first kept us warm,
> Green that first kept us well,
> Smoke around which we first shared community,
> Bless this space, this mother, and this babe.

The officiant takes red ochre and a small paintbrush, and traces the rune Othala on her belly such that her navel is centered in the middle of it. The officiant says:

> Hail to the ancestors,
> Who did what they had to in order to survive.
> We would not be here without them,
> And if sometimes they made poor choices,
> We can learn to forgive them this
> As we are sometimes short-sighted in our turn.
> From birth to death to birth again,
> We hail the bond of blood,
> Even as we come to sever it.

The officiant then cleans the paintbrush with the rag and water, and dips it into the soot. Above the Othala, the officiant paints an Algiz rune, and says:

> O Wisewoman of the Northern Mountains
> Of the coldest reaches of Giant-Home,
> A shadow lies on this bloodline.
> This mother would save her child from that shadow.

> This mother would free her child from that yoke.
> This mother would protect her child from that fate.
> O Hyndla, hear our plea!

The officiant cleans the paintbrush with the rag and water, and dips it into the white flour. On either side of the Algiz rune, the officiant paints a Wunjo rune, each facing outward, and says:

> May light shine through the shadow,
> May light glow in the darkness,
> May light break down the blade.

One end of each red cord is placed in each hand of the mother, and she holds them above her head. The officiant takes the other end and begins to turn them so that they ply together, in a clockwise direction. When they are entirely wound together and the mother is holding the two ends only a hands-breadth apart, the officiant brings the other end up over the woman's body and walks toward her feet, until the mother is holding the two ends over the Othala rune and the officiant holds the far end past her feet. The officiant says:

> The red cord of blood carries our life,
> And it carries the deeds of our ancestors.
> Those of us who draw breath carry the weight of those deeds,
> But this child draws no breath yet.
> We ask you, Hagia of the Northern Mountains,
> She-hound, Grandmother of all Bloodwalkers,
> Cut this life from the shadow that lies here
> Yet not from flesh and heart and love.
> Mother, how will you pay for this boon?

The mother speaks, and tells what she will pay Hyndla and the other Gods for releasing her child from this curse. Then the officiant takes the shears and cuts the twisted cord, right beneath the mother's grasp, and says:

> Hail to you, Hyndla! May it be so.

Then the mother is helped to her feet and her belly is covered, and she takes the cup of liquor outside to pour on the earth, preferably on some bare rocks that look like mountains, giving Hyndla her personal thanks.

Ritual for Elevating the Troubled Dead
Galina Krasskova

Ancestor elevation is a sacred practice that is done to help the soul of a dead family member who was troubled or angry or depressed in life, perhaps doing harmful things to themselves or others, perhaps never able to live a happy life due to their own inner demons. By doing this, we aid their souls in finding peace. It is an act of mercy, and can also be an act of emotional freedom for the living, especially if their own lives were negatively affected by that individual when they were alive. It is ironically a lot easier to do this work for someone after they are dead. Unlike the act of simply wiping them from one's life, this practice actually helps the problem at its root.

Begin by laying an altar on the floor. This is done in part because the ancestors are our roots, and in part because during the course of this nine day ritual, we will symbolically be raising the altar and thus lifting our ancestor up. Be sure to place this somewhere where it can remain out for nine consecutive days. If you have pets, that's OK. It's not going to harm anything to have them drinking out of offering glasses.

The altar should be white: white cloth, flowers, candles. Culturally for us, this color still speaks of faith, purity, and spiritual cleanliness. In doing an elevation for a particular ancestor, we are engaging in ancestral healing, in cleansing a tiny bit of mess, blockage, pain, strain, hurt from that particular line. White, representing cleanliness to us, is a good color to use for this.

Set up a picture of the dead person you wish to elevate centrally on the altar. (If you don't have a photo, write their name on a piece of white paper in your best handwriting.) It should be noted that an elevation can be done for a beloved ancestor just because you love that ancestor and want the best for him or her. While they are usually done in the case of troubled, aggressive, unhappy, unhealthy ancestors or conditions, they don't *need* to be reserved only for those cases. The only pre-requisite to doing an elevation is that you must already have a primary ancestral altar and an engaged ancestral practice.

Put out flowers. Prepare a candle, a glass of good, clean, fresh water, incense, and whatever other offerings you wish to make.

When you are ready to begin your ritual, set a candle at each of the four corners of the altar and light them, offering a prayer that fire will cleanse and consecrate this space, making it sacred, making it a place where clear communication may occur between you, the ancestors, and the Holy Powers. Call upon any God or Goddess whose help you might wish in this endeavor. Ancestral work is a very personal thing. It not only involves us and our spiritual connections but specific ancestors and *their* spiritual connections. Regardless of the fact that we are Heathen, Norse Pagan, or Northern Tradition, etc. we may find ourselves called to put representations of Deities our ancestors honored on the altar, or to call upon Them. This is not about us. If you have a grandmother who had a close connection to the Virgin Mary, and in the course of an elevation, you get a sense that you should put an image of the Virgin on the altar, I'd suggest doing it because really, who is better positioned to help elevate that grandmother than the God or Goddess to whom she prayed her entire life? Get over yourselves, people.

ଔ ଔ ଓ ଓ

Sit in front of the altar (on the floor) and call to the ancestor you are elevating. Light incense, then the main ancestral candle. Begin by offering the following two prayers on behalf of this ancestor (these are the ones I commonly use, but feel free to use others if you wish):

First Prayer:
>Hail to the Gods and Goddesses.
>Your grace illumines all things.
>Your gifts shine forth,
>Making fruitful nine mighty worlds.
>Blessed are those that serve You.
>Blessed are those that seek You out.
>Holy Powers, Makers of all things,
>Bless and protect us in Your mercy.
>Lead us along the twisting pathways of our wyrd
>And when it is time, guide us safely along the Hel-road.

Second Prayer:
>My Lord and My Lady, my Beloved Ones,
>May those You call always hear Your voice.
>May I always love You beyond trust and mistrust.
>May my surrender be complete and voluntary.

Give me this day the grace of Your presence.
When I fail You of Your kindness,
Permit me to make amends.
Use me and teach me according to Your will,
And deliver me from all complacency.[1]

Third Prayer:

Oh clement and merciful Gods,
Magnificent Holy Powers hear my prayer.
I offer these prayers for the soul of _____,
And for all good spirits
Who wish our prayers and recognition.
Please let _____ know that someone here on Midgard
Is stepping forth to speak for him/her.

Merciful Holy Powers,
And all other good spirits and ancestors
Who might intercede for the relief of this soul:
Grant him/her hope.
Grant him/her the awareness
That he/she is illuminated by the Divine Light,
That he/she is younger kin to the Gods,
Beloved of the Holy Powers.
Let her see those tangles in the wyrd,
Those hurts and imperfections
Which keep him/her away
From peaceful tenure in the realms of Hel,
From rebirth, from renewal.
Open his/her heart to understanding,
Grieving, repentance and restoration.
Let him/her understand that by his/her own efforts
He/she can make the time of his/her testing easier.
Wyrd unfolds always, and living or dead
The power to weave it well is in our hands.

---

[1] This prayer was originally written by Fuensanta Arismendi for the Gods she loved above all others, Loki and Sigyn, but you can readily adapt it to your own devotional connections.

> May the Holy Powers and other helpful ancestors
> Give him/her the strength to persevere in all good resolution,
> To meet the tests of his/her wyrd rightly and well.
> May these benevolent and loving words
> Mitigate and soothe his/her pain.
> May they give him/her a demonstration
> That someone in Midgard acknowledges, remembers
> And takes part in his/her sorrows.
> May _____ know that we wish him/her happiness.

At this point, offer the glass of water to your ancestor. Put your ancestor's picture and the glass of water on a book (cover it with a pretty cloth so it's aesthetically pleasing). Remain meditating and praying for as long as you wish.

When you are ready to end the ritual, you may leave the candle to burn for a bit, or blow it out. Thank the elemental power of fire for holding and consecrating the space as you blow out the four corner candles. Thank the Gods and ancestors and then your ritual is over.

Repeat this for nine consecutive nights. Each night, clean, fresh water should be offered and the water and picture lifted by the addition of a new book. After the ninth day, the picture and offering glass of water can be placed on top of the main ancestral altar.

ଔ ଔ ଓ ଓ

A few caveats: if the candle or the glass breaks, you should do three things:

- Start the entire elevation over.
- Call upon your disir, and other strong and protective ancestors to guide and watch over the ritual.
- Put pieces of camphor in the water. In traditional folk magic, and in spiritualism from which the concept elevations originally evolved, camphor is protective. It keeps destructive spirits away. If you want to use a more traditional northern herb, sprinkle dried Agrimony.

If the altar is very active, change the camphor or Agrimony every day and do not use the candle. Usually your strongest ancestors will come forward to help with the elevations anyway.

I have found that the dead like to be remembered with food, drink, and offerings, but also with music. It would not be inappropriate to offer music during this ritual. At the end of the whole thing, when the elevation is complete, it is always good to make an offering to all your ancestors, and to make an offering to the Gods upon whom you called for help.

You may do elevations for the same ancestor multiple times. It does not hurt. In fact, with particularly damaged or angry ancestors, or tangled wyrd, you may have to. It's not a bad gift to give a beloved and healthy ancestor though.

Ritual for Frith
Assembled by Raven Kaldera

This ritual was created by a group of people who saw all the verbal warfare, vicious rumors, hatemongering, and unhelpfuness that dogged the various denominations of Northern religion. We have many gods and goddesses who are combative, it is true, but we also have a surprising number who have aspects as frith-bringers. (For those who are unfamiliar with the word *frith*, it means both peace and social order. A frithful space is one where everyone is made to feel welcome and hospitable, and conflict is resolved peaceably and maturely.) The very creation of the ritual was an act of power to bring about change, as each one of its thirteen pieces – dedicated to thirteen different deities – was written by a different individual. The creators ranged all over the planet, making a web of intent that spread wide. This rite does not belong to one group, but was an act of frith and cooperation in its own manifestation. Every time this ritual is performed, it energizes that web of intent and makes it larger. We would like to see it performed at least yearly by many different groups all over the world, because our world could certainly use more frith.

It is inappropriate, for this entire ritual, for participants to carry weapons of any kind with them into the sacred space. While it is assumed no one is planning to need a weapon during the ritual, some people have ritual items that could be considered weapons, and some habitually carry a knife or handgun or pepper spray for self-defense. Depending on the participants, there may be different opinions as to what counts as a weapon, but a good guideline is that if a participant thinks of it as something they could use as a weapon, or if they think of it as a symbol of a weapon, then they should not carry it, but someone who doesn't think of the same item in that way could carry it.

If any participants have ritually important weapons they feel they must carry for spiritual reasons, even these should be set aside for the Frey section of the ritual. If that is not possible, omit the Frey section of the ritual rather than excluding that person. The writer of the Frey section feels that it would be entirely contrary to the point to use this ritual to divide participants over an issue, and it harms no one to omit it.

Your group can have one speaker for each of thirteen Gods, plus one for opening and closing, or any number of people can speak, including only one. This rite is best done outside because of the great number of libations that will be poured out onto the earth, but for an indoor ritual someone can be sent to pour the libations outdoors at the conclusion of each section. Sacred space is created in whatever way the participants feel is appropriate; we suggest a recaning with mugwort. Altars can be set up for all the various Gods, either in the center or around the outside of the circle, or one large altar can be set up with cloths and items of all thirteen Gods of Frith. Refer to each section of the ritual for specifics of what is needed, but in addition to whatever items you have for the altars, you will need the following items:

For Frigga:
- A drop spindle with many pieces of handspun thread wound around it.
- A horn of mead, as libation.

For Snotra:
- A handful of local sacred plant matter.
- A offering of food for the land-spirit.
- Locally made fruit-wine, as libation.
- A bottle of water, as libation.

For Frey:
- Either homemade beer (enough for all), or one bottle of a local craft beer (as libation).
- A loaf of homemade bread, enough for all.

For Gerda:
- A pot of chamomile tea, and enough cups for all.

For Freya, either:
- diabetic lancets and alcohol wipes, enough for all.
- A rich red port wine, mixed with honey, as libation.

... or:
- A golden necklace.
- Fruity mead, as libation.

For Sif:
- A glass cup.
- Any light liquor, as libation plus enough for all.

- A hank of lightweight breakable red yarn of some natural fiber, sufficient to surround the entire gathering.
- An archway decorated with rowan leaves.
- A large lit candle, in a large fireproof bowl or pot. Alternately, a bonfire or hearthfire.

For Forseti:
- A clear vessel of pure water, as libation plus enough for all.

For Iduna:
- A bottle of good cider, either alcoholic or not, as libation.
- A basket of apples, with some cut up to share.

For Bragi:
- A basket of paper slips printed with ways to promote frith, more than enough for all.
- A horn of mead, as libation.

For Aegir:
- A tray of small pieces of finger food, enough for all.
- A tray of small shot glasses of beer, enough for all.
- A bottle of home-brewed or locally brewed craft beer, as libation.

For Sigyn:
- A container of stones, enough for all.
- An attractive sturdy bowl, large enough to hold all of the stones.
- Hibiscus tea or white wine, as libation.

For Njord:
- Blank slips of paper, enough for all.
- A small paper or wood model of a Viking ship, large enough to hold the slips of paper.
- A container of pens, enough for all.
- A large lit candle, in a large fireproof bowl or pot, large enough to burn the ship in. Alternately, a bonfire or hearthfire.
- A mug of rum, as libation.

For Hela:
- A bowl of ground chalk.
- A small cauldron of hot herb tea, as libation.

To begin, one of the officiants steps forward and says:

> Hail to you, O Gods!
> We gather here for a holy purpose,
> To take the fire from the anger in our world,
> To take the wind from the quarrels in our halls,
> To take the tears from those bruised and battered,
> To take the earth out from beneath the cycle of vengeance.
> We call upon you, O Gods,
> To bring frith to the spaces between each of us,
> And between our communities.
> Let eyes be opened, let hearts be quieted,
> Let hands be joined, let horns be shared,
> For we know in our hearts
> That we work better together
> Than when we are separated
> By our own shortsightedness.
> We come to you today open to your wisdom,
> And we hail you in this great and painful task.
> Hail!

All shout, "Hail!"

Frigga[1]

Frigga's officiant steps forward and says:

> Hail Frigga, Frith-Keeper,
> You who welcome all to your hall, Fensalir,
> Your hospitality and kindness turn foes to friends.
> Weaver of Orlog, Spinner of Wyrd,
> Keeper of Hearth and Home,
> Keeper of the Keys,
> You who sit in the high seat,
> Teach us to have compassion and open hearts,
> To see beyond our prejudices
> And our small-mindedness.
> Lead us, Lady of the Hall,

---

[1] Written by Janine Marie Gorham, Maine Heathen, USA, in service to her Lady.

To show all whom we meet respect and graciousness.
Beloved of Odin, may our words bind us
And our deeds strengthen us.
Hail Frigga, Queen of the Aesir.

Frigga's officiant walks around the circle with a drop spindle full of handspun white yarn, cut into long lengths and rewrapped on the spindle. Each person is given a piece of yarn, and is instructed to tie their piece to that of someone else, until it is a great yarn web. Any person can tie their piece to that of multiple people. This weaves and binds Wyrd together. The web of yarn is then rolled back onto the drop spindle and placed on the altar.

Finally, a horn of mead is poured out for Frigga.

Snotra[2]

If this ritual is being performed in North America, Snotra's officiant should have a handful of organic tobacco in their hand. If it is being performed on any other non-European continent, they should have either a handful of a locally-grown sacred plant or some dish of local traditional food. If it is being performed in Europe, they should have a dish with any food offering. Regardless of the venue, they should additionally have bottle of locally-made fruit wine.

ભ ભ ૭ ૭

Snotra's officiant steps forward and says:

> I am a guest of my parents,
> Who have welcomed me to this world.
> I give praise to my ancestors
> For the blessings of my blood,
> And give honor with drink.
> Please shout this word after me: Honor!

All shout, "Honor!" The officiant raises the vessel as the people repeat, then pours the libation. If the ritual is being performed on European land, the officiant says:

> I honor this land whose roots lie beneath me,
> Whose earth brought forth so many,

---

[2] Written by Linda Demissy, Lokabrenna Kindred, Montreal, Quebec, Canada.

And took them back again.

The officiant lays down the food offering. If, instead, the ritual is being performed on non-European land, the officiant says:

> I am a guest on this Native land,
> Whose bounty feeds my body.
> With a gift of sacredness,
> I show respect to the Native spirits.
> Respect!

The officiant raises the tobacco or other sacred plant matter as the people shout "Respect!", then sprinkles it. Putting down the vessel, the officiant takes a bottle of water out of a pouch and opens it, and says:

> I am a guest of this community, who has welcomed me in their hearts. I give honor to those who listen with words of inspiration, and offer water in understanding of those who do not drink. Understanding!

The officiant raises the bottle as people shout "Understanding!" Then the officiant pours the libation, and says:

> By my words and deeds you have taken my measure, without needing to know my name. I am host now and welcome Snotra to our rite, with open words of honor, open hands of respect, open heart of understanding. We are hosts and we welcome the goddess of hospitality within us. The low we raise, the high raise higher, with our words and deeds.

Someone in the circle, previously prompted, steps forward, saying: "I was not invited, and I am angry!" The officiant says:

> Then I welcome you as my counselor, and give you honor, for anger is a warning of wrongness. By your outburst I know that you care about bringing balance. I welcome your anger, and praise your warrior's courage. Take my hand, together we shall restore balance and bring peace.

Speaking to the people, the officiant says:

> Please hold hands and shout this word after me:

Honor!

The people repeat. Someone in the circle, previously prompted, steps forward, saying: "You are my enemy, and I shall not take your hand!" The officiant says:

> Then I welcome you anyhow, and give you comfort, for my ways are not you own. In our difference, I give you determination. In joining against us, I give your people unity. May your people be united in caring for each other, and become a shining example by how kindly the least loved among you are treated. Do not take my hand. Separately we shall restore balance and bring peace.

Speaking to the people, the officiant says:

> Please drop your hands and shout this word after me:
> Respect!

The people repeat. Someone in the circle, previously prompted, steps forward, saying: "You are strange, and I do not trust you." The officiant says:

> Then I welcome you as my teacher, and give you honor, for ignorance is the slayer of peace and prosperity. Teach me how to respect and give you comfort, show me how you give honor to your guests, and I shall treat you with the honors you desire. Welcome me into your home, and I shall welcome you into mine. Taking turns, we shall restore balance and bring peace.

Speaking to the people, the officiant says:

> Look at how different we all are, yet we can learn to work together. Understanding!

The people repeat, "Understanding!" and the officiant continues:

> Please shout after me:
> Honor, respect, understanding bring frith!

The officiant has the option of having them repeat a few times with increasing conviction.

Frey[3]

At this point, Frey's officiant steps forth with the trays of bread and beer. At least one loaf of bread and some quantity of beer is required for this ritual. The bread and beer should be made by someone either in the ritual or personally known to someone in the ritual, and should be made in a loving way. If no one in the ritual knows anyone who can make either bread or beer, one of the participants should visit a local bakery or brewer, and personally help in some way with the making of these things. (The idea is that someone involved has a personal connection to the yeast.) If handcrafted beer is not available, share the handmade bread and use a local craft beer for just the libation.

Everyone in the ritual, including officiants, should consume at least a small amount of one of the things shared, so check on the dietary restrictions of all who will be attending. Bread made with barley is ideal, but any yeasted bread is fine. Similarly, a traditional barley beer is preferred, but any yeast-fermented, grain-based drink is acceptable, including non-alcoholic. More than one variety of bread or beer can be used. (If there is any question at all as to whether the bread or beer turned out well, test it before ritual.)

It is the custom in some groups that when food or drink is ritually shared, participants can pour some as a libation or throw some in the fire rather than having it themselves. However, for this section of the ritual, participants should either take some for themselves or pass, so all of the shared food is actually eaten by participants. If it is not practical to finish all of the blessed bread and beer during the ritual, it can be eaten afterwards but it should not be thrown away or given to others, so only bless a reasonably sized portion.

ঙ	ঙ	ৎ	ৎ

To begin, the officiant says:

> Hail Frey, Golden One, Lord of the Grain,
> Frithmaking God who gave up your sword for love,
> Lord who bears no weapon, and in whose hallowed spaces
> No weapon can be carried, O Bringer of Light.
> We come together in the spirit of friendship,
> Setting aside all our weapons.

---

[3] Written by Joshua Tenpenny, a Freysman in Massachusetts, USA.

The officiant then blesses the bread and beer, saying:

> By gathering together and sharing food and drink,
> We nourish our bodies and nourish the bonds between us.
> With this bread and beer,
> May each of us find Frey's blessing,
> And may each of us share that blessing with others.
>
> May we find shelter with each other,
> May we take nourishment together,
> May we work together towards our common goals,
> May we learn from each other,
> And not quarrel amongst ourselves.

Setting aside one bottle or glass of beer for a libation, the remainder of the bread and beer is then shared among the participants. In a large group, one or more assistants may bring the bread and beer around. In a small group they can be passed around, or shared less formally. The officiant and any assistants should join in sharing the bread and beer. While the bread and beer is being shared, the officiant says:

> You nourish our bodies and bonds with bread and beer,
> Yet even with grain, no bread nor beer can be crafted
> Without the sacrifice of thousands of tiny lives.
> The yeast, which is so important to its making,
> Gives up its life, like you, Lord Frey, to feed us.
> And the secret to this sacred alchemy, it is said,
> Is that one must treat the yeast like a guest in one's home.
> No voices can be raised in wrath or fear
> Around the brew, lest those fragile lives die off too soon.
> This is the lesson you teach us, Sacrificed One.
> That which nourishes the people cannot be sustained
> Without respect and care for all who surround us.

After everyone (including the officiant) has gotten at least some of the bread and beer, the officiant pours out the libation, saying:

> O Frey, help us to create the perfect warmth
> Where all are welcome, whether they agree,
> For peace is always better than righteous wrath.

Gerda[4]

Then Gerda's officiant steps forward and says:

> Hail to Gerda, Etin-Bride of Frey,
> Lady who married across lines of race and war,
> Whose very marriage-bed was a cry for peace,
> Who will bear no children to be hostage in games of war,
> But who speaks for her husband's people
> In the councils of her own clans.
> Hail to the quiet goddess of implacable strength,
> You who can watch your lover die every year
> And welcome him back to life, glad of his sacrifice
> Because it serves the people, and feeds them well.
> Bride of fertility who chooses not to breed
> Until there is frith between your peoples,
> Teach us how to have a hope so strong and steady
> That we never waver in our peacemaking pursuits,
> Nor give in to despair, nor forget the joy in the working.

Gerda's officiant has a pot of chamomile tea and a number of cups, and goes about pouring a bit of tea into everyone's vessel. As the officiant pours, they say:

> Gerda understands the secrets of herbs, and she knows that chamomile brings peaceful sleep at night, gentle enough even for an infant. Its flower is as golden as the Sun, and it is the Maythen, one of the Nine Sacred Herbs. Take this sacred herb into your body and experience a little of its peace, and let your body be a vector from which this peace flows outward into the world.

Then the remainder of the tea is poured out as a libation.

Freya[5]

Then Freya's officiant steps forward and says:

> Hail to you Freyja, Sovereign queen,
> Fairest Vanadis in all things beauty finding,

---

[4] Written by Gudrun of Mimirsbrunnr, Heathen, BC, Canada.
[5] Written by Ember Leo, Vanatru Heathen, California USA.

Show us the beauty in ourselves and each other.
Lady of love, giving passion without prejudice,
Your power in the circle of Brisingamen is bound,
Which was traded fairly for a taste of your love.
For all that lives, you show respect and compassion.
For all that dies, you show honor and reverence.
Even as we sacrifice in faith to you,
So do you sacrifice to mysteries beyond,
And the blood which binds us each to another,
To gods and to ancestors, thus binds us to all beings.
Within that cycle, bound round like Brisingamen,
You show us that we each live and love and die
And in doing so, we are all much the same.

Freya's officiant has a choice of two separate ritual actions, depending on the nature of the assembled group in question. One, which is preferred, is to hand around small sterile lancets (generally available for diabetics in any pharmacy) and alcohol wipes, and bid each person to prick their own finger and add a drop of blood to a small goblet or cauldron which is passed around. The people are encouraged to say, "We are all of the Worlds, by shared Blood bound." This cup is then filled with a rich red port wine and a little honey mixed in, and then poured as her libation.

If those present would not be comfortable with this action, an alternative is to have a golden necklace which represents Brisingamen, and to pass it around the circle. Each person holds it in turn and says, "We are all of the Worlds, by Brisingamen bound." For this version, use a fruity mead as a libation.

Sif[6]

For this portion of the ritual, there is an archway set up on Sif's side of the circle, decorated with leaves of rowan, or if these cannot be found, with paper rowan leaves as the symbolism is important. If need be, this can be a small arch held up by two assistants. Sif's officiant has a glass cup (ideally a Norse or Saxon reproduction but any glass vessel will do) full of any light liquor, with enough left over to share with everyone.

---

[6] Written by Thorskegga Thorn, Thorswoman, Chiltern Kindred, England.

To begin, Sif's officiant steps forward with the glass cup and says:

> Hail to Sif,
> Golden wife of Thunder,
> Queen of Stormbright Hall,
> Cup-Bearer, Peaceweaver,
> Goddess of kith and kin,
> Spae-speaking Sybil,
> Come and share this cup,
> Let us know your love,
> And bring up your wisdom.

The cup of liquor is poured out for Sif, and then the officiant takes up the red yarn and says:

> Hark to the wisdom of Sif!
> A family or kindred is like a stronghold,
> Walled with trust and loyalty and shared passions,
> And this is a fine thing.
> But a stronghold divides you from the world beyond.
> Between the words "us" and "them" lies a great gulf,
>   like the ocean.
> It need not be so.
> Turn outwards and look beyond the garth.
> Come take this thread, and surround us.

The yarn is carried around the circle by volunteers, who encircle the group at about waist height, so that it is held up by the people in the circle. The officiant says:

> Now take the thread gently in your hands.
> Know it for what it is,
> The mistrust of all that is unfamiliar,
> All that is outside.
> Break it, and be open to the wisdom beyond your garth.

The thread is broken into small pieces, and the pieces are burned in the flame of the large candle, or other fire. Then the officiant says:

> You have opened your hearts
> To those beyond the boundaries of your hearth and kin.

> Now you shall be free of the ill-wishing spirits
> Who thrive on mean thinking and spite.
> The holy plant of Sif is the rowan,
> The protective tree with its berries of sacred red.
> The tree that is called Thor's salvation.
> It saved Thor from the anger of vengeful giantesses,
> Let it save you too.
> Pass beneath the rowan three times,
> And receive Sif's blessing.

The group lines up and walks three times beneath the arch, chanting:

> Rowan tree and red thread,
> Rowan tree and red thread,
> Wicked wights they hold in dread!
> Rowan tree and red thread,
> Rowan tree and red thread,
> Drive ill-thinking from this stead!

Repeat until everyone (including the officiant and assistants) has passed beneath the arch three times. Then the officiant says:

> Now drink from the glass cup and raise a toast to frith, as Sif did herself when she offered peace to Loki at Aegir's feast.

Everyone passes the cup, and drinks or pours out a little onto the ground, and says, "To frith!" The last of the liquor is poured out as a libation for Sif.

Forseti[7]

Then Forseti's officiant steps forward and says:

> We hail you, Forseti, Stiller of Strife,
> Son of Baldur, in ancient times
> You were worshiped on an island set apart,
> A sacred place
> Where the cattle were never slain.
> A spring flowed on your island,

---

[7] Written by the author of the Lagutyr blog, USA.

Its waters holy and pure.
The people drank from its waters
In complete silence,
Honoring you,
Honoring your peace.
Water binds all of us together,
Interweaving all life;
No life may be without it.
Water heals the blistered soul, mind, and body,
And smoothes down the sharpest stones,
Keeping all in balance.

Forseti, we now pray for your balance.
Please bless those here,
And bring us together in gentleness and wisdom.
May we keep the peace that is holy,
Honoring each other and honoring you.
May our dealings be open
And grounded in integrity.
May we truly listen,
And may we truly hear.

The officiant holds up a clear vessel of water and says:

In reverence, in joy,
In connection to each other,
We ask that you bless this water.
As we share this gift together,
May we share in life and hope.

Each person drinks from the vessel of water. Silence should be maintained during this action.

Forseti, we thank you for hearing us,
We thank you for blessing us.
May we always drink deeply of your peace
And be a blessing to each other.

The rest of the water is poured out as a libation for Forseti.

Iduna[8]

Then Iduna's officiant steps forward and says:

> Idunn, fair goddess, we greet you who grant
> The life-giving apples to mortals and gods,
> Restoring the youth of body and mind,
> That quicken our limbs, and brighten our minds
> With the bliss we once knew, but which we forgot
> In the grey grinding days amidst all our strife.
> Let us find peace, and let us make peace
> With ourselves and each other, as you among Gods.
> You counter old age, which equals us all,
> With the essence of life, the gift we all share.

Iduna's officiant then holds up the basket of apples, saying: "With this bite of immortality, we see the future and understand how important frith is to our survival. Take these apples and eat, and let love of life flow through your body." The basket of apples is handed around, and all eat. Then a libation of cider is poured for Iduna.

Bragi[9]

Bragi's officiant has a basket of small paper slips, each with a phrase written on it about where one could be of the most help to bring frith to the world. Time should be spent inventing these: "Start with your own home; bring frith there first." "Go to a faith group you disagree with." "Go to a faith group entirely different from your own, and learn something." "Work within your own faith group." "Talk to prisoners." "Write what you feel, where people can see it." Make two to three copies of each one, and have three times as many as there are people present.

ଔ ଔ ଓ ଓ

Then Bragi's officiant steps forward and says:

> Hail to the Skald of Skalds, Bragi the Bane of Boredom!
> Long ago when the Gods quarreled
> They made Kvasir with their spit and blood,

---

[8] Written by Michaela Macha, Frankfurt Asatru, Frankfurt am Main, Germany.
[9] Written by Ari, Norse Pagan, Ottawa, Canada.

> And he walked from home to hall to home
> Throughout the Nine Worlds, and was always welcome.
> But things being as frithless as they are,
> Kvasir was murdered, turned into sacred mead,
> Filtered through Odin's veins,
> And reentered Gunnlod's womb,
> And now you, Bragi, walk the Nine Worlds,
> Welcome from home to hall to home,
> Proof that frith cannot truly be killed
> And stay that way; it will sneak into our hearts
> Sideways, inevitably, when we are not looking.
> Now you walk the worlds for peace,
> Singing songs to lift sad and weary hearts
> No matter whose hearts they may be.
> Teach us the long slow path, Harpwalker,
> Roadsinger, Wordsmith, God of Eloquence,
> You who hold hope always in your heart
> When you go once more into the world,
> You who measure out your audience
> And find the words that they will best hear.
> Teach us this art, O Skald of Skalds
> That we might speak and sing across chasms of belief
> And find them not so uncrossable after all.

The officiant then passes around the basket of paper slips and says, "Hear Bragi's words about where your road must wander to bring your words to where they will create the most frith." Each person takes a piece of paper. The officiant may encourage them to sing the phrase aloud, to any tune they like, if they judge the group to be of the sort where this would be welcomed. If it would embarrass people, do not ask; no one should be made to feel uncomfortable during this rite. At the least, if singing the phrase is suggested, suggest also that it is all right to hold it silently to your heart as a promise to Bragi.

To conclude, a horn of mead is poured out as a libation for Bragi.

Aegir[10]

Then Aegir's officiant steps forward and says:

---

[10] Written by Suki Moyne, Australian Heathen.

Hail to Aegir, Lord of the Sea,
Brewer of beer whose foam splashes on every northern shore,
Master of Aegirheim where all are feasted,
Drowned sailors, children swept out to sea,
Aesir, Vanir, Giants, Elves, Duergar,
All who can come to your hall
Sit peacefully and share a drink with each other.
Your great cauldron, though once stolen,
Now redeems itself by brewing frith;
Every drink at your table, every morsel of fish and crab
Is imbued with peace so that none shall quarrel.
Master of Hospitality, you know how to manage
The difficult situation where warring parties must share joy.
Teach us this gift, that we might make our shared spaces
Into halls as hospitable as your own.

Two people come forth bearing trays, one of small bite-size pieces of food, and one of small shot glasses of homemade beer. They walk around the circle in opposite directions, saying, "Taste hospitality! May we all eat and drink in frith together." All who wish can take a bite or drink a shot.

To conclude, a libation of home-brewed or locally brewed craft beer is poured for Aegir.

Sigyn[11]

Sigyn's officiant has a container of stones and a large bowl. Each stone is somewhere between the size of a walnut and a bar of soap, so that it is possible to easily hold a bowl filled with all of them. The bowl is big enough to hold all the stones. Ideally it should be attractive and not easily broken (carved wood, etched copper, etc.). The bowl should be placed on an altar decorated with pink, lavender, pastel blue or green, or a brown altar cloth, with flowers – especially peonies, roses, daisies, carnations, lilac, honeysuckle, or other flowers that attract butterflies. White wine or a fruity hibiscus tea is set aside for a libation.

ଓ ଓ ଓ ଓ

---

[11] Written by Talas Pái of County Roscommon, Ireland.

Holding the container of stones, Sigyn's officiant steps forward and says:

> We praise Sigyn, Lady of Endurance –
> Though You have been tested,
> You hold strong without yielding:
> Like a willow bent in the wind
> Without breaking.
> Hail Sigyn, patient and wise!

The people repeat, "Hail Sigyn, patient and wise!" Then the officiant walks around the circle and passes out stones to everyone. The officiant then says:

> We praise Sigyn, the Loyal Protector;
> Your love is steady as a stone, as solid as the earth
> You tread, as deep as the cavern
> Where you follow and protect.
> Hail Sigyn, mother and wife!

The people repeat, "Hail Sigyn, mother and wife!" The officiant says:

> We praise Sigyn, Lady of Strength
> Whose name means Victory;
> Whose coming is the sweet breath of spring,
> Whose love is the brilliance of fire,
> Whose gentleness is the fading leaves on the wind,
> Whose pain is the iron grief of winter.
> Your wisdom, hard-won,
> And your bravery, tempered in loss,
> Teach us. Your innocence and joy,
> Your light and comfort,
> Warm us. Your constancy and indomitability
> Steady us.
> Hail Sigyn, lady of grace!

The people repeat, "Hail Sigyn, lady of grace!" At this point, the officiant begins to pass around the bowl with an explanation: One should place one's rock in the bowl silently while considering how one personally contributes to discord/strife/conflict, before passing the bowl on. The rocks pile up, the bowl fills and the weight reminds us of the terrible consequences of carelessly breaking frith. While the bowl is being passed around and filled, the officiant can extemporize on the nature and necessity of frith – in that frith is something we must all deliberately build, each adding our own contribution to the structure. Frith, peace and harmony are things we share. Frith is something we must deliberately cultivate. When the bowl has made the full circle, the celebrant holds it aloft and says:

> Sigyn, You who hold the bowl,
> You who protects and abides,
> Help us to mend the bonds of frith and spread peace.
> Hail to Sigyn!

The people repeat, "Hail to Sigyn!" Again, the officiant begins to pass around the full bowl, explaining that this time, one should remove a rock (any rock) while stating aloud how one could personally contribute to creating or sustaining frith. Specifics that can be followed through on in the future should be preferred to vague goodwill. As the bowl is passed, it is emptied, growing lighter, the result of bringing frith. The officiant says:

> May we be always mindful of Your gifts
> And Your burdens. May we follow Your example
> And match our strength with our compassion,
> Our love with our endurance,
> Our war with our peace.
> Hail, beloved Sigyn, Lady of Frith!

The people repeat, "Hail, beloved Sigyn, Lady of Frith!"
A libation of white wine or hibiscus tea is poured out for Sigyn.

Njord[12]

Then Njord's officiant steps forward and says:

> Hail to you, Njord, Consort of Nerthus,
> King and Diplomat who knows how to make peace
> Between prideful warring enemies.
> I speak this plain, no fancy words,
> As you speak plain, yet all who hear you listen.

---

[12] Written by Geordie Ingerson, Vanic Pagan, UK.

When the Aesir and the Vanir warred,
It was you who saw that there could be no winning,
That both peoples would destroy themselves
In stubbornness and pride, and it was you
Who decided that scorched earth
And poisoned seas were not worth the satisfaction.
It was you who raised the flag and called the halt,
And when it was decided to exchange hostages
You gave yourself and your two children
Into the hands of the enemy for that peace,
And to use your influence to change their ways
From the inside, on their councils.
You made yourself so crucial to them,
And taught your son and daughter to do likewise,
That when your people slew their hostages in wrath
Your enemies did not do the same for you,
For they had, by then, become your friends.
Teach us, O Ship-King, O Lighthouse God
Who shines your light for all communities to follow,
How to speak the words of diplomacy,
And follow them with actions that keep the peace.

Njord's officiant has a small paper or wooden model of a ship, holding enough blank slips of paper for all participants. Njord's officiant passes the ship around the circle, as well as a container of pens, and everyone in the circle takes a slip of paper and a pen. Then Njord's officiant says:

> We have all said things about those we dislike, things that are not true, or not entirely true, or true but the way in which we say them shows contempt, and to say these things is the opposite of what will bring frith. Choose the worst of these things that you have said, and write it down, and swear by the Ship-King's boat that you will endeavor never to speak it again. Choose wisely – choose the words that will have the most impact if they are not spoken, or spoken only with respect and appreciation. Choose the words that will be a struggle not to say, especially when you are angry, for this is the true sacrifice, and it is only true

sacrifice that provides the power to make real change in the world. Make your tongue your willing hostage for peace in those moments, as Njord is a willing hostage for peace.

When all participants have written, the officiant passes the ship around again and collects the papers in it. Then the ship and papers are set on fire with the large candle or other fire, and burned to ashes. The officiant walks around with the ashes and marks each person on their right palm, saying, "Remember what it takes to make real peace." To conclude, a libation of rum, the eternal sailor's drink, is poured out for Njord.

Hela[13]

Then Hela's officiant steps forward and says:

> Hail to Hel, Wisest of Wights,
> You who give final peace to a life of strife,
> You who take all who come into your arms
> And give their souls the healing of years,
> Decades, centuries, millennia,
> You who wait long in patience
> And see far in silence,
> May all that stands between us and frith
> Die a straw death and rot away
> Into the folds of the good Earth.
> Teach us all the long view that only Death can know,
> And let us understand, in the face of Death,
> What truly matters in this world.

Hela's officiant takes a bowl of ground white chalk and goes around the circle, saying, "Will you work for frith even to the end of your life?" If they say yes, they are marked on the left forehead and cheek and left hand with the chalk. A small cauldron of hot herb tea is brought forth, and poured out onto the ground as a libation for Hela.

---

[13] Written by Raven Kaldera, Iron Wood Kindred, Massachusetts, USA.

To Finish the Rite

Ideally, if people are able to learn it, the ritual should conclude with participants singing Groa's Fourth Charm. This is a shaman-song, one in a series by Raven Kaldera of the sung magical charms the ancient giantess Groa gave to her son Svipdag. This one is called "Foes To Friends":

> You see my heart, and I am seen.
> You hear my words, and I am heard.
> You feel my fears, my foes, my flight,
> You fathom deep my path and plight
> And friendship steals across your sight,
> And understanding steals your fight,
> And we will reach across this road
> And hand to hand we bring this right.

Groa's Fourth Charm: Foes to Friends

About the Editor

Raven Kaldera is a Northern Tradition shaman, dedicated to Hela, but a lover of all the Northern Gods. He is a devout polytheist and believes that ritual can be an amazing and uplifting thing, and not boring at all. He is the author of too many books to mention, and delights in bringing new ideas to the world. 'Tis an ill wind that blows no minds.

www.ingramcontent.com/pod-product-compliance
Lightning Source LLC
Chambersburg PA
CBHW031307150426
43191CB00005B/119